Ring Of Fire

W A Horsburgh

Published by New Generation Publishing in 2013

Copyright © W A Horsburgh 2013

First Edition

The author asserts the moral right under the Copyright, Designs and Patents Act 1988 to be identified as the author of this work.

All Rights reserved. No part of this publication may be reproduced, stored in a retrieval system or transmitted, in any form or by any means without the prior consent of the author, nor be otherwise circulated in any form of binding or cover other than that which it is published and without a similar condition being imposed on the subsequent purchaser.

www.newgeneration-publishing.com

New Generation Publishing

Contents

Acknowledgements 5
I Woke Up 7
The Primary Years 13
The Big One 32
Over the Rail 40
The Hangin' Boy 46
The Cruiser 50
Alcudia – Majorca 55
The End of School Days 61
A New Start 70
A Trip to Save My Sight 76
A New Direction 85
My New College 101
Blackpool 113
Tenerife 117
Back to College 120
The Blind College 134
On the Move 145
One of the Boys 153
My Twenty-First 162
A Joke Too Far 167
Amy 176
I'm Going Home 188
Right At Home 200
Visitors 210
Leeds 218
My New Friends 228
Premier Contact 237
A Visit to Shetland 249
Weddings, Funerals & Fall-outs 263
Neglected in London 282
Delighted, Devastated & Disciplined 300
I Woke Up 315

ACKNOWLEDGEMENTS

First of all, I would like to thank Mum, Dad and Michael for putting up with me over the years – through thick and thin. Without the support of my family, and their involvement in my life, there wouldn't be a story to tell.

To the rest of my family: my aunties, uncles and cousins - who have also been an influence in my life from childhood to the present day.

A special mention to all my grandparents, who if were alive today, would have been proud of my achievements. I miss you all. And also to my friends who are no longer with us today.

To my best friends for putting up with me over the years: Craig, Laura and Brian, John, Alan, Stan and Christine.

And to my friends in the community, the rest of Fife, Britain and across the world, I wouldn't have been able to produce this book without your involvement.

To Drew Lawson for his time and dedication in editing the book and choosing the appropriate words and phrases.

To the late James Howells for initially attempting to edit the book.

To Alasdair Bisset for helping me complete the final edits and corrections.

To Paul Johnson from the Sunday Post for advising me of the words to say from the published Article.

To Campbell Deane for providing me with a Defamation/Liabal/Privacy read of the book.

To Stephen Gunn for designing the book cover.

And Finally, New Generation Publishing, and everyone involved for publishing the book – without New Generation Publishing the book would not be available.

This book is an honest account and all characters are real people, however, some names have been changed to protect their identity.

No injury to any individuals is intended in this publication and if so is entirely coincidental.

A number of company names and buildings have closed down, changed hands or changed ownership prior to this publication. The chronology of the book should be viewed in light of that.

The information regarding medical Conditions and procedures may not be completely accurate and individuals with similar conditions should always seek their own medical advice.

Chapter 1

I WOKE UP

I woke up after my second major operation. I was very thirsty and I was choking from the oxygen mask, pulling it off all the time - not realising that it was there to help me breathe. I can remember my mum asking how I was feeling and my auntie May giving me sips of 'Tango', and trying to listen to them through the grogginess from the anaesthetic. I was so tired I fell into a deep sleep, and when I woke again it was just my mum and dad that were still there. I was able to talk to them a little, as the anaesthetic had worn off a bit by this time. My mum asked me how I was feeling.

I said, "I feel a lot better but I can hardly move and I'm still in a lot of pain." It was a long day. I had a number of visitors and I tried to keep myself awake and aware of what was going on around me but I just wanted to sleep. When night came and all my visitors had gone I took in my surroundings, listened to the nurses bickering back and forward to each other, cuddled up to my Garfield teddy that my granny had given me when I was eight, and fell fast asleep.

The following morning, I was feeling a lot better so the nurse got me sitting up in bed. I had a single room to myself so I had my own television and my own toilet facilities. As I sat watching the television it suddenly occurred to me that I hadn't heard anything from Neil. Neil was a boy that I knew from my days at the clinic. That's where we went, with a few other kids, to get physiotherapy. He was in the hospital at the same time as me, to have the same operation. I remember, the night before my operation hearing this strange noise. I decided to leave my room and check it out. As I got closer I began to realise what the noise was. It was coming from Neil's room. I knocked on the door and went in and called his name. He couldn't answer me from crying so much. I still couldn't find him though! I followed the sound of the crying and it was coming from the toilet. Reluctantly, I walked in. I found Neil sitting on the toilet. When I asked him what was wrong, he told me he was frightened about having his operation and he didn't think he could go through with it. I tried to give him some words of encouragement and talk him round. You see, Neil was like me, he had cerebral palsy but his was worse than mine. He was in a wheelchair and he couldn't talk very well. Because I had cerebral palsy too, I had some understanding of his situation. While I was sitting up in bed thinking about Neil, curiosity got the better of me, so I called for a nurse, on the buzzer, and asked where he was. She told me that he had gone home because he couldn't go through with his operation.

The nurse tried to get me on my feet that afternoon but I couldn't manage. The pain was like someone digging a knife into my hips when I tried to walk; like carrying a load of bricks on my legs. That night I had a dream that someone was cutting my arms and legs open with a very sharp knife. I was glad when I woke up in one piece but I was still in pain. I can't remember many visitors the day after my operation except for my mum and dad again and my little brother Michael. This time it was only during visiting hours though. After that it was quite boring, as I had nobody to talk to and nothing to do, apart from sit and watch television.

After my nightmare, I woke up to find a different nurse looking at me. I thought I'd landed in heaven! The nurse's name was Patricia. I know this because she had seen me wake up and introduced herself. She was a good-looking nurse, tall, with long brown hair and a nice friendly smile. I saw a Zimmer frame sitting at the bottom of my bed and I was wondering why this horrible thing was there. Zimmers were for old grannies and granddads. I said to myself, 'this isn't for a twelve year old boy' - but - sure enough the nurse said, "The Zimmer frame is for you". She said, "It's about time you started trying to walk again." So she got me on my feet and onto the Zimmer frame but I couldn't move an inch. After all, I had just had a major operation on my hips. I started to cry when I couldn't move because I thought, 'Am I going to be like this for the rest of my life.'

Cerebral palsy is a condition - not a disease. If a person has cerebral palsy, it means that part of their brain is not working properly. The cause of this may occur before they are born, around the time of birth or in early childhood. The affected area of the brain is usually one of the parts which control particular muscles and certain body movements. In some people, cerebral palsy is barely noticeable. Others can be more severely affected. The condition is more common than most people realise and it can affect people from all backgrounds. It's currently believed that about one in every 400 children is affected by cerebral palsy, ie. about 1,800 babies are diagnosed with cerebral palsy in Great Britain each year.

My mum had cheered me up that day though, by bringing me in a pizza. She had to ask the nurses if I could have it, first. The pizza was my favourite kind, ham and mushroom. I finished the lot, as I was so hungry after trying to eat the dreaded hospital food. I'd had a few visitors the first few days I was in hospital. My granny and granddad came to visit me on the third day and this was the sorest day. My granddad asked me how I was feeling and I told him I was very sore and he said to me, "The third day is usually the worst but it gets better after that". I think he was trying to make me feel better but it didn't help, I was still in a lot of pain. During that first week I had a lot of visitors. As well as my mum, dad, little brother, granny and granddad a lot of my aunties, uncles, cousins and my auxiliary from school came to visit, which was really nice. Cheryl, one of my cousins, brought me a plastic ring to go on my finger. She told me to squeeze it, and when I did, water came squirting out. She had one too and she was squirting water back at me. We had so much fun we soaked half my room. Still, it was only a little bit of water and soon dried up.

The operation was to straighten my upper body. It had been quite bent for some time. I had to get physiotherapy every day afterwards and that was extremely sore. The physiotherapists put sand bags on my feet and I had to lie on my stomach. I then had to try to bend my legs. I was also in the swimming pool for a few days during the two weeks, to try and develop movement in my legs again. To get in the pool I had to be lowered by a lift mechanism. I enjoyed this. Before I went to the pool the nurse had to change my dressings for waterproof dressings but the water still got through.

I was in hospital for two weeks, but I did get home at the weekend and watched World Cup 94 the whole two days. On my first night home, the stitches on my left leg burst open overnight. It wasn't really very sore but it was strange and off-putting looking at a gaping wound in my leg. My mum phoned the hospital. "What should she do?" They told her that it should be fine until morning and then to go to the doctor and he would re-stitch it for me. So we did – and it turned out okay. The reason I got to go home at the weekend was that there was no physiotherapy then so my mum did my exercises with me. After the few days at home it was back to hospital first thing Monday morning.

The few happy days I had in hospital were great because there was a special nurse. I can't remember her name but she was so beautiful. She had long blonde hair and cracking features. I still think about her today and wonder where she might be now. When I was able to walk better I chased her all over the ward, waiting for her at the lift because I knew when she started her shift, but I was only trying to be friendly. She played games with me if I was bored and walked and talked with me. This didn't last long as she got moved to another ward to do a training course. She was really upset when she got moved. She said she was going to miss me. When she'd gone I had a chat with one of her colleagues, Morvan. She told me a lot about nurses and how they work. That's when I realised that she couldn't get too friendly with her patients or she could lose her job. So, I decided to leave nurses alone after that. Thinking back, I've been a bit of a Casanova all my life, liking so many girls at one time. My first girlfriend was in Primary 3 and her name was Diana, I kissed her behind the waste bin, in the playground, so no one would see me. At the time, it felt as if the relationship lasted for ages but it was probably more like a fortnight.

One night, Top Gun was on television, so I decided to watch it. I had nothing else to do! Morvan came to see what I was up to and decided to join me. It's one of my favourite films. I think it was one of Morvan's too, though she may have watched with me *because* I was the only one that had a coloured television and a single room.

I needed the toilet one night so I buzzed for a nurse to come and take me. Neither Patricia, nor the other nurse was on duty so I had to make do with one of the night nurses. I didn't like this because she was very fat - and very rough. When she arrived, she brought a wheelchair with a hole in it, so it could fit over the toilet. By the time she came and we got to the toilet I was about peeing myself. She pulled my trousers down so fast and so roughly that she pulled my dressings off so they had to be replaced. She wasn't nice at all – but I didn't pee myself!

When it came time to go home, I couldn't wait - but I had to take the dreaded Zimmer frame home too.

The night I got home, it was a nice evening so I went out into the back garden with my Zimmer frame and played Frisbee with my dad. This was a bit boring because I could never catch the thing and Dad always had to go and fetch it for me so I went back in the house. I was glad to get back inside and give my little legs a little rest.

The school trip that I was supposed to go on, in Primary Seven, earlier that year, was to Broomlee. It was a week's camp for all Primary Sevens in the area, where they could meet and do activities with other children who were all going up to High School together. I never went on the trip. Mum didn't want me to hurt myself, as I was due for my operation in a few weeks. I was deeply upset that I didn't get to go. It would have given me a better chance in life, mixing with other people, but I just had to put the disappointment behind me and accept that I would meet up with them when I got to High School.

It was after my hip operation that the full realisation of my condition hit me - the rest of my life was going to be tough and it wasn't just cerebral palsy that was going to affect me.

Chapter 2

THE PRIMARY YEARS

I was born in a small, one bedroom flat in Cellardyke, one of the loveliest old fishing ports in Scotland. I lived there for a few years with my parents. My mum and dad both had four siblings. Mum had two brothers and two sisters while Dad had a brother more and a sister less. All the brothers and sisters on both sides had two or three children each. So I belong to quite a large family. We moved from our one-bedroom flat in Cellardyke into a much bigger two-bedroom house about a mile along the road in Anstruther when I was still a toddler and my young brother was just an infant. Mum and Dad called my brother Michael, as they liked the name, whereas I was named after my dad. I can still remember living in that one-bedroom house and I have memories of it, which in later life became vital to me.

I remember a lot about my childhood - a lot more than most people, it seems. I have memories of when I was only four years old and at nursery. I remember going out the old iron gate with the class and into a very large park to have a picnic. I also remember what I had for my 'piece' one day - a biscuit and a cup of chocolate flavoured milk. In toddler days everything seemed massive but looking back now everything was tiny. I also remember playing with a spinning top and some kid trying to steal it from me, and the nursery assistant telling them off. Everyone who has asked me what I can remember is surprised that I can remember this. A few years ago I spoke to a girl called Tanya who worked in a pub and told her that I remembered her from playgroup, before nursery. She was amazed that I remembered her from so long ago. When I was five, I wore spectacles but couldn't understand why – none of the other kids wore them. I just accepted that I had to wear them - and that was that! I was born with fair hair so because of my fair hair and glasses I was often nicknamed The Milky Bar Kid.

I started school a year later than everybody else because of my Cerebral Palsy. This didn't bother me but it did mean I was always the oldest pupil in class. I think the delay was also because Mum and Dad were concerned that kids would make fun of the way I walked. I remember my very first day at school. It was such a good day the class sat outside on a carpet and I remember eating a packet of fruit pastels during break time. Primary One classroom was full of bright colours, all the colours of the rainbow. There was a banner that ran along the full length of one wall. It had all the letters of the Alphabet on it. It started with a large A then a small a, large B then a small b and so on until it reached Z, z. The classroom had a sand pit with toys in it. The classroom desks and chairs *looked* enormous, but were probably so small I'd have to kneel on them now. The exercise books were colour-coded. The colour of each pupil's book depended on their progress. I remember Blue, Yellow, Red and Green books. These were for numbers and sums. Every time it was someone's Birthday in Primary One, the Teacher played a tune on a music box. It was made to sound as if it was playing Happy Birthday to that person. Everyone was so shocked that it sounded like their name when it played. We all, including me, thought it was magic. Everyone loved story time at school, especially me. I only vaguely remember most of the stories that were told in Primary One but I do remember the Chicken that thought the sky was falling down.

Although I had Cerebral Palsy, I did try to mix with my classmates and during break times I tried to join in the games in the playground. This was difficult as they all played hopscotch and ran about a lot, neither of which I could do. The best thing that I could do at break times was sit and watch.

Primary Two was quite different: a big step up from Primary One. Everything was getting harder, but I learned a lot of new things. There was a time when we had to make models out of wood. I made a model of my dad's van and it was very impressive, considering my age. I wrote 'Boats Van' for the registration plate (Dad was a fisherman) and couldn't understand why I was told off for it. I made a lot of them and finally discovered why I was always getting a telling off. I was spelling Boats wrong. I was saying 'Boots Van' instead and the teacher wouldn't let up till I spelt it correctly.

We had a project in Primary Two called insect week. We all had to go out into the school garden and look for as many different insects as we could find. We then had to put them all in a tub and take them back to the classroom and look them up in books to find out what they were. There was a blue beetle and we couldn't identify it in the books we had. When we returned in the morning the beetle was gone. The container the beetle was in was deep but didn't have a lid, so we came to the conclusion that the beetle had wings and flew away. We never did find out what kind of beetle it was.

I managed a lot better during breaks in Primary Two as I was a year older and now had my younger brother at school with me. I was able to join in games a lot more as I got older. We used to hog the train set every day and play with it until it was time to go home.

Nineteen-ninety, and Primary Three was a very rough year for my family and me as I had my first major operation on my heels. At the time I never thought I would be able to walk again. The operation was on my Achilles tendons. This was to lengthen them and allow me to put my heels flat on the ground. I don't know if I realised why I was in a hospital for an operation at eight years old. I probably didn't know what an operation was. All I remember really was playing with some children and thinking I was just there to play. When I went in later, to get my hips operated on I realised that it was the same ward as I had this operation in. The only difference was that there were now two sections to the ward - a children's section and an adult section on the same level.

I don't remember going downstairs for my operation. I remember people in white coats sticking things all over my body and my mum standing beside me. And I remember being told to count to ten. I only got to 3. I remember waking up in the recovery room and hearing a lot of people crying with pain - but I was fine.

I remember seeing white things on my feet and I didn't know what they were. Later, I found out that they were called 'stookies' – plaster casts. I was quite comfortable lying in the recovery room. When I got back to the ward I tried turning over but couldn't. Moving my legs was too painful. I can still remember the male nurse's name; he was called Gary. I remember this because I got a teddy from my granny while I was in hospital. It was 'Garfield', and I re-named him 'Gary' after the nurse. I used to wonder about Gary being a nurse. I actually thought he delivered letters. I still have 'Gary' today.

I needed a drink of juice one night but Mum had put the bottle on top of my bedside cabinet, just out of reach. I tried to call a nurse but the buzzer wasn't working so I decided I'd have to get it myself. It was quite difficult, and painful, but after a lot of stretching and straining I managed to get to my knees and reach the juice. After taking a long drink, I placed the bottle above my pillow and fell into a contented sleep. I was very proud the following day when I told Mum what I had done. She was not so pleased. Not quite homicidal – she didn't demand blood - but she insisted on having the buzzer fixed *immediately!*

I remember a girl in the next bed. She was the same age as me. She used to cry all night after her parents went home. Her dad would lie on the bed beside her until she went to sleep. Sometimes he fell asleep himself. I don't know why she cried all the time. Maybe she was frightened. I was supposed to go home after a few days but that didn't happen. My ankles were so painful I couldn't stand up so I had to stay another few days. The girl went home before me. Then I got a good night's sleep.

When I got home I was off school for weeks because I couldn't walk yet. I thought I would never walk again. I had never walked with my heels on the ground before and I was finding this very hard to cope with. Before this time my balance was quite poor and the operation seemed to make it worse. However, with perseverance and a lot of help from the physiotherapist this soon improved greatly.

I got Homework sent home for me from school to do. My cousin, Cheryl, helped me a lot with this. She's five years older than me so it was a piece of cake to her. I remember her helping me with my walking. She held my hand and walked me back and forth across the living room so many times I thought we would wear a hole in the carpet. With Cheryl's help and encouragement it wasn't long before I was able to 'go solo' and complete the course without holding on. Then it was back to school for more work - and play.

Before I went back to school, I had to get my 'stookies' off. The day I got the casts off, my feet looked tiny. As Dad was carrying me back to the car, walking along the corridor with me over his shoulder, I suddenly felt something wrong with my right foot. My stitches had opened up so it was back to outpatients to have it stitched up again.

My cousins - and me, all used to love visiting my grandparents. This was my mum's Mum and Dad. I saw more of them than Dad's side. We all called Granddad 'Dae', short for Granddad. Granny and Dae lived in a big house just up the road from us. It had two big living rooms, two bedrooms, a small box room, a bathroom, small toilet and a longish kitchen. It also had a large attic that used to be a bedroom for one of my uncles when he was young. The attic had a hatch and a ladder that had to be pulled down with a pole. We all used to play in that attic for hours at a time. The house had a beautiful big front garden with lots of different coloured plants. Alongside the house there was a big garage stuffed with all kinds of everything – except a car. That stood in the driveway. The back garden was even bigger than the front. The grass was beautifully manicured and a row of different shrubs stretched down one side. A swing, rhubarb patch and a tool shed completed the picture. My cousin John, who was a few years older than me, liked to read comic books. Books, like the Beano and the Dandy. He would always read the comics in the shed, as that's where they were kept. I began to wonder if he really was reading the books and one day I asked him, "Are you reading that book? You're not moving your lips." He said, "Of course. You don't have to read out loud. It's called silent reading". Well, that was a new one on me! We often used to play in that yellow shed with its many 'treasures' – and smells. Those were the days.

Granny was a lovely woman who liked a Sherry. My dae, a man that moaned a fair bit, liked a brandy. Dae would often sit in front of the television smoking his cigarettes and *often* fall asleep halfway through a programme. Sometimes we would ask, "Are you asleep Dae?" and he would answer, "No, just resting my eyes." Sometimes he didn't answer! Granny and me, we used to play word searches on her lap. I liked that. We used to play for hours. Other times, we would play *coconuts in the basket*. Actually, throwing a ball *very carefully* into a bucket so that it didn't bounce out.

For as long as my granny was alive, the whole family would come round for . . . now was it Christmas Dinner or New Year's Dinner? Anyway, there were so many of us I don't know how they got us all in! Mum and Dad would take us to Granny's every Christmas to write our letters to Santa. Michael and I would write a hopeful long list - with drawings - just in case Santa couldn't read our writing! Then we 'posted' it up the chimney. Mum had a clip-on Santa at that time. On the nights leading up to Christmas the clip-on Santa moved around the house, providing we were 'good boys', and when Christmas Eve came it would be on the front door, ready to open it for Santa. As I got older, my belief in Santa began to waver. One night, when we were at Granny's, Dad nipped home and moved Santa on to a new position. When we got home Michael and I noticed that Santa had moved, so I believed for a little longer! There was one Christmas when everyone but me got a Chocolate Santa. I was really upset. But then, one 'came down the chimney' just for me, the world started to shine again. Years later, I discovered that Auntie May had suggested to her son, Gordon, that she could give his one back to Santa and he would pass it on to me. I remember, it was Terry's chocolate. Well not really Terry's, not even Gordon's – it was mine, wasn't it. And – it was lovely. Ahh, Christmas – goodwill to all men - especially Gordon. I always liked that boy!

Granny and Dae both made great meals. One of their specialities was mince an' tatties. I used to mix mine together – still do, though I don't sculpt faces in them now or shape them into rows and say, "Dae is doing the Garden."

During 1990 the feeling around Granny's changed. Sometimes she would sit in the front room and put a band around her leg and pump it up. When I asked Mum and Dad what was wrong they would only say, "Granny's not very well". I didn't realise she was going to die. I didn't even know what cancer was, then. During the winter of 1990-1991 Granny was in and out of hospital a lot. Michael and I got to visit a few times but not very often. One night my other Grandparents came to 'baby-sit' while Mum and Dad went to the hospital. Mum was trying to give up smoking then but she ran out of the house with a cigarette in her hand. When I shouted, "Mum – you're smoking!" she got angry and threw it away. Michael and I were upstairs with my granddad, playing on a games console, when they came home. We rushed down the stairs to meet them and found Mum in tears. We were so upset we started to cry too. I asked her, "What's wrong Mum?" Through a great river of tears she managed to say, "Granny's passed away, boys." Granny died on the 17th of January 1991. She was only fifty-nine years old and the memory of her death is branded into my memory. The cancer she died from is often curable now – too late for Granny. Mum took it especially bad. She was the only one of Granny's children at her bedside and still wears her ring to this day. Michael and I stayed off school for a few days and I wanted to go to the funeral but I was only nine – and Mum said I was too young.

But I wasn't too young to feel the pain of a great loss.

I was in Primary Four when Granny passed away. My physiotherapist came to the house every second Wednesday afternoon to give me quite strenuous exercises. That meant I had to finish school early every second Wednesday. She was an older lady, about the same age as my granny, maybe even a little older. She wasn't very clean! She had an aviary in her garden and had six dogs. She always brought the dogs with her in the car and she would trail dog pooh into our house. Sometimes she would have birdseed in her hair. As much as I didn't like her, she was very good at her job – and very firm with me! She wouldn't let up until I did each exercise perfectly. I used to hate her visits because she was quite gruff but if it hadn't been for her I wouldn't be coping as well as I do today. However, every Wednesday was football training at school and it meant that every second Wednesday I couldn't go. She never did find out that I played football. If she had she would probably have killed me because I wasn't supposed to play. I enjoyed it though, so I never told her. I was never fit for playing outfield so I was always the goalie, which was fine as I was quite good in goals.

I rarely ever had school lunches. Mum always sent us to school with a packed lunch. One of my cousins had the same. That was Marissa, Auntie May's youngest daughter. She only stayed round the corner so we met up on the way to school. Everyone with a packed lunch had to pile them up on top of each other, next to the school office. Lunch was in the assembly hall. We ate our lunch away from the main tables where the 'school dinners' sat. The 'packed lunch area' was on the steps leading up to the stage. I remember eating lunch and watching ants crawling across the steps! Meat in your veg! Anyone? I had bananas for lunch so often that I became well known as 'banana man'. The nickname caught on and followed me right through Primary School.

At lunch time the boys played football in the playground – every day. For a long time I sat and watched but eventually they asked me to play. That was great. The playground was tar macadam so I didn't go in goals, as I couldn't risk diving about, which I loved to do on grass, so I tried playing outfield. If we had a corner someone would lift me up so I could head the ball into the goal.

I often hung around with the girls at school too, and some of my 'crimes' from those days have come back to haunt me. A girl who used to live at the end of our street reminded me, years later. When I bumped into her one-day she said, "Do you remember when we were wee and you used to tie us to the school gates with our school ties?" I had forgotten about that – honestly! The girl was called Elaine. She had a younger sister, Laura, and an older sister called Lisa. I went out with two of them. Not at the same time! My brother went out with the youngest one. This became a repeating pattern for us. The five of us played a lot together as we were all about the same age. Elaine was a year younger than me but was in my class as I started a year late. Lisa was the same age but a year above me; Laura was the same age as Michael.

Elaine often sat beside me at school and we got on well. But there *was* a time when I drank her milk by mistake and she turned into a madwoman! She was a real fiery character. I apologised – profusely. I enjoyed Primary Four and Five the best as I had my favourite teacher for both of them. I think Mrs Nee was in her early sixties. She specialised in mathematics but taught many other things as well. Like, how to keep us in line! I also had Elaine beside me for most of Primary Four and Five. This is when Sean kept running out of class.

It was so funny - he couldn't take a telling off. Any time Mrs Nee would tell him off, he would start to cry and run out of the classroom and down the street.

Mrs Nee always held a drama class for the older pupils in the school and entered us into a competition each year. About 20 different schools took part in the competition. The theatre for the event was huge and the stage was a lot bigger – and better than the one we rehearsed on. I always liked taking part but I enjoyed watching the other schools too. There was one show in particular that I liked. They were dancing to the 'Final Countdown' and climbed up on each other to form a tower. It was an amazing sight. I can't remember much about the shows *we* did – except that they were never very good. More of a 'song and a dance' than a drama! We tried our best but we were just not cut out to be thespians. Yet, we did get an award for being - the best-behaved school – and that was nice. On the way home from one of the shows I got into a bit of trouble. You see, on the bus there was a button that said, DO NOT TOUCH, so of course I pressed it! I thought it was hilarious when the bus driver did an emergency stop. Unfortunately for me, the driver didn't see the funny side and so I got three rows for the price of one – one from the driver, one from Mrs Nee and another when I got home.

In 1992, I won the school's bicycle safety test. I found the test quite easy, really, especially the 'slow cycle' part. You had to cycle as slowly as possible without falling off. Piece o' cake for me, as mine's was the only bike fitted with stabilisers!

I got on well with everyone at school apart from Sean. He never liked me and he used to do everything he could to tease me. One day in the middle of winter, it was very icy and I was standing next to a huge puddle. He took a long run and then slid into me so that

I fell into the puddle. I was saturated. Mum wasn't very pleased when she had to bring me a whole set of dry clothes. If she could have laid her hands on Sean . . .

From Primary Three to Primary five, I took my bike to school, the bike with the famous stabilisers. Because my balance was poor I had to use it to get around school, a fact that tickled most people. I even took it to the Christmas Parties. When my walking improved, I started walking to school, after all, it was only a couple of minutes around the corner – and that's when I started coming in late. One day, in maths, I overheard the teacher talking to someone about a wheelchair for me. Well, I freaked and ran out of the classroom because my mum told me she never wanted to see me in a wheelchair. Of course, they soon caught up with me and wanted to know what was wrong. So I told them. Nothing was ever mentioned about a wheelchair again.

I won a lot of prizes at school, including one for winning the 'Rabbie Burns' poem competition on two consecutive years. Speaking the Scottish 'twang' wasn't hard, and my brother Michael came second in the competition, both years. The winning poems I recited were The Kirk Moose and The Boy in the Train. I think I won because I emphasised the words and made hand gestures during the readings. No one else did that. I remember most of the words to those poems. Some of the words I remember from the Boy in the Train are:

> Is yon the mune I see in the sky?
> It's awfy' wee an' curly,
> See! there's a coo and a cauf ootbye,
> An' a lassie pu'in' a hurly!
>
> He's chackit the tickets and gien them back,
> Sae giy me ma ain wan, Daddy.
> Lift doon the bag frae the luggage rack,

For the next stop's Kirkcaddy!'

For this poem I was pointing to the moon in the sky and the coos in the field. The Kirk Moose was the first poem I did and some of the words from that poem that I remember are;

I'm a wee kirk moose and I havn't got a name,
But thon muckle kirk at the corner is ma hame,
Wi the cock on the steeple and the bell that gangs "DING!"
I wish that I was big enough to gaur it gie a ring.

I can sing aw the psalms, I can say aw the prayers,
and I whiles do a dance, up and doon the pulpit stairs.
I ken aw the texts, I can find them in the book,
and there's mony a human-bein' wi' nae notion where to look.'

A new boy came to our school in Primary Six after he was expelled from his previous school. He was a bit of a nasty guy and played a lot of tricks on us. One day he came into school and told us that he had played the 'Weegy' board and told us all the things that had happened. Sometime after this, my face started going bright red and he said, "The Weegy board says that if you see someone's face go red it'll go so red that it'll burst and they'll die" I believed him and ran to the toilets to try and cool it down. Eventually though, we grew to like each other and I landed up going to his house a few times for tea.

Some of us got into trouble with The Police in Primary Six. In front of the school there was a garden, which we converted into a gang base – destroying the garden in the process! We took saws and cut up branches we had broken off the trees to transform the garden into hideouts. The school, and a few police officers, held an assembly for Primary Fives to Sevens, to find out who was involved and some neighbours identified a few of us. Mrs Nee was shocked when I confessed to being involved. We were all given a very severe warning from The Police. It didn't stop us doing it all again, somewhere else though.

Primary Seven was the hardest year at Primary School because I was the oldest in the class, and therefore the oldest in the school (I was growing up). That was the year I missed Broomlee and had my second major operation. It was also the year I got dragged out of class for something I didn't do and got in trouble over girls.

I was sitting in class one-day working hard and someone had let off (broke wind). For some reason the whole class blamed me, but it wasn't me. It happened again so I got dragged out of class. My mum had something to say when I got home and she found a nasty bruise on my arm. She marched right back to the school and confronted the teacher who had done it. He hadn't been able to handle the situation himself and had dragged me to Mrs Nee's class. When he told Mum what it was all about she got really angry and told him that I would never do a thing like that. Luckily, the Headmistress intervened to calm things down before Mum could do any real damage!

I remember a whole lot of small things from Primary Seven. Like ringing the school bell. Everyone in Primary Seven took turns in doing this, on a rota system. Some of us used to try to outdo each other: each trying to ring the bell louder than the rest. Then there was 'Rounders'. We played this every Friday afternoon. I really enjoyed that because I was a strong batter. Maybe I developed my arm muscles more than other kids as a consequence of my leg problems. On the other hand, I couldn't run very well so it's just as well I kept battering the ball over the school wall - each one scored me a home run!

Being a bit of a Casanova I was never short of girlfriends, right through Primary School. But it backfired on me when one girl complained and made a big fuss when I asked her out. It developed into such a row that the teacher kept us in after school and made us apologise to each other before we could go home.

Before we went to High School I was asked if there was anyone I didn't want to be in the same class with. I said, "Just keep Sean away from me, please." Guess what! - Sean, was in all my classes!

Dad was away from home quite a bit over the years. He had his own fishing boat that he co-owned with Dae. They'd be away for about ten days and only home for four, every two weeks. Like Dad, most of Mum's brothers worked at sea and they also had their own boats. Mum would be left on her own most of the time, to look after Michael and me. A fisherman's wife has to be very good with money. Sometimes Dad would come home with loads of money; other times he'd almost be empty handed. That's what it's like for fishermen. Your pay depends on what you catch; plenty fish - plenty money, nothing landed - empty handed.

Like most married couples, Mum and Dad had their share of fall-outs. Dad would sometimes disappear down the pub and drink a bit too much, or go onto the boat and stay there for a while. Sometimes, Mum would storm out and go for a drive and leave the three of us with our faces tripping us. But that wasn't too often and most of the time we all got on really well. In fact, Michael and I felt very much loved by both our parents. Michael and I have always been close, no matter what came along. From an early age, Mum used to dress us in matching clothes; shell suits, school clothes, even pyjamas - always the same. Just like the proverbial 'peas in a pod' we were. One exception was shoes. I always had to have special shoes because of the Cerebral Palsy! I suppose all brothers fight sometimes and Michael and I were no different. In fact, *we* seemed to fight every other day. Being disabled, you might think I would always come off worse - not so. Michael would often try to pin me down but because of my upper body strength, I would always manage to wrestle out of his grip. One time I just threw my arms back and he ran away. Not really so surprising - as I'd just caught him on the nose and he was running to the bathroom to stop the bleeding!

As Michael and I were quite close in age, we often played the same games. One favourite game was building models out of Lego. We had a huge bucket of Lego - talk about a wheelie bin! We must have had a ton of bricks: years of presents from Mum and Dad. We built fire stations, police stations, treasure islands, pirate ships, cargo planes and many, many more. After we'd built them, we'd take them apart again - and build them again. Early lessons in recycling! When we took everything apart, the Lego bricks completely covered the floor of our bedroom. Mum liked the Lego too. She got a bit of well-earned peace when we were upstairs for hours building ever more complicated models. Sometimes we, and our cousins, would have competitions to see who could make the best model. To us kids, it was a fantastic hobby. The only thing we didn't like about the Lego was tidying it up when we were finished!

Sometimes I would get quite upset because of my disability. Michael would never show his emotions for me, but I think it upset him too. One night my heels were so painful that I couldn't even walk from my bed to our snooker table although it was only a few feet away. Mum was quite upset that night. She thought I should have managed with ease. For a long time I had to wear full-length splints in bed to keep my legs straight while I slept. I absolutely hated this, as I had to lie more or less in the same position all night – or I would have, if I'd kept them on. Fact is I'd often rip the bandages off because the splints were so uncomfortable. Strange to tell, Michael also had to be bandaged up at night as he suffered with eczema – and he too would tear his bandages off, overnight. Poor Mum and Dad – the floor of our bedroom was covered in bandages most mornings, after we'd undone all their good work.

Michael and I loved watching Thunder Cats on television. We often used to imitate the characters, wearing nothing but underpants. But not just one pair; we had about five pairs on. We would take all the towels from Mum's airing cupboard and lay them all over the house and jump from towel to towel, flashing our Thunder Cats swords.

Superman was another of our heroes and we both wore Superman pyjamas when we were little. One day Michael decided he could fly. Imagine Mum's surprise when she got a phone call from a neighbour telling her that her son was standing on top of the garage preparing to fly. Luckily Mum got to him in time otherwise it wouldn't have been a rescue but a disaster.

Hide and seek was a popular game in our street. We'd always play when it was dark as it was harder to be found. There must have been twenty to thirty kids played. I used to love playing hide and seek but never could get back to base in time, as I couldn't run fast enough. Often, I found really good hiding places; so good they would give up looking for me and start a new game. That would really annoy me. "That's not fair,"

I'd say, "you should find everyone before you start a new game." I'd as well have been playing Man Hunt for the time that it took to find me.

Through the years the movement in my body became easier thanks to my physio and my determination. I was supposed to do my exercises with Mum between my physiotherapist's visits. Sometimes I didn't feel much like it but I always got them done. I had no choice, Mum made me do them. One day, the physio brought a set of parallel bars along, which sat in the hall for ages; a hideous eyesore. Eventually I did use them and got a great benefit from them. Sometimes, the physio would get one or two dogs to chase me through the bars, knowing I was petrified of dogs. Not fair! One of the exercises I had to do involved putting two tins of beans in a bag and tying the bag in the middle so the bag could hang over my foot, with a tin on each side. I then had to lift the makeshift weights off the floor, lying flat on my back. It was hard work but the exercises made me more supple so that I was able to do a lot more of the things I wanted to.

As my legs got stronger I was able to play more football. I was never strong enough to play outfield so it was always goalie for me. I was always picked first as I was a really good goalkeeper and rarely let a goal in. I never liked an opponent hitting the ball low along the ground as it was difficult for me to get down that low but a level shot or just above my head was no problem. We would play throughout each summer up in the local park and it was really good to get involved. As well as playing football, a crowd of us would go to watch our local football team, East Fife, either in my dad's van or my uncle's van. There must have been about eight of us. We would go along each week when Dad was home from the sea. We wouldn't just go to home games; we would support 'The Fifers' at away games as well. When we were young, we wouldn't really pay attention to the game, we would just play instead but when we got older we stood and watched the game. All the younger fans like me would stand behind the goals and throw chewing gum golf balls at the keeper's legs. We'd pop across to the local shop to buy about fifty of these balls and then waste them, by throwing them at the opposition keeper. If East Fife scored, which wasn't often, we would jump around like idiots. Those were the days.

When I was about eight, I started to go regularly to Auntie May's house, to play with my older cousin, Gordon. I didn't really think of Gordon so much as a cousin, more as an older brother. We would play football on his games console most of the time. I hardly ever won; he was too good for me. One game we used to play was International Superstar Soccer on the Nintendo. I sometimes beat him but not very often. Sometimes I would panic and kick the ball out accidentally. Gordon thought this was hilarious and would rag me for hours afterwards. I loved Gordon like I did all of my family.

Chapter 3

THE BIG ONE

No one knew if I would cope in a mainstream High School but I had no intention of attending a special school. Some people thought I wouldn't manage in mainstream but there were others that thought I would. I was wrong about High School. It was a *lot* different *and* it was bigger than Primary School. It had stairs and long corridors. It had lots of classrooms and over fifty teachers. Yeah - it was different. I think this is why some people thought I wouldn't cope with the sheer size of the place. But I wanted to go to Waid Academy. Before moving up, all Primary Sevens had a three-day induction in the final term of Primary School, just to give them a taste of what was to come. This was my first time meeting people from other schools as I had missed out on the trip to Broomlee. I knew some of them from playing with them out of school. The idea of the induction was to get familiarised with the school layout, the classrooms and meet some of the teachers. It didn't take me long to find a girl I liked during the induction. That was Aileen. I don't know how but I seemed to know her from somewhere before and she knew me too. I couldn't figure out how we knew each other, as I didn't go to Broomlee. Anyway, I asked her out. No, come to think about it, I didn't; someone else asked her for me. She wasn't as gutless as me as she came to me herself and told me that she couldn't go out with me but wanted to be friends, so I left it there.

   I had an auxiliary all through Primary and I was still going to need one at High School. Her name was Anne. She would carry my bag from class to class and help me with my work. I didn't really want an auxiliary because I wanted to look normal in front of everyone at Waid, but I did need one. There was no lift in the school so when my class was upstairs, I had to walk up the stairs. The only classes that were upstairs were English, Geography, and Art and Design, so I would only be up stairs two or three times a week. All the other classes such as Music, Science, Physical Education, Mathematics, Modern Studies, 'Techy' and History were on the ground floor. In fact, History and Modern Studies were outside in huts and I had to walk quite a distance to get there. There was also a separate part of the school across the road which was called South Waid and had Business Studies and Home Economics. It did look a big school, but there are far bigger schools in the area, with more of everything - more classrooms and teachers, for example. We had a very small swimming pool, which we called 'The Puddle' because it was only twenty metres in diameter. I knew the school fairly well before going there because it's also a Community Centre. It opened at night for night classes and at the weekends for other activities. Every summer there was a play scheme in the town, for children. I used to attend it with my brother and some of my cousins. The Waid's pool was made available for the play scheme and we'd use it most Friday nights; Michael, Hayley, Marissa and me. I must confess our unruly antics often annoyed the pool attendant. Jumping and bombing were frowned on as safety risks but what really wound the attendant up were the times when we boys would pretend to get changed, then after a few minutes we'd run into the pool area and jump in, in the nude, just for a laugh.

When I got to High School I was amazed to see so many beautiful girls - I thought I had landed in heaven. There was one special girl. She did a lot for me. She often asked me, "Will you be able to walk properly when your legs are straight?" I'd always say,

"We'll see, Louise." I knew the answer but I didn't want to disappoint her. We sat together for the most part of First and Second year, especially in Science. A few of my cousins were already at High School when I arrived, like Hayley, Kev, John and Gordon, but I think Cheryl had left school by then. It was very reassuring to have them there to look out for me when I was troubled or sometimes bullied. They all had their own friends but I knew that they would always be there *for me*. Kev and Dave, my brothers age, but a good friend of mine now, would help me in the canteen with my food. I think they offered to help because they always got to jump the queue with me – and they were allowed to leave their classes early. We often sat at the same table at lunchtime, which made things much easier for me.

A lunch club was held every day by some of the Learning Support staff, including Anne, Brenda, Linda and Jenny. The club was supposed to be for people with learning difficulties, but I was allowed to go. The Learning Support staff were in place for pupils that had difficulties reading or writing and although I didn't have learning difficulties it was nice to know that they were there if I needed help with my class work. I became quite attached to Brenda and Jenny. Brenda, I think was in her early fifties. She was quite small and slightly deaf. Jenny was probably in her early forties, with dark hair. She was a giant, over six feet tall but a big softy who had enough time for everyone and rarely raised her voice or told you off. They both had hearts of gold. After Christmas in First Year I did need quite a lot of support because just before Christmas, I went for major operation number three, and that was extremely uncomfortable.

This operation was one of the most promising, but

also one of the most painful. The one I had on my hips, the previous year, gave me a lot of pain but – worse was yet to come. The operation came roughly two weeks before Christmas and was on my hamstring muscles. I was in the same ward as the previous time but in a different part. This time I was in a room with three old men - and one television! The old man in front of me was very grumpy. The one next to him didn't say much at all but the man beside me was fine and we talked quite a lot. I don't remember much about preparing for the operation apart from lying in the ward doing nothing all evening, the day before. In the morning I was quite thirsty so I reached out to grab my bottle of Coke and it wasn't there. All my drinks and sweets had been moved and I wondered why. The man beside me saw this and called for a nurse. While we waited, he told me that I wasn't allowed anything to eat or drink before the operation. When the nurse came I told her that I was thirsty and she brought me a little water.

I remember this operation as if it were yesterday; this time they didn't ask me to count to ten, just told me how they were going to put me to sleep - and did it. Mum was beside me all the time. So off to sleep I went, saying goodbye to Mum. I think I fell asleep before I got all the words out.

I woke up in the ward screaming my head off. My left leg was fine but the pain in my right leg was so bad I wanted to cut it off. Emergency! The doctor ran downstairs for some instruments and then ran all the way back up again. After he cut the plaster off I felt a great relief - and so did everyone else. Mum had dissolved in tears - she didn't understand what was wrong. Happily, it was just that the plaster was too tight - panic over. After a short rest I was back in the plaster room getting a new plaster fitted. When I was returned to the ward, I was given a machine with a button to press in the event I had severe pain – turned out that this was most of the time!

In hospital, I had some magazines and a television that I had to share with the grumpy old men. One day I was watching Gladiators on the tele. In the slow bits, I was reading my magazines when the old man in front of me suddenly got up and changed the channel. I said, "Hey, I was watching that!" He just curled his lip. "No you weren't, you had your head buried in that Magazine!" Mum came in a few minutes later so I told her what he had done and she said, "I'll show him!" She marched to the television and put it back on to Gladiators. The man got even grumpier and said, "Your boy wasn't watching the programme." Mum got quite angry, "Yes he was," she said, "and he wants to watch it now!" The man sitting beside me piped up, "He was actually watching it - and so was I." Mr Grumpy just turned his head away.

I was very sore from time to time so I had to keep pressing the PPA system but even this didn't completely relieve the pain. I don't think it was working properly. This time in hospital was very different. Maybe because it was close to Christmas, I didn't have as many visitors – and I was bed-bound. I had to be washed in bed and when I needed the toilet it was a case of using a bottle or a bedpan. Sometimes I would fall asleep while I peed in the bottle and then I got in the habit of keeping the bottle between my legs until it was full. When the nurse finally got around to collecting it she would say, "You must have been bursting!" I would just smile.

I couldn't chase the nurses round the ward like I had done previously. I was in bed for over a week but it was when the doctor got me on my feet again that I got pain like I had never experienced before. I really thought my legs were going to burst. It seemed like I had grown a few feet taller. I couldn't believe how straight I was - the straightest I've ever been. I actually reached the height that I was supposed to be - five foot six inches. I was in hospital for just under two weeks and got home on the 23rd of December. Before I went home, I had to walk around the ward. That was very difficult but the nurse tried me with elbow crutches and then I managed fine. It looked like I was going to be using crutches for the rest of my life. My physiotherapist wanted to see me, so we popped round on the way home. She was delighted with the outcome but noticed that my ankles were swollen so told me to spend plenty time with my feet up. She put me through hell to get me mobile again. She would do anything to help and every hospital appointment I had to see the doctor, she was there too.

The next four weeks were a nightmare. That was because I had 'stookies' on *both* legs for the first time and so I didn't have the same freedom. I had to go backwards up stairs, pulling myself up, one step at a time. When Christmas morning came, at first I couldn't be bothered opening my presents. I found it difficult in my two-stookies state! When I finally did open them I was delighted. I got a Nintendo game – a silly racing game but I enjoyed it. A few days later I got severe pains again. This time it wasn't in my hamstring muscles. The stookies had been rubbing against my knees and they were very sore. I couldn't sleep at night. I had to try sleeping, sitting up but I couldn't sit up forever. So, back into hospital again, immediately after Christmas, to open up the stookies and insert foam pads to prevent the rubbing. When I finally got rid of them, wasn't I glad to see the back of those stookies but then I wished they were back on again because the pain that was to come was worse than ever.

After New Year it was straight back to school again. I didn't cope well, although the full-length stookies were now off. I wasn't allowed to bend my legs; I had to try and keep them straight. I had to sleep with 'half stookies' on and then go to school with them as well because without them I would have collapsed. After I got the 'half-stookies' off I had to manage without any support. One day in Maths, my right leg gave way and I started to fall. The teacher caught me and with all of her strength she managed to keep me up. Everyone in class was worried about me, but I knew that I would be fine, eventually. There was a time when I was at home, playing Nintendo with Michael. I was standing with the remote control and my legs suddenly gave way. As I fell, I was hanging between a desk and Michael's bed and screaming in pain. Dad was in the next room and ran to my rescue. He lifted me up and slowly and carefully stretched my legs out again. I felt much better after a lie down but it was a frightening experience.

After a number of weeks with my legs straight I couldn't bend them. The physiotherapist gave me a hard time getting me to bend them again. It was a very painful experience but it paid off in the long run. The same physiotherapist worked with me through all my operations. Her exercises helped me to cope much better with life. I didn't want to do them but I had no real choice. For some reason, she's never been back since I turned sixteen. The idea of this latest operation was to lengthen my hamstring muscles so that I could fully straighten my legs. To do this the muscles had to be cut and rejoined. It was painful but worth it. The difference was quite amazing.

The operation was performed by Orthopaedic surgeons. Surgery is often recommended when spasticity and stiffness are severe enough to make walking difficult or painful. For many people with cerebral palsy, improving the appearance of how they walk – their gait- is also important. A more upright gait with smoother transitions and foot placements is the primary goal for many children and young adults. In the operating room, surgeons can lengthen muscles and tendons that are proportionately too short. First of all they have to determine the specific muscles responsible for the problem. This can be quite difficult. It makes more than thirty major muscles, working at the right time and using the right amount of force, to walk two strides with a normal gait. A problem with any of these muscles can cause an abnormal gait.

As the body makes natural adjustment to compensate for muscle imbalances, these adjustments could appear to be the problem, instead of compensation. Doctors have to rely on clinical examination, observation of the gait, and the measurement of motion and spasticity to determine the muscles involved. A Diagnostic technique, known as 'gait analysis' is now used. Gait analysis uses cameras that record how an individual walks, force plates that detect when and where feet touch the ground, a special recording technique that detects muscle activity and a computer program that gathers and analyses the data to identify the problem muscles. Using gait analysis, doctors can precisely locate which muscles would benefit from surgery and how much improvement in gait can be expected.

It's recommended that the operation be carried out when a patient is a child or young adult, as recovery time then is shorter – typically, up to a year. I recovered from the physical effects in about six months. However, I don't think I will ever fully recover psychologically, from the operation, as I think about it all the time. It was quite an ordeal.

Chapter 4

OVER THE RAIL

In Second Year at High School we went to Edinburgh Zoo. The Science and English departments arranged the trip. When we got there, they wanted to put me in a wheelchair provided by the Zoo, to get me about quicker. I wasn't too keen but eventually I agreed because it was only for a few hours. It wasn't so bad because I had Louise to push me around the Zoo and also the auxiliary, who at that time was Graham, a good friend of mine now. The reason I didn't want to go in a wheelchair was because I didn't want to undo all the good work that I had gone through to get on my feet. We had great fun that day. There was a point when I tried to wheel myself but I was on a hill and just about in the bear pit before Graham caught me. We wandered away from the rest of the group and explored the Zoo on our own. From time to time we bumped into the rest of the class. At the monkey house we were amused at the antics of a group of small monkeys. And even more amused when it turned out one monkey's intentions were to catch the female and take her from behind.

It was a super day out – a scorching day with a clear blue sky. I think many people go to the Zoo to see one thing in particular – the Penguin Parade. I had never seen this before and it was quite magnificent watching hundreds of birds marching in a line. It's a pity we couldn't get women doing the same. I was quite sad when the day ended.

We went on another trip to The Discovery in Dundee in the same year. I found this trip very boring.

The only good thing about it was that they had a special director's area downstairs on the bus where I got to sit with Graham. This had its good points and its bad points. Yeah I was happy sitting with Graham, but I would have liked to spend it with my classmates too. The trip was all about a ship called Discovery anchored at Dundee's waterfront. It's supposed to be famous for Captain Scott's trip to the South Pole and we were there to learn the history behind it, but Graham and I weren't really interested.

Every year at school there were three discos held in the main assembly hall. These were to mark Valentine's Day, Halloween and Christmas and I went to most of them. At one of these parties, I was shocked to catch Louise kissing someone passionately, in the cloakroom. There was obviously a bit of jealousy there. I hated seeing Louise kissing another guy when I thought there was something between us. The guy she was kissing was a bit of a troublemaker too, so I thought she was getting in with the wrong crowd. It turned out that it was just a fling and I ended up going out with her for a while after that. It didn't last long though, like all the other girls I went out with, but it was good while it lasted.

I was quite a popular guy at school and went out with several of the local girls. But in the summer of 1995 I went out with one particular girl - and this time it lasted quite a while. The only thing was, she was only ten years old. But she was stunning. I was thirteen by this time and it was great. Although she stayed in Pittenweem, only a mile away, we hadn't met. We only got together because my cousin, Cheryl, was going to cut her big sister's hair and I went along with her. I had gone with Cheryl to see my friend but didn't realise he had such a good-looking sister. I went out with her for a year but it eventually ended in misery. It got to the stage I no longer wanted to live; I wanted to commit suicide. Everything had been going great with my operations and things, but my love life wasn't. I didn't think anyone could stop me ending it all – but I was wrong. My cousin Marissa came to my rescue.

I was all set to go over the cliff railings at Pittenweem braes. I had a lot of girl trouble and wanted my legs perfect like everyone else's, but I am glad that Marissa was there for me and brought me out of it. I would have put so many people through so much pain and sorrow and I wouldn't be here today if it wasn't for her. I was 14 years old by this stage. As I was coming round, my foot slipped, but I managed to grab the bottom rail. I was hanging there not sure what to do, I was getting tired and Marissa and my girlfriend were trying to pull me up. I was getting really worried and losing my grip, but I managed to use all the strength that I had left to pull my self up and get a foot hold and climb back over the rail. Once back over the rails, I collapsed with exhaustion.

When people heard that I was going out with the Pittenweem girl they started picking on us – name-calling and that sort of thing. At the time, we thought it was the real thing but looking back now I realise that it was a terrible mistake and I think she does as well. We really liked each other a lot and although we both agreed to end it, I was devastated. I remember the day we broke up, she and Marissa came to see me at my house; she was all in pink with her long blonde hair. We went out for a walk and that's when she ended it. She only came along to tell me it was over and then went off to catch the bus home again.

In Third Year I met a guy called Phill. He had seen me around but never thought to come and say hello but this day he did. Phill was from Edinburgh. A lot of people saw him as a geek with his long dark hair and thick, black-framed glasses, but I saw him differently; I gave him a chance. I began to hang around with him more than anyone else at school. He sat next to me in classes such as Art and History and I would go along to his house and he would come to mine. He was a nice, friendly boy who was trying to fit in to the community. We had a lot of fun together and he started to hang around with Dave and me at lunch times. He started to go to the lunch club with us as well. The club was getting quite big by this time. I liked going to Phill's after school and at nights I would often walk along to get some exercise. Phill lived in an upstairs flat. All the houses in his street were upstairs and downstairs flats. Some of the upstairs flats had their attic converted into a bedroom. In Phill's house this was his bedroom. His mum and dad's, and sisters' rooms were on the lower level. Phill was never a football fan; he was into motor racing. I tried to get him into football but it just never happened. Sometimes we would play games on his Playstation, racing games and fighting games and he would always win.

One day, when I was fourteen, I was outside with my family, in the back garden when I noticed that my dad seemed to be checking my hair. When I asked him why he was staring, he said, "I'm staring because I think I see some dark roots coming through." That was the start of me losing my Milky Bar Kid looks. Mum, Dad and Michael all had dark hair. I was the only blond and I was pleased that my hair was finally getting darker. I was getting a little bit tired of being called the Milky Bar Kid.

Phill and I were at a disco one night and went outside to get some fresh air. We sat on the steps for a while talking to a couple of girls. After a while I went back in to the disco and asked a girl for a dance. Her name was Cherie and she was very nice. She accepted my offer and we stretched the one dance to four, before the disco ended. Cherie was not very tall but with long blonde hair and a lovely smile. She was a very friendly girl. I thought we were very attracted to each other and I did something I shouldn't have; I started going for walks around by her house when one of my cousins told me where she lived. After about a week I plucked up the courage and went to her front door and asked if she would like to come out for a walk. She said she couldn't because she had homework to do but I didn't believe her. Some of her friends found out about my interest in Cherie but couldn't believe that I was walking round by her house and told me to prove it. When I drew them a picture of her house they changed their mind but then started to call me a stalker, which I suppose was true - but with the very best intentions.

I still went for walks but on my way one night, I saw some of my friends playing football so I stopped to watch. I was just about to walk off again when they asked me to play in goals so I did. I played really well. I think I only let in one goal, the whole night so they asked me to come again. I was quite pleased at that and said "Okay then, I enjoyed it tonight. See you guys later". I went along several times but eventually I got a bit tired of playing football so I would start my journey but then turn around and go home again. I seemed to be missing a lot when I was playing football, even my favourite team, Arsenal, playing live on television. I was still walking on crutches, of course.

A lot of my friends went to a youth club on a Friday night so I started to go as well. We mostly played pool and snooker all night. We ran a competition every week, with a can of juice for the winner. I didn't win much! There was another club on the same night, from eight till ten so we would go to it at about half past eight, after an hour at the earlier one. I was chuffed when I discovered that Cherie went to the second club. I confess I made a fool of myself more than once. I was often there before her and when she finally came in I would pretend to faint. What we do for love!

I decided to back off a bit when the summer came. I still liked her a lot but I decided to play it cool. I drew her pictures in Art and made her a dolphin in Home Economics and kept giving her small presents. We became friends more than anything else and eventually, after a while, started hanging around with each other. I'm glad we became good friends as I was really getting obsessed with her. Michael had a weights bench, which I would often lie on, in the bedroom, on my own, and listen to a song that made me think of Cherie. The song was, 'I Need You' by 3T. I used to put it on repeat and listen to it for hours - and feel sorry for myself. When Mum would shout on me for tea I would take ages to come down, as I had to get myself together first. When we became good friends we would play badminton and do a lot of things together, which helped me get over the feelings that I had for her.

Chapter 5

THE HANGIN' BOY

It was a lovely warm, summer evening and I decided to get the bus to Pittenweem to visit Phill. He wasn't in when I arrived but because I didn't think he would be far away I sat on the kerb outside his house – and waited. After a while, I was beginning to get a bit weary when a car pulled up. Phill and his mum got out and Phill asked if I'd been waiting long.

I said, "A fair bit - I was just about to go home."

Anyway, it was good that he turned up and we decided to have a kick-about in his back garden. His dog had other ideas and kept stealing the ball from us, running away with it. The dog was a little black Manchester terrier, bred for hunting rats. Phill once told me that Merlin would never harm anyone; that she would be okay with anyone already in the house but got a little bit upset when people knocked on the door. I took him at his word and, anytime I visited, always made sure I was standing well back when Phill answered the door. After a while we gave up trying to outwit this little black and tan thief and went inside to play some computer games.

It was still a beautiful evening so, when I decided to go home, I set off on my own, on my crutches. It was roughly a mile from Phill's house to mine and I'd walk the distance quite regularly to keep myself fit. It would usually take me around half an hour to forty minutes, depending on how fast I walked - and how energetic I felt.

By the time I reached the half-mile point, the sun was starting to go down so I decided to take a short cut, on a rough path, through the golf course. This meant walking between the fields and across the seventh tee, and then on to a footpath again. Short cut - so I thought. Some short cut! As I walked, I was getting stung by nettles and jagged by thorn bushes. Not being especially fond of nettle stings and thorn pricks I decided to change course again. The rocks looked a good bet so I started heading towards them, and suddenly I changed my mind about going home. Instead, I began to climb the rocks. The view from the top of the rocks went on for miles. As well as being able to see clear across the Forth Estuary I could see the whole of Anstruther harbour. What a beautiful sight. The view brought back memories of when we were kids. We used to climb the rocks all the time then, and we were never scared, although the top was a fair distance above the shore. The rocks were known to us as The Johnny Doo's and the story goes that a minister used to preach from the top of Johnny Doo's in the long distant past. True or not, the high rocks would certainly have made a good pulpit. I was feeling quite happy up there, on my own, looking at the sights, savouring the memories of long ago and was in no hurry to go home.

Eventually, as the light started to fade, I decided I should start heading home. But as I turned to go, my foot slipped, I stumbled and I dropped my crutches. The sky and the sea changed places as I lost my balance and tumbled over the edge of the cliff. By a combination of fast reflexes and sheer luck I managed to grab hold of the nearest solid object and found myself clinging to an overhang of rock. I very quickly realised how heavy I had grown as my arms began to tire from the effort of taking the whole weight of my body. The sky darkened and I began to feel the chill of the sea breeze as the sun went down. I was quite close to panic when I noticed a large rock over to my right, just about level with my feet. It was close but just out of reach. It formed a narrow ledge and led on to a series of other ledges, which I thought might provide my escape. I started swinging my body from side to side, very gingerly. I didn't want to risk losing my grip on the overhang above me. Very carefully, I built up a bit of momentum and took a chance. After about six swings, and with my feet heading in the direction of the ledge, I released my grip and prayed for a safe landing. As luck had it my feet landed solidly on the ledge and I grabbed desperately for another rock, higher up. I made it – just. I was mighty glad for that, because it was a long way down! With a good bit of sweating and straining, I scrambled back up to the top and, having retrieved my crutches, headed for home.

On my way home I realised how lucky I'd been. If I had fallen, there was no one about; it was dark, cold and windy. I might have been stuck there with broken bones for hours and nobody would have had a clue where I was. Mum would obviously have been in a bit of a state if I hadn't turned up by bed time and I would have been likewise, if I'd had to lie there till morning. To say I was mightily relieved to be safely back on terra firma is an understatement. Even though I was on crutches, I almost ran the rest of the way home, and then I went straight to my room, after telling Mum I was back. I had to lie down. The stress I was feeling was more than just physical exhaustion. Yet, I realised that in a bizarre sort of way the disability that made walking difficult had indirectly also given rise to my escape. You see, having the problem with my legs, I had worked extra hard for years, doing exercises to build up my upper body, and it was the exceptional strength in my arms that had ultimately saved me. Isn't it a funny old world?

My mum never found out about 'The Hangin' Boy'

and I didn't tell many people about it, either. It was something that could have been very serious, but thankfully, wasn't. I sometimes look back on it and think how stupid I was, but I'm still in one piece and that's what matters. After that night I never walked home by the golf course again; I stuck to the main road or got the bus back. Both were much safer options than solo rock climbing by a boy on crutches.

Chapter 6

THE CRUISER

I wanted to become more independent and also relieve my mum from the job of driving me to school every morning so I decided to get some transport of my own. I originally thought of a little quad bike so Mum took me to a place that sold them to see if they had anything suitable. However, the salesman advised that a quad bike wouldn't be the thing for me as they were too fast and too dangerous. The man then suggested that a mobility scooter might be better so I had a little think about it and I looked through the brochures for mobility scooters and decided I would give it a go.

I got in touch with a place that specialized in mobility aids. At this place I saw a couple of salesmen that knew their stuff about mobility scooters. I had a look around their warehouse and the two men were advising me on the best kind of scooter for me. I had a look at a couple of four-wheeled scooters and a few with three wheels. The men suggested that the three-wheeled scooters might be more appropriate for someone of my age. I picked out one that I liked, called a Rascal, and had a little test drive outside in the street. The men suggested that I should go quite slowly since I had never used one before. I had no trouble keeping to his advice. The scooter was anything but fast. After a few runs up and down the street, I decided to get that model. I then went back in to the showroom with Mum and Dad to discuss payment details. One of the men suggested that I could pay it through my mobility money as that's what a lot of his customers did. I didn't want to do that as I felt that I needed that money for other things so I decided to take out a loan instead. That way I was able to have regular payments, which I could afford myself. The Rascal was available in cream, green and red. I didn't really like the cream or red scooters but I was really taken with the green one. So it was decided, and a green scooter was placed on order. It was to be delivered in two weeks time. I was so excited on the day the scooter was due and I invited Phill around to check it out. We had been told that it would be delivered mid to late morning so Phill and I went up the street to get some things from the shops, for Mum. We thought we would have plenty of time but when we got back, there was the van with my scooter, sitting outside our house. Again, as before, I was told to go at a slow pace on the scooter and then when I got used to it I could speed up a little. I had a chat with the two deliverymen about possible accessories, like a headlamp for when the dark nights came in. I said I would get in touch if I decided to go down that route. When they left I jumped on the scooter straight away and Phill walked along by my side. As I knew they had gone I cranked the speed up to maximum and off I went with Phill running now along behind. The scooter only managed about 4 miles per hour but Phill still struggled to keep up. The battery had to be charged regularly, with a full twelve-hour charge. The battery was fixed to the scooter so Dad arranged for power in the shed in order to charge it.

I was now independent, with my own transport to get me to school. On the other hand, I was now late every morning! I didn't use the main road route as it was too dangerous. I decided to take the safer option, which was a little bit longer. That was through the park and around the back of the school. During the school day I would chain the scooter up at the front of the school so that no one could run away with it. However, this seemed to attract a lot of unwanted attention so I got a bit wary about leaving it there. I asked the janitors if there was any possibility of keeping it in their shed, which was also at the front of the school. In there it would be out of sight, as well as locked up. One drizzly morning, I was heading for school on the safer route but this still involved crossing a road. There was a Land Rover quite a bit behind me so I thought I had plenty of time to make the crossing. I stuck out my arm and began to cross the road. Suddenly I heard brakes screeching behind me. When I looked round the Land Rover was inches away from hitting me. The driver was quite shocked and got out to see if I was okay. It could have been a terrible accident and she was in tears. I wasn't in tears, but I was badly shaken and couldn't understand why she hadn't seen my hand signal. Maybe I overestimated the nippiness of my scooter. Anyway, I went much more cautiously, the rest of the way to school. Lessons learned the hard way tend to stick.

There is a fair in St Andrews, every August. It's just a few nights, with lots of rides, lots of stalls and lots of people. In the summer of 1996 I was at this fair when I noticed another scooter, almost identical to mine but it had a plate on the back saying, 'Speedy'. I took this on board and decided to get a plate of my own. I wanted mine to read, 'Cruiser'. I went to the shop to get a plate made up. I thought it would be quite pricey but it turned out that I got it for the modest sum of only seven pounds. Next, I paid a visit to one of the local garages to ask if they could fix the plate on the scooter. They told me to come up one Sunday afternoon and they would do it while I waited. The best bit was that when we finally got the 'Cruiser' plate on the scooter I didn't have to pay anything – the man said, 'It was only a two minute job, son, so you can have it for free.' What a nice man. I had a lot of friends who liked to cruise about town in their cars so I wanted to do the same on my scooter. They also had music blaring from their cars so I thought, "How can I make this happen for the scooter?" So I bought a couple of speakers and a compact CD player. I put the CD player underneath the battery case and wedged the speakers under my seat. I was now fully 'wired for sound' – just like all the other cruisers! The first batteries I got for my new sound system must have lasted a full ten minutes. Buy cheap - that's what you get! So, straight back up to the shop I went and splashed out on a decent set that gave me a stereophonic presence on the street for up to a couple of weeks at a time.

I was able to park the scooter and walk if I wanted because it had a rear rack to carry my crutches. However, one day, when I arrived at Phill's house I discovered that my crutches weren't on the rack. I shot off, back to Anst'er as fast as I could, with no recollection of what I had done with the crutches and – when I got home there they were, lying against our garage. Obviously, my memory was having a rest day! When the nights started to draw in, I decided that I should get lights fitted on the scooter so that I could use it in the dark. I contacted the suppliers and they came to fit them, the following week. Now I was able to ride the scooter at night as well as through the day. But night riding was more difficult as I had to concentrate much harder on the road. I would always ride on the road but stick close to the kerb and follow the double yellow lines as much as possible. I would never go further than a mile or two at a time in case the scooter ran out of power. If it had, I would have to flick the lever onto 'freewheel' to allow me to push it home – and I didn't fancy that! The scooter main battery was supposed to be good for 20 miles but as Anst'er has lots of hills, it ran out a lot quicker than that. Most of the time it only managed about ten miles, sometimes less, before it needed charged again.

I would often go up to the Community Centre at the school on my scooter to hang around with friends. The Centre held a pool competition every Monday night that I liked to play in and when it finished I would jump on my scooter and head over to the Youth Club that I mentioned earlier. One night, when I got to the Youth Club someone pointed out that my battery cover was missing. That was strange. Several screws had to be undone to remove the cover. Reluctantly, I came to the conclusion that someone might have stolen it. But why would anyone go to that trouble for a battery cover? The following day, I had a word with the janitors at the school and asked if they could check the security cameras for me and see if there had been any suspicious activity around the scooter in the past few days. They discovered that there had been a couple of people hanging around the Cruiser while it was sitting outside. The images weren't too clear so they got the police involved to see if they could help but neither the battery cover nor the culprit were ever found.

A lot of people loved hanging around with me when I had my scooter; in the hope they would get a ride on it. I wasn't too keen and only allowed it if they agreed to sit on my knees. Some of them were fine with that but some of the girls didn't fancy the idea. Oh well, c'est la vie! I think the two-up trips may have been why it would run out of battery power quicker as it was only designed to carry one person at a time, not two. The scooter gave me a lot more freedom in my life. I thought it was the best thing since sliced bread. I could go where I wanted, when I wanted without having to depend on other people. Now, the world was my oyster.

Chapter 7

ALCUDIA - MAJORCA

Mum, Dad, Mum's brother Uncle Jock and his wife, Auntie Karen, my cousins Kev and Carra, my brother Michael and I decided to go abroad on holiday to Alcudia in the summer of 1998. This was during the time of the World Cup in France - one of the times when Scotland qualified. We had never been abroad for a holiday before so we were really looking forward to it. Mum, Dad, brother and I had never even been on a plane. The holiday was booked for two weeks before the end of the school year so I missed those weeks at school, but I wasn't bothered as I was going on an exciting trip abroad. I had no idea what to pack for a holiday abroad so I did what any normal person would do; I got Mum to pack it for me. The Flight left Glasgow airport at six am, but we had to be there two hours before departure, so we were all setting off at midnight. It only takes one and a half hours to get there so we would be there in plenty of time. The phone rang and it was my uncle asking if we were ready to go; this was just before eleven. We were all ready so we just left an hour earlier than planned and got to the airport mega carly. My auntie and uncle drove in front and we followed behind. As my dad is a slower driver he struggled to keep up with my uncle.

There is only so much you can do in an airport departure lounge while waiting for your flight. Michael, Kev, Carra and I tried to keep ourselves occupied by looking in the shops and playing in the arcade, while our parents had a few drinks at the bar. They were all quite tipsy before they even got on the plane. We were the last families to board. Apart from Dad and me, the rest of our group all fell asleep on the plane. I couldn't sleep, as I was so excited about flying and enjoyed looking out the window although I had to stretch over Michael to get to it. Breakfast was served on the plane while most people were still sleeping. Dad and I tucked in and everyone else's food was left on their trays for them to get when they woke up. It wasn't the best food in the world but I was hungry so I ate it and stole a few things from Michael's plate while he slept. Everyone was awake by the time we landed at Palma and they all cheered when the captain announced that we had landed safely in Majorca. Dad and I let everyone else off the plane first and when I finally got to the door, the heat was so intense, I almost collapsed. After we'd collected our luggage we made our way to the coach that was taking us to our resort, Alcudia, in the north of the island. The bus journey took about forty-five minutes - more drinking time for our families.

As soon as we had checked in and dumped our bags, we headed for the beach. My uncle wanted to take me for a swim in the sea. I agreed and in we went. I'm quite a strong swimmer but I'd never been swimming in the sea before and never swam with someone who was drunk. We were enjoying the warm water and had swum out quite far when suddenly we heard the sound of a loudhailer. "Ahoy, two swimmers – you are heading for dangerous currents – please turn around and head back toward shore immediately!" Of course, it was us. We'd just arrived and had already managed to breach the local swimming rules. We kept our heads down as we headed back towards the beach! By the time we got back to the shore we were both very tired and spent the rest of the afternoon relaxing on the beach. We went back to the hotel for a couple of hours then Mum, Dad, Michael and I went out for an evening meal. I don't think the rest of them had the inclination -

or the strength – so they had an early bed!

Michael hung out with Kev for most of the holiday while Carra and I tended to go out together. This arrangement suited all parties. Michael and Kev liked to keep up a fast pace but Carra had a lot of time for me and didn't mind going at my, much slower, speed. By hanging around with Carra I began to get quite attached to her. We would go down to the pool together and go for walks to explore new places. One time, when we were in the pool, pushing each other under the water and just messing around, I clung my legs round her waist and started to get an erection so I quickly released myself from her and tried to forget about it. Carra was very sporty – and pretty, with long blonde hair. She was a bit of a tomboy that liked to do things that boys did, like play football and hang around with the guys.

It was the opener for the World Cup 98, Scotland's opening game against Brazil. We looked around for a pub that was showing the game. We found a Scottish pub not too far from us so we went to watch the game there. We coloured our faces with face paint; I had a blue face with a white cross and my glasses on top. I couldn't read the line up for Scotland so Carra read it out to me. The atmosphere was superb with Scotland supporters from all over Scotland crammed into this one pub watching the game. I sat with a lager and Carra had a juice as she was under age whereas I was sixteen. Although it was a great game and Scotland put up a good fight, we eventually lost 2 – 1. Most of the Scottish supporters left the pub quite drunk - and disappointed. As Carra and I were walking back to our rooms, I caught sight of a fantastic looking girl standing near the lift. She had face paint on as well, was about my height and had long black hair. She smiled at me and I smiled back. She seemed to be having an argument with her dad. I was quite fascinated by the girl and didn't notice the lift arriving, so that I jumped when I heard Carra's voice. "C'mon, Billy – the lift's here. What's wrong?" I just said, "Nothing," and got in the lift. That was the first and only time that I saw that dark haired beauty. I didn't even know her name, just that, because of her accent, she was probably from around Glasgow somewhere. I couldn't help thinking of the Cinderella story as I wondered if I might recognise her later, without her face paint. I never did. But there was a girl I did manage to hook up with on holiday. Her name was Kirstie, and I also spotted her while I was waiting for the lift. She was English and had longish blonde-coloured hair. We went out together several times but it was just holiday stuff and we didn't keep in touch when we got home.

Water polo was held in the hotel pool a few times a week while we were on holiday and Michael, Kev, Carra and I all joined in. It was great fun. I was a lot smaller than most of the people that played but I was quite good at throwing the ball. We all tried to be in the same team, but it didn't always work out that way. I was often on Carra's team and Michael was on Kev's team. One time I was surrounded by people on the opposite side, I dunked the ball on Michael's head so it would bounce to a teammate. He wasn't amused and went ballistic. He was so mad, he tried to fight me in the pool. There was another time when I had the ball but with my back to the goal, so I threw it over my head and turned round to see it flying into the net. I tried to manage without my crutches round the pool but one day I lost my balance and grabbed the arm of the nearest person to me. The woman was one of the holiday reps and got a bit of a shock before she realised it was me, but knew I couldn't help it. After she regained her balance and her composure, Michael threw her in the pool - for a laugh. Funny guy Michael!

One of the highlights of our holiday was a boat trip round the island. The boat left from the jetty on the beach. As we walked along the very narrow jetty I was scared I might fall in. I didn't. The excursion rep for the trip was a young man called Juan. We thought he was a bit of a 'cissie'. But he was brilliant, what a laugh we had with him. Mum, Dad, Auntie and Uncle as usual started straightaway on the drink and were quite 'blootered' by the time the boat got back to shore. On the way back we stopped for a while, to let people dive off the boat for a swim. Everyone went in - except me. I was frightened for sharks. My Mum was sure that a shark brushed her while she was in the water but none of us believed her. On the way back, while the parents were getting quite drunk, Mum went to the front of the boat and tried impersonating the girl in 'Titanic' by shouting, "Look I'm flying." Well, that started a chorus of laughing and a crowd of passengers came to the front to find out what all the fuss was about. I was a bit embarrassed. Juan just lay on the top deck, sunbathing in his Y-fronts, laughing along. When we got back to Alcudia we thought Mum and Auntie were sure to fall off the gangplank into the sea as they swayed along – 'singing a song, side by side'! What a laugh we had that day.

Nobody could ever find Carra and me during the holiday; we were always out somewhere enjoying ourselves. Sometimes we were in the arcades and sometimes in the pool. Other times we would be playing football or hanging out with Kirstie. There was an Austrian man who had a penalty-shoot game that I spent a lot of time at. The aim of the game was to score points by kicking the ball into the goal from the penalty spot. The number of points scored, depended on which part of the goal the ball hit. Sensors on the goal allowed a computer to immediately flash up your score. If you scored over 68 points with three kicks you got a gold trophy. Everybody got a gold, silver or bronze medal depending on their score. I went home with heaps of medals. The man was amazed that someone like me was able to take part. A lot of people went around to his stall just to see him do head stands. He was about sixty but headstands seemed effortless for him. He was incredible.

Towards the end of the two-week holiday we went to the beach for a ride on the banana boat. Carra and I hated it. As we surged into the waves the boat bounced so hard we felt sick and thought we were going to fall off. There were six of us on the boat. When it was time for us to come in, the speedboat did a wide turn and tipped us all off. Carra and I were in the middle and as we came off, we banged our heads together. I was okay but she screamed so loudly I thought my ears were going to burst. Happily for both of us, no lasting damage was done to head - or ears.

It was a great holiday but at the end of the two weeks, most of us were sunburned, skint and ready to go home. Still, everybody agreed, it was money well spent.

Chapter 8

THE END OF SCHOOL DAYS

I didn't really enjoy the last two years at high school because I had a lot of ups and downs - more downs than ups, actually. It all started with my dad's fortieth birthday party. Families on both sides were invited to join in the celebrations in the small town hall. We had to provide our own entertainment and I had taken a few CDs along but thought of another one I wanted to play so, with a couple of my cousins, I popped home to collect it. The cousins were Carra and Lisa and at the time I was beginning to fancy Lisa. She is a cousin on my dad's side of the family. When we got home I tried to get close to her and I asked her out on a date. I'd already had two or three Alco-Pops and not surprisingly Lisa said, "No." That didn't put me off, though, and I became quite keen on her over the following months. But she wasn't interested. I found it quite hard to bear, especially as we were in the drama class together. Brenda talked to me about her quite often and tried to console me but that didn't really help. I was in love with my cousin - and I knew, I shouldn't be. It took a long time before I got over her.

I passed all my standard grades with flying colours but I needed a reader for almost all my exams. This was because of a partial loss of my eyesight. I didn't study very much for any of my exams, except Art. I went round to Phill's house to study for that and he was able to choose the colours for me. I didn't really have to study for the rest, but I still got better grades than Michael.

During Fourth Year a very lovely girl started at

Waid Academy, her name was Rachel. She came from Hull, in England but was now living in Pittenweem, where Phill stayed. She was really friendly, with dark curly hair. Phill and I started hanging around with Rachel and as she lived in Pittenweem, I now had two friends to visit there. I started visiting Rachel at her house and she would come to mine. The three of us became really good friends.

Michael and I were getting older and needed our privacy so Mum decided to convert our bedroom into two bedrooms. She arranged for a local joiner to come and do the work and at the time my cousin, Gordon, was doing his apprenticeship so he helped. As the last bit of board was put in place I said to Michael "Well Michael it was nice sharing but - see you later, pal". As I became a big fan of Arsenal I decided that I wanted my bedroom done in Arsenal colours. I had Arsenal bed covers and curtains, an Arsenal rug, a lamp, an alarm clock and a few more items all associated with Arsenal Football Club. Michael just wanted plain colours of Mum's choice. I couldn't wait until it was all finished so I could sleep in my Arsenal room. Just before the room was ready we went for a day out to do some shopping and have our Tea. There was Mum and me, my auntie May, Cheryl and Marissa and Auntie Julie and her girls. It was a great day out but I just wanted to get home for Mum to put my Arsenal sheets on the bed so I could snuggle in and go to sleep.

This was around the same time that Dad decommissioned his boat. Michael and I were allowed one last trip on it before they started breaking it apart. When I saw that, I had a tear in my eye because we'd had great fun on it over the years. Every year, for the Pittenweem festival, Dad would take disadvantaged children out for a trip to the May Island, a few miles offshore. The family also got to go on the trip including

Michael and me. Dad was always worried about me on these trips because my balance wasn't good and he was afraid I might fall over the side. He would be especially concerned when I would climb up on the shelter deck and whaleback and through the wheelhouse window and so I would always have someone looking after me when I was up high.

Most Saturdays, I would go to the harbour with Dad. While he pumped the boat out and checked everything was in good working order, I'd clean the wheelhouse for him and he would give me a couple of pounds for doing it.

Every year, the boat had to be painted from top to bottom and Michael and I were always asked if we wanted to help. I always did. Mind you, I wasn't very good at it, but I did it anyway. Dad often had to touch bits up for me. One day, Sammy the seal was in the harbour while the boat was being painted. Forgetting about the wet paint, I patted the side of the boat, startled Sammy, who promptly swam away, and left a glaring handprint on the side of the boat. Another bit for touching up for Dad! After the boat was decommissioned Dad sailed with my uncle.

Soon after this, the school lost a member of staff in a car crash. She was a very good teacher and a good friend to me. It was a tragedy for all of us. I stayed off for a week. I don't think she ever got angry with anyone; she certainly never got angry with me, anyway. The accident happened while she was on her way to work. It was December and the roads were a bit slippery. I knew this because I had noticed the ice when Mum was driving me to school. While we were in registration class, we heard sirens but I didn't think any more about it until I looked at my watch, much later. 'Regi' was only meant to last ten minutes but we were there for about forty five so I asked my 'regi' teacher the reason for the delay and he said there had been a car crash involving a teacher but he didn't say which one. I later found out that it was Jenny and I couldn't work for crying. The rest of the year went on and into the next year and a lot of people seemed to forget about this tragedy but not the people that were very close to her, including me. I'll never forget about her. I went to her funeral and our head teacher read a poem that she had written. I took a copy of it and will keep it forever. Whenever I am down in the dumps I think of her.

Fifth Year, my last year at school wasn't a good one for me. That's why I decided it was going to be my last year. There were a number of reasons why I wasn't enjoying Fifth Year. For one thing, all my cousins had left school so I no longer had anyone to look out for me. Another reason was the death of my favourite teacher and I was really missing her. I was missing the laughs we had together and I could talk to her about anything, anything at all, and I knew that she would try and help me in any way she could. The last thing she said to me before she died was "I'll see you later". Of course, I never did see her again. I do, however, talk to her a lot - in my prayers, whenever things get difficult and I need someone to talk to.

Throughout Fourth and Fifth Year I had extended treatment at the dental hospital. I was fitted with 'train tracks' to keep my teeth straight until my final remaining tooth would come through. Well, that tooth was never coming through and while I was sitting in the waiting room with Mum one day, I was talking about Jenny's replacement; how I didn't really like her. It turned out that the new teacher's son was in the treatment room and his dad was sitting next to us – and quickly made us aware of this! I was deeply embarrassed when I realised how I had blundered.

When it was my turn in the treatment room, I was

told that there was still no movement from my reluctant tooth; that it just didn't want to come through, so they said I would have to have an operation to help it. I didn't really want to have another operation but after some persuasion I agreed to go through with it.

The operation was to be done in Dunfermline's Queen Margaret Hospital and I was told that it wouldn't take long and I would be home in no time at all. Like all my previous operations, I would have to be put to sleep for this one too, as they couldn't do it under local Anaesthetic. When I went along to the hospital several different doctors explained to me what would happen during the op. I was then taken down to theatre that same morning and as always Mum was by my side.

When I woke after the operation, my mouth felt really weird. It felt like my mouth had collapsed. Well, in a way it had because my gums were shrivelled up. I also had a surgical pack stuck in the roof of my mouth. The surgeon had made an incision in my gum to allow the tooth to come through and the pack was there to prevent the hole closing. The pack made it really difficult to eat or drink anything and the state of my gums didn't help! They said I would have to stay in hospital for a couple of days but I really wanted home by the Wednesday night because Arsenal had a game being televised on Sky. When I mentioned this to a porter he promptly went around the hospital hunting high and low for a room that had Sky TV. It was a nice gesture and I felt very grateful. As it turned out, I got to go home the very day that the Arsenal game was on and so I got to watch it at home after all. That night, when Mum asked what I wanted for Tea I said, "Ham and Chips, mum." Mum looked surprised and said, "Is that not a bit rough for you just after your operation?" I said, "Maybe – but that's what I really fancy." And so, that's what I got – and I scoffed the lot. Yeah, the Tea was great but the match was a big disappointment. After all my excitement in the build up, the floodlights failed after half-an-hour of the match and the game was abandoned. Ah well, at least I was home and in my own bed again.

I slept really well that night - at first. When I woke in the middle of the night, I felt something rolling around in my mouth. I screamed when I discovered it was the surgical pack. Mum came through, checked me over, told me to go back to sleep and said we'd go to the hospital in the morning. When we saw the surgeon, the following morning, he put another pack in and said if it happened again that the hole would take a day or two to heal over so not to worry about it. That night, it fell out again!

I'd had enough and said to Mum "I can't deal with this any longer!" We let the Dental Hospital know what I was feeling and they arranged to take the train tracks off and leave the hole alone, to close up. An uncomfortable operation for absolutely nothing - what a waste. I had to go back a couple of weeks later to have the stitches taken out, and that was it. I didn't eat very well for a few weeks afterwards and stayed off school for a few days but after that I got myself together, got my school clothes on, got my scooter out - and went back to school!

After our holiday together, I became quite attached to Carra and I began to hang around with her more and more. We would go to the arcade and the shows, and she would hang around with me on my scooter and play football with me. Dave seemed to be always around us, trying to get me away from Carra, as he knew that I was strongly attracted to her – and I shouldn't have been. Eventually, I explained this to Carra. She took it quite well and admitted to having strong feelings for me but didn't want to do anything about it, as we were first cousins. Yet, she didn't want to spoil our really good friendship. My auntie and uncle found out about our 'attachment' although they never said anything to me. It was my cousin, John, who told me they knew, some time much later. I broke down a few times, later that year, because of Carra, but some good friends and my guidance teacher helped me eventually get over her.

I got extra help that year from support staff because my eyesight was deteriorating badly. Before the help materialised I was hardly going to classes; I just wanted to leave school. I was sitting in the cloakroom one day, skiving from Maths, when my Science teacher spotted me. We talked a bit and he suggested that I go to the Assistant Rector and explain to him how I felt. So I went straight to the Assistant Rector's office and told him I wasn't happy, and why. He said it would be best if I could make the effort to go to all my classes but if I ever felt so bad that I really couldn't go, I should make my teachers aware that I wouldn't be in class.

The Assistant Rector arranged for some extra support and I started going to classes again. I can't remember the details too clearly, but I must have been struggling with my eyesight for some time without realising it. Obviously, I had fallen a bit behind but the extra support helped me to make up some ground. However, the extra help didn't change my mind about leaving. Some weeks later I went to the Rector and told him how I was feeling. Part of my problem was that I was worried about my eyesight; by this time I had noticed a huge difference in it. The Rector was very sympathetic and told me that he had some difficulty with his hearing. He said he had always loved music and was concerned that he might lose this pleasure some day. He said he treasured the hearing that he still had and tried to listen to music as much as possible. He said he found listening to music very enjoyable and relaxing and suggested that I should try it. I thought about what he said and realised that, if I ever lost my sight I would still have my hearing and could still listen to music. After that conversation I felt a good bit better and I began to appreciate my music much more.

I couldn't have a lot of the subjects I wanted to do at school. I wanted to take PE because I loved sport but for me the course wasn't really feasible. However, I did get one subject I really wanted, though – Biology. The reason for this choice was that Dad loved animals and he knew a lot about them - and I wanted to be like my dad. The course was a lot harder than I thought it would be and I had no extra support for it. The teacher was very good though and gave me as much individual help as he could. When November came I was still struggling but I was leaving school at Christmas so I just muddled along. A major meeting was held for me, in the school. As well as Mum and myself there were also some learning support teachers there, a teacher from the college I was going to and someone from the travel department. It lasted for about an hour. A great number of arrangements had to be made such as travel, support staff and what subjects I would take at college.

When end of term came everything was in place, but then I didn't want to leave. I was told that I was so well known and liked that I was going to be missed by a lot of people. The lunch club decided to throw a party for me so I wouldn't forget all the people that had been close to me. The speech I gave at that party meant a lot to me because everybody that mattered was there; friends and support staff that I had been especially close to, pupils that went to the lunch club and a whole lot of teachers. After the speech I realised that although I'd had a really hard year, I was still going to miss The Waid.

The final day of term came and it was church day. Everybody had to go to church because it was the end of term - and it was Christmas. I don't think a lot of people liked this day, not because they had to go to church, but because it brought back too many memories of the year just past. When we got back to school I couldn't find the Rector and I badly wanted to see him before I left. Eventually, I did catch up with him and we spoke for a little while and then he shook my hand and wished me the best of luck.

That was it; I was no longer a high school pupil!

Chapter 9

A NEW START

I had now left school and was looking forward to Christmas and New Year. I really enjoyed the festive fortnight. I always read the tags on my presents on Christmas Morning, to see who they were from but this year it was very difficult; I could barely see the tags. I was pleased at what I got but soon I was getting extremely nervous about going to college on the fourth of January. When the day came, I got up at seven, had my shower and went down for breakfast. By eight o'clock I was thinking, 'Just ten more minutes'. The taxi came a little bit early but I got in, waved to Mum and Dad and off I went. The journey was almost silent. Although the driver and I knew each other really well, we hardly spoke; I was very nervous. The journey took about forty minutes but we got there on time – and now there was no turning back.

When I got into the college I went straight to the reception desk and told the receptionist my name. The young woman made a phone call and within a few minutes a lady came and took me away to sort out my bank details, national insurance number and a few other necessary details. She then introduced me to my auxiliary who's name was Jim. He was a nice man and really knew his stuff. I knew right away that we were going to get on just fine - he was a football physio with East Fife!

The first day was spent just getting to know everybody. This was essential but quite boring. The second day, I didn't go to the college. Instead, I had to go to a rehabilitation centre for visually impaired people run by The Royal National Institute for the Blind. I didn't like this. I had just started college and they send me to another completely new place - it didn't help my confidence. It took all day for them to assess what I was and wasn't able to do. The good thing about it though was that lunch and coffee breaks didn't cost anything! The day was very strange for me because I had never before been around people with eyesight problems - I didn't like it. I was also taken to the low vision aid clinic. This was to assess me for magnifiers that might help my vision. I was given a few hand-held magnifiers and a small hand-held telescope. The telescope was to help me read bus numbers and, the excellent news – it could be helpful at football matches!

On the third day I only had one class – Communications. Great! I had always enjoyed English at school and this class didn't let me down. Jim helped me by reading things from handouts and the black board, and he also scribed for me. In the afternoon I had to do extra study with a visual support person who's name was Elisabeth, I think. She would give me some work to do then come back a few hours later to see how I was getting on. I did this in the library, where it was quiet and the librarian would sometimes assist me if I needed some help.

I spent the whole of the fourth day, the Thursday, in the switchboard room with Melissa. All I did was just sit there and listen to Melissa explain how she operated the switchboard. That's why I was there! Melissa was a very nice person, blonde and fairly young but I didn't fancy her – which might surprise you! I sat there, with my shirt and tie, bored out of my face, but somehow I managed to keep up a good front, chatting constantly with Melissa.

Friday was a full day, with Maths all morning and

Internet Studies in the afternoon. Everybody got away early on a Friday – except me - I had to wait until four, for my taxi. I didn't mind this; I just went to the canteen and waited. Well – that was my week.

The following Monday I had Information Technology in the morning and Flexible Learning in the afternoon and this was to be the pattern every Monday. My Tuesdays and Thursdays were to be in the switchboard room with Melissa, for a number of weeks, because the Central Admissions room, where I should have been working, was being decorated. Once this room was ready I wasn't with Melissa anymore. I don't think I learned much during my time on the switchboard anyway, although, sometimes I was taken away for training on the phones. On these occasions I was given a sheet of paper with every extension number in the college on it and I had to phone them all, just to test the line. It was good practice but took ages. Then – I was told I had to memorise them all. Panic! How was I going to remember a whole bucketful of telephone numbers? Then it turned out that someone was just having a joke. Well – wasn't I relieved!

While I was at college I was part-time staff, part-time student so I had to wear a shirt and tie on Tuesdays and Thursdays while I worked in Central Admissions - then they supplied me with a suit! When I started going to the Student Development Staff Room I got friendly with some of the auxiliary staff and in particular, Marion, a middle-aged woman. She was very nice and started to help me with my classes; Information Technology (IT), Flexible Learning, Maths and Internet Studies. My only other subject was Communications, which Jim helped me with. Communications wasn't my favourite just because I liked it at school. No, I was the only male in the class! There were about ten girls and yours truly. About six of them were veeeery nice looking but I can only remember the names of three - Amy, Nicky and Barbara. I got on really well with them. They often walked me to class, which was a real treat.

Working in Central Admissions, taking general enquiries about courses, sending out prospectuses and supplying interview times and dates to the Course Tutors, was to help familiarise me with working in an office environment, - my aim for future employment, and IT was to help me learn to touch type. I had great fun with this because Marion was with me. We often took a break from typing to play 'hang the man' which helped me relax. Marion and I got on really well and she eventually became more of a friend than a helper.

As I said, I started the College in January. Like school, the college held a lunch club for people with learning difficulties, so I went along one lunchtime, - to check it out. It was much different to school; some of the students had quite severe learning difficulties and some also had troublesome behavioural problems. I stuck with it for a while to see if I would eventually fit in. My Birthday came in that first month and they held a small party for me. I wasn't keen to celebrate my seventeenth birthday with people I hardly knew but they insisted, so I didn't complain.

The Student Development Staff Room was next door to the Lunch Club so I would often pop through and have a chat with Marion. I would just punch in the code (which Marion had given me) and walk in. Marion was always pleased to see me and the arrangement worked fine - for a while – until another member of staff asked me not to come in; at any time they could be discussing other students and that might be confidential information which they wouldn't want me to overhear or relay elsewhere - as if I would do that. That was a bit of a shock and of course I stopped going to that staff room, in fact I didn't even go to the main staff room after that, I stayed out of staff rooms altogether!

Before I left high school I had asked if I could work at the Waid Centre, as I didn't want to be away from Waid altogether. The manager told me that there were no vacancies available but he said I could work there on Friday nights and help out with the disco, if I wanted. It would be unpaid and the disco was for Waid pupils up to Third Year, so they would be quite a handful. After a short pause for thought, I took up his offer so then I was not only at college five days a week; I was also working on a Friday night, too. I went to work most Friday nights on my scooter and as there were a lot of people coming into Waid through the front entrance, I asked the Janitor if I could bring my Scooter in through the fire door, round the side, so it was out the way. I really enjoyed working the Friday nights as it meant I was still involved at the school. Sometimes I manned the hall door and made sure everyone had a stamp on their hand so they could get in. You could say, I was a bouncer or doorman. Other times I helped out in the canteen and reception as well. It was great fun. I spent most of my time in the reception talking to Kathryn, the receptionist; we got on really well. I was also able to see everyone coming in, including Aynsley, who I'd had a little crush on, when I was still at The Waid. Aynsley was too young for me then but Phill and I would often admire her in Art, from a classroom across the corridor. She was about the same height as me with long blonde hair, quite slim and very good-looking. At that time, the closest we got to friendship was when she, and her friend, who Phill fancied, would ask for a shot on my Scooter!

I wasn't a great help in the canteen as this involved operating the till, something I found very difficult with my failing eyesight. Although Friday nights were mostly fun I got a bit fed up of false fire alerts. One of the times the alarm was set off, I was up at the swimming pool chatting to the pool attendant. He panicked and wasn't sure what to do, so I helped him. I told him to get everyone out the pool, and outside, through the school gym, as fast as possible. With my help it went well and we managed to get everyone out successfully and safely. I was proud to be of assistance that night but when it happened again, the same night, I gathered up my belongings and walked out. There's just so much you can take! I was so annoyed, I was back again the following Friday - I enjoyed it too much to stay away.

Chapter 10

A TRIP TO SAVE MY SIGHT

Towards the end of School and the start of College my eyesight was failing badly. I had numerous trips to the hospital for check-ups. The doctors had trouble establishing exactly what was going wrong. Eventually, I lost the sight in my right eye completely, although my left eye wasn't too bad. Although the internal pressure in my eyes checked out fine the doctor thought there was significant damage to the nerves in the back of my eyes. He suspected Glaucoma, but couldn't be certain, so he asked me, and my family, if we fancied a trip to London's Moorfields Eye Hospital, one of Britain's top specialist eye hospitals. At first, I wasn't too keen but when I realised that this might save my sight, I was all for it.

It wasn't long before the appointment came through – sometime in February 1999. As it happened, we had relatives in London - Auntie Anne, Dad's sister, her husband, Uncle Jose and their two children, Monica and Jose Luís. Auntie Anne was a housewife in her early forties; Uncle Jose, Spanish and in his late 40's was a chef at one of London's top restaurants. Monica was about twelve and Jose Luis was 6 years old. Auntie Anne let us stay with them while we were in London and that made our stay easier.

While we were preparing for the journey I was playing pool with a friend and I said to him, "I don't know if I'll be able to do this much longer as I am losing my eyesight." My friend was shocked at this remark and he got in touch with his granddad that was on the board at East Fife to see if I could be mascot for one of the Fifer's home games. I was 17 years old by then and thought I might be a bit old to be mascot. By the time the day came though, I had no qualms and I took the opportunity to run out on the pitch with the team I'd supported since I was a kid. Before the kick-off, I got to meet all the players in the dressing room and then I made my way out onto the pitch, ahead of them, to save time. When the team came out I wandered over to the penalty box to take a few shots at the keeper, but by the time I got there, there wasn't enough time left. The team captain called me to the half way line to toss the coin. Having completed my mascot duties, I ran off the pitch towards the Players' Tunnel. You might imagine my feelings, as the routine applause from the crowd became a standing ovation for me. I felt really proud and very pleased that my friend had made the effort to arrange the day for me. To complete a perfect day, I had predicted a 1-0 home win – and I was spot on!

So, off we went, Mum, Dad and me, on the train to London - and what a long journey it was. On the way, looking out the window and taking in all the sights as best I could, I was thinking, 'Will I be able to see all this properly, soon?' When we got to Kings Cross Station I was amazed to see so many people. In some areas it was so packed it was difficult to move. After a bite to eat we took a taxi to Auntie Anne's, which wasn't very far from the Station. When we arrived, Jose was at work and my cousins were at school so we sat and had a long chat with Auntie Anne. Soon, Anne started preparing tea for us and insisted that I help. I was 17 years old, disabled, losing my sight and had never touched a cooker in my life! Still, I thought it would be good manners to try so I made an attempt to do what I could. Unfortunately, that didn't last long as I quickly scalded my hand on a boiling pot and was quickly ushered out of the kitchen where I would be safe from hostile domestic appliances! I wasn't used to anyone else's cooking apart from Mum and Dad's and didn't know what to expect from Anne. I can't remember what we had for tea that night but it was something Spanish - quite nice really, but not something Mum would make. After Tea I had an early night but Mum and Dad sat up for a while and had a drink with Anne and Jose. I slept in little Jose Luis's bed, Mum and Dad were in Monica's and Anne, Jose and my two cousins all slept in Anne and Jose's bed - a bit cramped but we all got by.

As we were only in London for my eye examination, we didn't get to see much of London's tourist attractions. Uncle Jose drove us to the hospital the morning after our arrival and the traffic was horrendous. He told us, "You can never leave in plenty of time to beat the traffic in London - it's pretty much like this wherever you go." Being from a quiet little town, we were amazed at the amount of traffic. We got to the hospital all right – but half-an hour late.

My internal eye pressure was monitored all day long, for two whole days. The doctors discovered that the pressure was constantly changing. I was also seen by the dermatologist and then had a brain scan and photographs taken of my eyes and face. The lady photographer took photographs of Mum and Dad, too. I think this was to see if the facial images could cast any light on my eye problems. The dermatologist was concerned about my lack of facial hair. He noticed that I had no eyebrows or eyelashes, facts that I was already aware of. He thought that the lack of facial hair might be linked to my failing eyesight. He said, "First of all we need to find out what is causing your eyesight to go." That first day was long and hard – with all those tests, different experts and constant eye pressure monitoring, with no decisive results. After all the tests were completed, it was off to Anne's again for a good night's sleep before doing it all again the following day. Anne advised Mum and Dad to get a Black cab home, as the mini cab drivers would take the longest possible route and charge more money.

The next morning, we left the house a lot earlier and this time we did make the hospital in plenty of time. This day was very different. I didn't see the doctors and specialists I had seen the first day. We sat all day in what was called the luxury lounge. It had comfortable seats, a television and tea & coffee facilities. Over a period of ten hours, someone came to take my eye pressure every two hours. After two long days I was finally diagnosed with glaucoma. I was given four different types of eye drops to take four times a day for the rest of my life. I wasn't too keen - but the treatment was going to save what sight I had left so I very quickly accepted the regime.

Glaucoma is a group of eye diseases which in most cases produce increased pressure within the eye. This elevated pressure is caused by a backup of fluid in the eye. Over time, it causes damage to the optic nerve. Early diagnosis and treatment of glaucoma can help prevent blindness. The reason for the long trip to London!

That night, we all went back to Anne's and had a celebration – at least I was going to have my sight. Mum and Dad had some of Uncle Jose's homemade wine, I had a beer and my cousins tanked up on juice! We listened to music, danced and talked for most of the evening. We were all sad to part in the morning. Unfortunately, we don't see our London relatives very often – mostly just at funerals and special occasions. Anne had ordered the taxi to the Station, which turned out to be a smart BMW. It came highly recommended as Anne was in the habit of using it herself and knew the driver - and it also worked out cheaper! Mum and Dad had very sore heads on the train on the way back, as the previous night's celebration caught up with them. I was just so traumatised by the whole experience that I just wanted to get home.

Once we were home again, it was back to college on the Monday, for business as usual. After a month I had to visit the consultant again for a check on my eye pressure. The news wasn't good; the pressure had risen again, so the drops had stopped working. The doctor told me that an operation was the only way of keeping the pressure down. I asked him what the risks were and he said "you could lose all your sight during the operation, you could lose a little or you could lose no sight at all". The situation was deteriorating and I had to decide quickly; it was all or nothing, so I had to say "go for it, I've nothing to lose".

In the run up to the operation no one knew how I would be afterwards so Mum asked Dad to take a couple of weeks off his work to help her look after me. I think she feared the worst and to be honest, so did I. I was getting extremely nervous, as there was a possibility I could be left with no sight at all.

Finally, the day arrived. I was trying to concentrate on the possible benefits of the operation, but couldn't help thinking about the worst. I took a couple of home comforts to the hospital with me, including my CD Walkman. I seriously needed something to help me relax and take my mind off the operation. It was mostly love songs I took with me and one track I remember playing over and over again was, 'I Believe I Can Fly', by R Kelly. When the doctor came to my room to discuss the operation I told him I was terrified, but if there was a chance it was going to help, I was happy to go for it. 'Happy', was stretching the truth a bit! After this, Mum and Dad went away for a while, promising to be back in time to go down to theatre with me. All alone now, I decided to listen to some CDs but this was short lived when the nurses came in to get me ready for theatre. Resplendent in my glamorous theatre gown, I went back to my CDs again and promptly fell asleep – until Mum and Dad returned. We played the guessing game, 'Who am I' for a while but all too soon it was time for theatre. We still carried on with the game while I was wheeled along the corridors; Mum knew I was really scared. She made it into the operating theatre with me but they closed the door before Dad got there. Lying on the operating table I tried hard to stay relaxed while the staff connected me up to all the shiny instruments and equipment. Finally, I was informed that I'd be helped off to sleep in a few seconds. It was a very strange feeling as I began to feel as if I was floating; I turned to Mum and said, "See you later" – not knowing if I would or not. And then, I was asleep.

When I woke up I was alone. At least, I thought I was. I couldn't see a thing. But there was someone there; sitting beside me was a nurse. She asked if I could see anything, and, disappointingly, I had to say, "No." She then said, "There's an eye-patch over your eye; it's got small pin-holes in it. Try and move your eye and look through the holes". I tried but still could see nothing. I was so upset; I started to cry and asked where my parents were. The nurse said they were having something to eat downstairs, but they would be back soon and so would the doctor. When she left to attend to someone else I lay there in darkness, listening to what was going on around me. I heard nurses chatting at the reception desk outside my room and the sound from television sets elsewhere in the ward and then - I heard Mum say, "How are you doing?" Dad was right behind her and asked, "How's the eye then?"

I had to bite my lip – and then I said, "I can't see!" As they sat down beside me, there was a long silence. Then Mum said, "It's okay, son, you'll manage!"

Some time later the doctor came round to assess my eye. He tore the patch off, saying, "You've been left in the dark long enough, pal!" To my delight and amazement, I was able to see. Maybe my eye was just too tired when the nurse put the question. I told the doctor, I could see just about the same as I did before the operation. He said, "That's great. We'll get a few more tests done shortly, to see what your eye pressure is like".

After the tests, I was allowed to sit beside my bed in the afternoon. Brilliant! The operation was behind me now and things seemed to be going well. Mum and Dad kept me company until late but eventually set off for home, promising to bring Michael in to visit, the following day. As the evening wore on, I became bored out of my face. When I passed this gem of information to a nurse, she asked if I'd like to borrow a ghetto blaster. I declined the offer, as I already had a Walkman beside my bed. She suggested that I could save my batteries if I borrowed the ghetto blaster and eventually I gave in. "Okay," I told her, "if you can find one, I'll gladly play it." Five minutes later she returned with a CD player and that relieved my boredom – for a while.

I was supposed to get eye drops every two hours. Several hours later I was still waiting but no drops had come. Then a nurse finally arrived. When I told her I was supposed to get the drops ages ago, she said, "I know. I've been really busy!" I wasn't amused. In fact I was very not amused! I was very uptight. Poor girl – she got both barrels. I didn't want to lose my sight - and I made that very clear. It was about eight o'clock before someone came to check the pressure in my eye and I was still sitting about in my lovely theatre gown. As he led me to the test room, my behind was waving to everyone we passed. A few wry comments from other patients drew his attention and he told a passing nurse, "When we're finished, can you get Billy into his pyjamas, please!"

Once he got me settled in front of his instruments, he found it very difficult to carry out his tests as my eye would hardly open. It seems it was very tired from the operation - and very gooey. We persevered. He managed to get the required readings but when he was finished he looked quite concerned and said, "The pressure's a lot lower than we would expect but it should sort itself out." He walked me back to my room and made sure that the nurse was on her way to help me with my pyjamas. Once I was more comfortably dressed, I switched off the television and my light and immediately fell asleep.

Next morning, I woke to find a nurse standing at the bottom of my bed. Not for the first time, but nonetheless welcome. She was checking my notes. She wanted to know if I'd like something to eat. I don't usually eat breakfast but after a little friendly persuasion, I agreed, saying, "Okay, then. Actually, I do feel a bit peckish." She brought me two crisp slices of toast, a glass of fresh orange juice and a small packet of butter and jam. It wasn't much but it was lovely. Later, Mum, Dad and Michael arrived to see how I was. It was good to see them all, especially Michael. He had been very subdued before my op. I think he was very worried that I might lose my sight completely and now he was pleased that I could still see. In the afternoon I was bored with watching snooker on the tele and so, when my Dad went outside for a cigarette I asked to go with him. I didn't smoke but I wanted some fresh air. The nurse said it was okay and I went out with Dad and

Michael. It was good to get outside for a while. The sun was beating down on us; a very hot day for April but I wasn't complaining. When we got back to the ward we found Auntie May and cousin Cheryl had come to visit. They had brought a present for me – a football jersey – the Scotland 'away' strip. It wasn't a great seller – at that time the 'away' jersey was pink! Not very popular, but coming from Auntie May I treasured mine.

The doctor came round in the afternoon to check my eye pressure again. This time it had risen a little but was well within the comfort zone. He was happy with the progress and said I could go home the following day if everything was still okay. I had to have eye drops daily and go back to see him in two weeks time. Two weeks later he was very happy with the operation. My eye looked healthy and the internal pressure was perfect. I was told to gradually reduce the drops and go back to see him in six months. At seventeen, I was the youngest patient he had treated for glaucoma, and also, due to my Cerebral Palsy, thought it caused the glaucoma. He had no name for it, so he called it 'Juvenile Glaucoma'.

So, it was back to reality; back to college and back to all my friends. I never wanted to be in a wheelchair, but no one knew what to expect when I got out of hospital so when a wheelchair was suggested, just temporarily, I thought it was quite a good idea and agreed. The wheelchair turned out to be quite useful but it wasn't powered and so someone always had to push me. I only used it for two weeks but decided to hang on to it. After all, it might be very handy at football matches.

Chapter 11

A NEW DIRECTION

Because the operation went really well, I was able to return to college earlier than expected. The first few days were just 'guest appearances', to let staff and friends know that I was ready to come back. For the first of these 'appearances' I wore my Scotland football top and shorts that I had got from Auntie May. Everyone was amazed to see me back so soon.

My first proper day back, I was working in the Central Admissions Department, so it was back to normal dress code. I had my own computer there and was given my own telephone and extension number so that my name now came up when I called someone. Supernova software had been installed for me, on the computer. This provided a speech facility and extra magnification, both of which made my work much easier. I'd never used Supernova before but I soon got the hang of it. The people who had been at school with me were doing different courses at college and so none of them were in any of my classes. My cousin was doing a course in Catering and a few of my schoolmates were doing Horticulture and Green keeping.

At lunch times, some of us used to hang around the reception area, chatting and generally having a carry on. That was where I first met Donna - a lovely, petite girl with long, brown hair tied up in an eye-catching pony–tail. I thought she was gorgeous, in her white Lecoq Sportif jacket. At first she was quite shy with me but after my friends filled her in on some of my background she soon came around.

About this time, Rachel started travelling in the taxi provided for me. I suppose the driver could have been awkward, if he'd wanted to, but he was very good about it. He said the fare went by the mileage, not by the number of passengers, so it wasn't a problem. One up, for common sense.

I didn't have long with Jim as my auxiliary. He didn't get along very well with one of the other support staff and decided to move on to pastures new. He'd worked with this woman before and told Marion and me, "She won't take your job, but she'll work her way up until you don't have a job!" Jim's moving left me with no help on my Communications course so I asked if Marion could take over from him. No luck! The powers that be said no and I landed with the Auxiliary that had caused grief for Jim!

Life at college was only good because I was going to classes and mixing with other people. I began to hate Central Admissions when they started getting very bossy towards me. However, while I was still there, I had to deliver the mail to the switchboard where Melissa worked but on one particular occasion, it was a different girl – and how! Jenny was so blonde with long hair and lovely blue eyes. She was very charming. What a stunner; I was soon wishing I'd been in with her when I was learning the switchboard. I wanted to deliver her mail everyday after that.

Once I had my own computer and phone I spent a lot of time dealing with enquiries for prospectuses. Loading the prospectuses and cover letters into envelopes and applying sticky labels was easy work but soon there were so many envelopes, I needed a huge bag to carry them to the mailroom, several times a week. I didn't mind, as I got to see Jenny.

Towards the end of the School term I was invited back to 'The Waid' to present the medals on Sports

Day – an opportunity not to be missed. The college gave me leave for the day and so back I went to renew fond acquaintances with former teachers and friends. Everyone was pleased to see me and I had a great time. I gave out the winners' medals for each event under a scorching June sun. On that very hot day, everybody got a handshake and a "congratulations – well done," from yours truly but as the girls were 'hotter' than the boys they got a kiss on the cheek to go with their handshake. As I said, I had a great time. Well, apart from a sunburnt scalp that remained painful for days.

After my visit to The Waid I became quite unsettled at college. Don't get me wrong, there were plenty aspects of the college that I liked but not Central Admissions – and I did miss my friends at The Waid. A week or so after Sports Day I got an invite to Waid's Summer Ball. I would need to hire a kilt but this time the college wouldn't allow me time off to make the necessary arrangements and eventually I landed up having to go for the kilt on the very day of the Ball. As it turned out, they had only one suitable kilt left by that time. Did I say suitable? It was far from what I wanted but I had no choice - so Royal Stewart it was then! The kilt was the least of my worries. I didn't really enjoy the Ball as much as I'd expected; my friends had moved on – and so had I. Even my best friend, Phill wasn't giving me much attention and I struggled to get around in the dimly lit marquee. My cousins, John and Gordon helped me more than my school friends. Most of us were still under age but we all managed to get drink down us. The teachers were more concerned that we should behave in a civilised manner, which, amazingly, we all managed to do. Phill had intended staying overnight at our house but decided to go home instead. That left me to get the bus and find my way home in the dark, by myself. Not the most successful night I've ever had!

I was only allowed two weeks holiday a year from the college. I wasn't happy about that. During the summer, when the rest of the students were off, I had to stay on and do my two days a week in Central Admissions. This soon increased to three days a week and I began to worry how much more would be added before the holidays were over. One week I told the college I wasn't going in on the Friday. I thought, and said, they couldn't stop me taking the time off. How wrong can you be! Someone much higher up than me said, "I wouldn't want you to do that, Billy, as it wouldn't be right and you'll be marked down as an unauthorised absentee, so have a good hard think about that, eh?" So I thought about it - and did it anyway. I told them that I'd be in college all day Friday but I ordered my taxi to pick me up at lunchtime and sneaked away home. I spent the afternoon with Phill but I got in a lot of trouble the following Monday when I returned to the college and had to complete an unauthorised absence form. By then I wasn't too worried – I'd passed all my course work, Jenny had gone, Marion had been made redundant and I just wasn't enjoying myself at college anymore. I managed to hold on until August, just over six months, but I was fed up and wanted to go home. So I left College never to go back. I didn't leave on bad terms though. I said friendly goodbyes to most of the staff and I kept in touch with a number of friends, including Marion.

The College transferred me to the Rehabilitation Centre for the Blind - the place that I hadn't liked, before. It was a residential centre where people from all over Britain came to do different subjects and to interact with other people who had sight problems. I think I was placed there to get to know people like myself, as I hadn't managed too well at College.

Personally, I think it was too soon to go straight to college after school.

The Centre wasn't a big place. It had a few rooms - I think about twelve in total. I didn't live in as I stayed quite close - just down the road, in fact – so I got home every night. There were three lounges, two quiet rooms - one with Sky Television and the main lounge, where most of the clients sat. It also had a television. This room was a smoker; if there were anyone that didn't smoke, they would sit in there anyway, just to be in the company. The Centre also had a kitchen, large dining room and a games room with some weights, and a pool table. The Games Room also had a television. At the top of each staircase was a gate to prevent any blind person falling down them. Subjects on offer were: Woodwork, Information Studies, Job Seeking, Gardening and Office Preparation. I did Information Studies, Job Seeking and Office Prep to start with for a few weeks, and my computer, which I had at the college, came with me. This way, I was able to get proper training on the Supernova Software. I found out how to use the software properly and was getting really into it. The computer talked to me with each letter I typed. It also read out menus, icons and some things on the Internet; things I never knew it could do when I used it at the college. With intensive training I also learned to touch type much better. I listened to a tape and typed the text into the computer. I did all my typing in a room on my own; I didn't mind, as there were no distractions and the quietness allowed me to concentrate. I started to think that the Centre wasn't too bad after all. I was meeting new friends, actually learning to cope without my sight and finding out what it was like to be regularly in the company of people with similar handicaps.

During mid-morning breaks on a Monday one of the

cleaning ladies would ask each of us what we would like for our lunch and tea for the rest of the week. As I didn't stay at nights I was only concerned with the lunches. I started to put some weight on, as every lunch was a three-course meal. As with the college, my taxi picked me up every day to take me there and back. I was only supposed to be at the Centre for six weeks but I liked it so much I asked for an extension. My stay was extended by another three months, which took me up to Christmas. This was great as I was getting to know everyone there and most lunch-times we would try and finish our lunch as quick as possible so that we could rush up to the top flight to play pool. Some nights I would decide to stay and go to the pub with some of the residents – unfortunately that hurt my pocket; not being a resident, I had to fork out for bed and breakfast.

One day, two people arrived at the Centre who didn't have any eyesight problems and that set me wondering. It turned out that they were on placements from school. Susie was doing office work and Craig was there to do gardening. We had a lot of fun with Craig; like myself, he wasn't used to being around blind people. By this time there was a group of us; Tony, John, Craig, Colin and myself, who all got on really well together and were amongst the ones that played pool at lunch times. We used to call John 'So Funny' because when he tried to tell a joke, we never really found it funny but he would always say, "that's so funny" and laugh at his own jokes. We would all laugh, just to keep him happy and we couldn't resist the nickname. One time, when we were playing pool he caught his trousers on the pool table and tore them, accompanied by a loud ripping noise. He was quite annoyed when we burst out laughing and he yelled, "That's not funny!" but we just laughed harder and said, "Oh, yes it's *so funny*, John!" Tony and John stayed in the Centre but Craig and I went home each night. Colin stayed there permanently as he had his own flat within the Centre; he only went home to his Dad's during holidays such as Christmas and Easter. Oh, and I nearly forgot Simon! Squeaky Simon. We called him Squeaky Simon because he had a really high-pitched voice and quite often, out of the blue, he would come out with, "I'm Blind you know!" Although we were all partially sighted, our little group would often take the piss. During my three months extension I expanded my timetable to take in Woodwork and Gardening. John, Simon, Tony, Craig and I would sit in the green-houses or in the old engineering room throwing earth at each other, making a good old mess, but only when Colin wasn't there as it was his garden. Craig was a quiet guy who didn't come out of his shell much but after his week's placement he had enjoyed The Centre so much he asked for an extra week's placement – and so did Susie. After Susie and Craig's extra week Colin arranged for all the clients to go for a night out to the Bowling Alley. Susie and I had become quite attached so we sat in the front of the Mini-bus together. The Centre had it's own RNIB Mini-bus with a voluntary driver. Colin, Craig and I became close buddies while we were there and Colin helped Craig and I, who were both under age, get steaming drunk at the Bowling Alley. It was a fantastic night-out with my new found friends and I stayed in The Centre that night to avoid going home too late. I got Susie's telephone number before we dropped her off and I kept in touch with her and Craig, after they left the Centre.

Life at the Centre was quite different without Craig but we had to go on with our own lives. After I had sufficient learning with IT I decided to concentrate on Woodwork and Gardening. I discovered that I could use my hands for more than just crutches and a keyboard. I didn't think it would be possible for a blind person to do woodwork, but I was wrong. The woodwork teacher taught us to use our sense of touch instead of our eyesight and with plenty guidance so that we didn't cut our fingers off! We used saws, drills, planes, sanders and plenty more. We were taught to work using templates so we couldn't go wrong. I built a clock out of wood, which was beautifully sanded and polished. This took ages to finish but was worth it and sat proudly in the wheelhouse of my uncles' boat. I also made a holder for my computer games and a few Christmas decorations as it was coming up to that time of year. We had to pay a small charge for the things that we made to cover the cost of materials but I did alright; I sold the Christmas decorations at £1.50 a go.

About six months after my eye operation I had to go back for a check up. The doctor was very impressed. He carried out a thorough examination and told me that everything was fine. I wasn't so sure and said, "I'm a bit concerned about a lot of visions I've been having during the night."

He asked, " What kind of visions?"

I said "All kinds of visions and I'm awake when they happen. I sometimes see dead people floating towards me; sometimes I see skeletons and lots of other strange things."

Once when I was staying at Phill's, I woke during the night and saw a skeleton at the bottom of my bed and another one sitting beside me. I got such a fright, I shot bolt upright and banged my head off a shelf. The next thing I knew, I woke up early with a shelf, and everything from it, on top of me - but no skeleton! I felt so embarrassed I left everything lying and walked quietly out the house and over to Dae's, hoping he would be up. After I told Dae what had happened, we sat in silence for a long time. Had I had a nightmare or was I going crazy? Now the doctor and I sat and looked at each other for a long moment.

Then I said, "What's happening to me Doctor?"

He said, "I think you have a bad case of Bonnet Syndrome." I didn't have a clue what that meant and so he explained that Charles Bonnet Syndrome (CBS) is a term used to describe visual hallucinations sometimes experienced by people with sight problems; they see things that they know aren't real, including images of people and buildings.

A Swiss philosopher named Charles Bonnet first described the condition in 1760 when he noticed that his granddad, who was almost blind, saw patterns, figures, birds and buildings that weren't actually there. Although the condition was recognised all those years ago it's still largely unknown by ordinary doctors and nurses. People experiencing it tend not to talk about it for fear of being thought mentally ill. The syndrome mostly affects people who have lost their sight later in life, but can affect people of any age, usually following a period of worsening sight. The hallucinations often stop within a year to eighteen months.

At the moment little is known about how the brain stores the information it gets from our eyes and how it uses this information to help us create the images we see. There is some research that indicates that the information transmitted from the eyes actually prevents the brain creating its own pictures. When people begin to lose their sight, their brains are not receiving as many pictures as they used to, and sometimes new fantasy pictures or old pictures stored in our brains are released and experienced as though they were being seen. These experiences seem to happen when there's not much going on, for example, when people are sitting alone somewhere quiet or when they are in lying in bed at night.

It's normal for people who start 'seeing things' to worry about there being something wrong with their minds. 'Seeing things' is often a sign of mental illness. People often keep quiet about their hallucinations for fear that others will think they are losing their minds. For sufferers, it's important to realise that failing eyesight is causing the hallucinations and not any other mental problem.

There are other medical problems that can cause people to hallucinate; Parkinson's disease, Alzheimers, strokes and other brain conditions that affect that part of the brain concerned with seeing. Having CBS doesn't mean that you are more likely to develop any of these other conditions.

Another difference between the hallucinations seen by people with mental health problems and those with CBS is that in CBS people quickly learn that the hallucinations, although vivid, are not real. However, people with a mental illness have trouble telling the difference between their hallucinations and reality, and will often come up with complicated explanations for the things they are seeing (sometimes called a "delusion").

There seem to be two different kinds of things people see. Each type can be in black and white or in colour, involve movement or remain static and each may seem real or unreal. Firstly, there are the hallucinations of patterns and lines, which can become quite complicated like brickwork, netting, mosaic or tiles. The second type are more complicated pictures, such as people or places. Sometimes whole scenes will appear such as landscapes or groups of people. These are often life-size but sometimes may appear much larger or smaller than in real life. The images appear "out of the blue" and can carry on for a few minutes or sometimes several hours. Many people begin to recognise similar things appearing in their 'visions' such as distorted faces or the same tiny people in particular costumes. Generally the pictures are pleasant although the effects can be scary.

For most people, just knowing that the cause is poor vision rather than mental illness is enough to help them come to terms with the condition. As I said above, the images tend to disappear after about a year or eighteen months but this is not the case for everyone. For those with persisting hallucinations, a number of medications are available. Unfortunately, none are effective for everyone.

As Christmas approached, my time at the Centre was coming to an end. The handy man of the Centre dressed up as Santa Clause for Christmas dinner and gave us all presents. Most of the male clients received an aftershave set, but I got a Drill set. A small selection of ex-clients was invited back and so were Susie and Craig. It was nice to see them again. I kept in touch with a good few of the staff and clients at the Centre, and before I left I went to a nearby pub with Colin and Craig. When we got back to the Centre most of the clients were in bed but Colin and I stayed up and talked for a while. Colin lit up a Cigarette and not to feel left out, I asked him for one. As I smoked it, Colin said, "I didn't realise you smoked."

"No," I said, "I don't usually. I just fancied one".

It didn't feel too great but I smoked it anyway. Nobody else would know, as they were all blind! That night, I had a nightmare and pulled the curtain off the curtain rail. The night warden went crazy at me and if it hadn't been for Sandie, one of the cleaners, I could have been in big trouble. Sandie and I got on really well and she was always looking out for me. Just as well or I might have come to a really sticky end!

After Christmas, I spent a lot of time lazing about,

pubbing with Phill and bashing a football around. Friday nights were okay as I was still working at the Waid Disco but otherwise life was becoming a bit of a drag. The dull routine was broken one night when I arranged to meet up with Craig. His sister collected me in her car and took my wheelchair along too. Craig's mum made us a slap-up tea and then Craig wheeled me down to the local club for a game of pool. He set the balls up and I broke off. I hit the pack so hard; the cue ball bounced over the triangle of balls, hit the bottom cushion and flew back at me. I had to duck smartish to avoid a nasty injury. I don't think I could play the same shot again if I tried – and maybe that's just as well! It was a great night, reminding me just how important good friends are. Unfortunately my very good friend couldn't avoid winning six frames in a row and I eventually decided to quit while I was behind. When we got back to Craig's house his mum served up huge cups of hot chocolate and a heaped plate of biscuits. When we thought we were all talked out Craig's mum drove me home. Craig came along too and it turned out we still had more to talk about!

I celebrated my 18th birthday in January 2000 and what a night it was. I invited everyone I knew and held my party in one of the local pubs that had a function room. Naturally, my two best pals were there; Phill and Craig. Craig's sister came too and brought Craig over in her car. She was almost the same age as me but not eighteen until August. I also invited the Friday night staff that worked with me in the Waid Centre. When I first started drinking, I drank lager shandies, which were quite easy to drink so I had quite a few of them that night. I had so many that Craig's sister made me drink a whole pint of water to try and sober me up. I didn't think I was that drunk but maybe I wasn't the best person to ask! As well as a disco and a buffet, I arranged a pool competition for that night. Guess who won. And I didn't even have to play my famous trick shot! The night was great and we all had a good laugh. Pity you're only eighteen once.

After a short period of doing next to nothing I made an appointment with a Careers Advisor. She agreed to visit me at home in order to save me the travelling. We discussed all the reasonable possibilities for me and decided, like everyone else had, that an office-based job would be best. I still didn't want to take that route and in fact didn't feel that I was ready for employment. The advisor then mentioned the possibility of a training centre and as there didn't seem to be any better prospect I agreed to give it ago. She arranged an appointment for us at a training unit in Buckhaven, run by the Council and a few weeks later we went along for a familiarisation visit.

I was quite impressed with the set-up in Buckhaven and agreed to start on some general SVQ work (Scottish Vocational Qualifications) until a fully integrated course could be organised for me. Now I was a full-time student and was expected to dress appropriately – shirt and tie was the order of the day! I treated myself to some new ties and a few fancy striped shirts. This was new ground for me, having never worn anything but plain self-coloured shirts in my life. Maybe it was a sign of brighter things to come? Transport could have been a problem but a taxi was provided by Access to Work, a government department set up to help disabled people into work and training. The department also provided other assistance such as computers and software.

When I started at Buckhaven there were only three other students there; two boys and a girl and we were all about the same age. Other people did join the course after me and so the numbers gradually grew during the time I was there. The plan was for me to do an SVQ in Administration but as my sight wasn't great I was only going to do selected parts of the course, not all of it. It was very different to my previous experiences in education. Most of the course was done on the computer. I became much more proficient on that machine and got quite interested in graphic design. I'd often work away for hours with the drawing software on that subject. One of the boys who was there when I joined was very quiet and always seemed to have a funny smell about him, not unpleasant just unusual. I never did pluck up the courage to enquire what it might be even though we did work very closely for quite a while and he often helped me with my drawings. On one occasion we created a good likeness of Britney Spears on the computer. It wasn't bad, by all accounts. In fact our supervisor liked it so much that she framed it and hung it in the staff kitchen. Food wasn't supplied at the training unit – we had to provide that for ourselves. Mine consisted of Mum's sandwiches – different every day – a touch of home from home while I worked my way through quite a demanding course.

After several months I held another meeting with my careers advisor and a few other people to plan my next move. It was decided that my best interests would be served by moving to Glenrothes College, a much bigger and more highly equipped place. I had really enjoyed my time at the Training Unit, but I wanted to make more progress and I was going back to college.

I was registered Blind before starting college in 2000. I had a meeting with my social worker from the Blind Society and she said that my eyesight was so poor that I should consider being registered blind. She said being registered would entitle me to certain benefits such as the severely disabled benefit, and that claiming this was well justified in my case. As I didn't have a wage coming in, disability benefit would also be helpful when the time came for me to start college. I agreed to her suggestion and so she contacted the consultant who had performed the surgery on my eye, to arrange for a 'blind certificate'. This was made out by The Blind Society and countersigned by the consultant. That was it - I was now registered blind.

Now that I was back in College, I didn't want to work Friday nights at the Waid any more. A lot of teenagers had been turning up to the disco already drunk and some of them made a real nuisance of themselves once they got inside. I decided to give it up – but not before I had a very special experience.

One Friday night, the lovely Aynsley asked me if I would get some drink for her and her friend. I knew I shouldn't and I didn't want to but I really fancied Aynsley so I agreed. But, first of all, I said, "I'll get it for you but only if I get a kiss from you." Not the most gallant of offers I suppose but, hey, Aynsley was truly gorgeous. She accepted, without any hesitation. I hopped on my scooter and left the building, leaving the fire exit open so that I could get my scooter back in. A few minutes later, I met Aynsley and her friend down the town. They gave me some money and I went to the off-licence and bought the drink for them. I didn't want to make the hand-over too obvious so we agreed to meet down a side street. And, that is where I got my payment! However, I hadn't counted on a small bonus that came my way.

Before I got to kiss Aynsley, she asked me to kiss her friend first. She said Kirsty fancied me – a bit! So what could I do? I just had to kiss Kirsty. I have to be honest – it was quite nice. But then – the thing I had dreamt of for ages – I kissed Aynsley and that was fantastic. It was warm and soft and lingering. If this is what the forbidden apple tasted like, no wonder Adam gave in! It was great but it was over all too soon.

Before I left them I warned them not to take the drink up to the Waid and not to get drunk. Could have saved my breath – they did both. Still, mission accomplished, payment had been received in full – I couldn't grumble. I scooted back up to the Waid, parked my scooter and slipped back inside. They hadn't even noticed that I had gone.

Chapter 12

MY NEW COLLEGE

The day finally arrived for me to start my new college. Unlike the previous time, I wasn't nervous at all. Having said that, the first day didn't go all that smoothly. First off, there was a misunderstanding about my transport. I had been told earlier that a taxi wouldn't be provided for the induction day so I arranged for my Dae to drive me in. However, just as we were about to leave, a taxi turned up. Yes, it was for me, and yes, I had to send Dae home. The taxi driver was a nice friendly man called Chic and he talked all the way to the College. When we got there, Chic took me into Reception and got me settled, and then told me he would pick me up again at two o'clock.

Having met our tutor, she took the class along to a classroom for our induction. I trailed along behind with my auxiliary as I couldn't see too clearly. When we got there I was being guided to a seat when I heard a voice say, "Are you not speaking?" I was delighted to find that it was my friend, Neil. The last time I had seen Neil, I was only twelve and in hospital, having my hip operations. It was great to see him again. On the other hand, my eyesight was so poor now that I couldn't check out the talent of the girls in the class - but they sounded nice.

The next step in our induction was to have our photographs taken for our student cards. Having given the camera my best smile I had to rush back to Reception to meet up with a mobility officer from the Blind Society. She was going to help me familiarise myself with the College layout, something I would have struggled with and taken a long time over, by myself. Doing it with the mobility person was a great success though and very soon I was racing round the college on my crutches completely unaided.

When the term started the following week, everything was in place; my computer equipment was all set up for me and so was my Auxiliary Support. As the first week went on, I began to make a lot of friends, not something that I'd managed to do in the first week at my old college. Two of these friends were girls - and guess what? Yes, I started to fancy one. Yvonne was a really kind person and she was very pretty, with long, brown, shoulder length hair, and a nice friendly smile. I fell for her like a ton of bricks. After a few days I managed to get her mobile number from a mutual friend and started to text her. In one of my messages I wrote, 'I know someone that fancies you!' Later on that same day she came running across to one of my Auxiliaries and said, with a big smile on her face, "Look at this message I got from someone!" I reckoned she knew that I had sent it, and I was standing right alongside her at the time. So – she was leading me on, was she? I certainly thought so. I bought her a lovely bunch of flowers and a necklace, with the chinese symbol for love. She seemed to like the presents but all she ever said was, "Thank you," nothing more. I got a bit annoyed when some students suggested that she was just leading me on – and nothing more! Sad to say, they were right and I soon discovered that she was already going out with someone else. I was gutted – I thought she was fantastic. I couldn't help being upset. I was sitting at the Refectory table when she came up and asked what was wrong. When she started talking, I just broke down in tears. She tried to comfort me but got dragged away by one of her friends – I suppose to give me some breathing space. Despite this we became really good friends and got on really well together.

Yvonne and her friends had a habit of hugging each other. Seemed like a nice habit, to me. One day, after Computer class, she introduced me to one of her best friends, Claire. Bad idea! Claire hugged Neil and then said to me, "I don't know you but I'll give you a cuddle anyway." She was lovely, quite petite and had long brown hair. I tumbled head over heels, all over again.

The College held a welcoming disco for the new students. I wasn't going to attend, but was talked into it by Yvonne. My Dad drove me along and Yvonne and Claire met me outside the college, and took me in. There were a few Auxiliaries working that night to help the disabled students so I was with one of them all night. Her name was Fiona. She helped me buy drinks and get about the dimly lit hall. She was a cracking lady and really friendly. I think Yvonne was eighteen but Claire was still only seventeen so I bought the drinks for both of them. Later on in the night, Fiona wanted to take a picture of Yvonne and me. We agreed, but we didn't know that she wanted a kiss for the camera - and it had to be snogging. Yvonne didn't really want to but she did anyway. It was great! And it was a good shot for the camera. Yvonne left shortly after this but I wasn't alone for long. Claire suddenly appeared out of the flashing lights and spent the rest of the night with me. Before the disco finished there was a terrific fireworks display outside on the college lawn. Well, so they tell me - I was too busy to notice. Just as the first fireworks went off, Claire started to snog me. No one forced her; she just did it – out of the blue - because she wanted to. I wasn't complaining, it was one of the best kissing sessions I've ever had. Now I didn't want to leave but, just like Cinderella, my carriage had arrived and my taxi driver, Chic, wasn't for waiting. Still, it was nice while it lasted.

While I was at Glenrothes College, the computer I used at home, for projects and homework, was provided by a solicitor. When I finished the course I would have to return the computer. I badly wanted a computer of my own. Problem was, I didn't have a lot of money and it was going to cost a small fortune for all the equipment I wanted so I asked the Blind Society if they could help. They were very sympathetic and arranged some applications for grants. In the meantime, I started thinking of fundraising events.

After Yvonne leading me on, it was Claire's turn next. You'd think I would learn but this time Claire didn't have a boyfriend, so I thought I had a chance. During College time Yvonne and Claire stuck to me like glue. Claire was always leaning over my shoulder and I thought she was after a kiss so I kissed her but was embarrassed when she seemed surprised. I kept trying my luck with her time and again, but disappointingly, got nowhere. She said she needed to get her head out of the clouds and sort a few things out – but, actually, she was after another guy. Even so, she kept holding my hand and taking me up to my classes. This didn't help matters; it just made my feelings stronger for her. To make matters worse, she always kissed me before she left. A lot of the girls thought she was going out with me, but I always told them, "No, we're just friends." She did say to me a few times, "I'm sorry it has to be this way, but who knows what could happen? We could be together someday." I decided to lay off her for a while and get my act together and get on with my course work, but it wasn't easy. I kept passing her in the corridor chasing this other guy.

At the same time as all this was going on I had another special friend. Her name was Kendal. She was a very nice person and when I first met her, on Induction, I thought she had no legs, but it was because they were so small I didn't see them! She was only about 3 feet tall and her arms and legs were tiny, but that didn't make her any different, she was a lovely girl and she whizzed about the College in her little Bob Cat. That was so nippy that I struggled to keep up with her. She went out with Neil for a while but got fed up of him chatting up other girls so she shortly finished with him. He was a bit like me with the women. I thought I was bad but Neil was ten times worse although he would never get upset the way I did. The five of us use to have a ball, hanging around together in the Student Common Room. Despite my latest girl trouble at the College, life had to go on but I was still dropping hints to Claire. One night I was listening to the local radio station and decided to phone in a dedication to Claire from 'her secret admirer'. The next day one of her friends came up me and asked if I had phoned in the dedication. I told her that I might have done! Sad to say, even that heavy hint didn't change things. One night, soon after that, I was at home thinking about Claire and I got out all my love song CDs and put together a selection on tape. When I gave the tape to Claire the following day, she started to cry and gave me a cuddle. She said it was a lovely gesture and she would keep the tape forever.

I'd thought about my fundraising events quite a lot and decided that I would do a sponsored walk with Phill, early in November. Phill and I went round all the pubs in Anstruther to gather sponsor money. Almost every pub was packed that night and I received a hell of a lot of money. The sponsored walk was from the start of Pittenweem to the end of Anstruther, which was exactly two miles. Mum drove us to the starting point and when I was nearly finished I phoned her to come and pick me up. It took me around an hour and a half but it was well worth it. The same month I was invited to the Wheelchair Appeal at the Craw's Nest Hotel in Anstruther where I received a £500 cheque towards my computer equipment. That was a massive help.

Christmas was approaching fast and I was thinking about presents for my friends at College. I bought them all little teddy bears - and most of them bought me Lynx packs. I think they were trying to tell me something! The College holds a Christmas Disco every year at the end of term and this year was no different. Again, I didn't intend going - because of all the problems I'd had with Yvonne and Claire but again – I went. I wish I hadn't. I was dancing with Claire and my Auxiliary when my head started to spin and I nearly fainted; I don't know why because I hadn't had much to drink. I had to go and sit down and when I did, Claire came and sat down beside me. And what did she do, she started to snog me again. I knew I still had very strong feelings for her and I thought she must have the same for me so I told Neil that I was going to ask her to marry me. He told me to go for it so I got someone to go and find her. When she came I told her to sit on my knee and when she did I said, "Claire, will you marry me?" She got up and ran away, crying her eyes out and I sat and did the same, thinking to myself, 'what on earth have I done?' I wasn't in the mood to do anything after that, but wait on my Dad coming for me, and even when he did, I didn't want to move, so he carried me back to the car. I never, ever told my family that I had asked her to marry me. They knew I was miserable that Christmas but I never told them why. How could I? All I could think about was Claire.

During the journeys to College I began to build a good rapport with Chic, my taxi driver. To begin with, Chic only picked me up but later he started to pick up other students. These students went to the Special Needs Department at the College. One of them was a girl called Christine. She was a lot older than me and was a right pain in the ass. I didn't know it, but Christine had also gone to the clinic with Neil and me, when we were younger. She fancied the pants off me but there was no way I would ever have got involved with her. After a while I started to speak to Chic about Claire, as we were comfortable talking about anything. He said he thought I was 'off my head' on that score. Well - I didn't take that too well and just wanted to finish up for Christmas. I got through Christmas and New Year okay but I wasn't looking forward to going back to College again. At the beginning of the new term Claire and I started to stay out of each other's way for a while. That didn't work too well. We liked each other too much as friends and eventually she became one of my best friends.

My nineteenth birthday was approaching in January and I started thinking about another fund-raising idea. I decided to hold a disco at the Craw's Nest Hotel and charge for entry. I walked along to the 'Craw's' and asked the manager if I could hold the disco there to raise money for my computer. She said that would be absolutely fine and she didn't even charge me for using the function room, which was even better. The event just happened to fall on my birthday so I not only organised a fund-raising event, I celebrated my birthday on the same night and that night I raised all the money I needed for my computer equipment.

After my birthday I went, on the rebound, looking for another woman to get my mind off Claire and found a beauty. I was sitting next to this girl chatting her up and trying to be funny and have a laugh when she got up to get something to eat. Kendal grabbed me and said, "What are you doing? Just ask her out, because she's already told me that she fancies you." "Oh – right!" I said, "I'll ask her at the next break." So I did and she said, "Yes!" At last I had a woman again. But it didn't last for very long; she was messing me about and cheating on me so I ended it after a few weeks. She kept asking me out again and again but I kept turning her down. She also had learning difficulties but she was very nice, she was very tall, blonde with big breasts. I still would have liked to go out with her but I didn't want to be let down again.

While Fiona was helping me at the college, she knew I was an Arsenal fan - my Arsenal tops were a dead give-away - and she tried to arrange tickets down to London to see a match there. She told me that her son was a season ticket holder with Celtic but would be happy to take me to London to see Arsenal. As it turned out, he couldn't get tickets so he said that he would take me to a Celtic match instead - if I wanted. I took up his offer and we went to a European game that Celtic had, against Bordeaux. The stadium was enormous, and the atmosphere was superb. The whole place was packed. Celtic went ahead through a Henrik Larsen penalty but Bordeaux came from behind to eventually win 2 - 1 and put Celtic out of the cup. I wasn't too bothered about the result but I thoroughly enjoyed the match and that was me hooked; I was a Celtic supporter from then on. I bought a Celtic scarf outside the ground that night and although they lost, I wore it to the college the next day.

It was getting to the end of my course and I started to finish subjects sooner than expected, so I had to hang around college until four o'clock every day until my taxi came. This was extremely boring. I did have the company of Neil most days but Kendal had her own taxi and no one to share with, so her taxi could come for her any time she liked. Neil and I had to wait on ours. Neil introduced me to Tasha, quite a quiet lass with dark hair and it turned out to be Christine's cousin.

One day, Tasha said to me, "Whatever you do, don't let Christine get a hold of your phone number or she'll never leave you alone."

It was too late - Neil had already given Christine my number and; right enough she kept phoning me and wouldn't leave me alone.

Neil said to me "What do you think of Tasha then?"

I said, "She's alright!"

Next thing, Tasha and I started to hang around together a fair bit.

When the course finished, I didn't think I would see all my new friends again, but then we all applied to go back. I applied for the higher course, which meant I wouldn't be in Kendal and Neil's classes. The last day came and it was time to say goodbye until the end of summer, at least. But we all got each other's numbers so we kept in touch over the holidays.

During that summer I hung around with Phill a lot and we started to go to the gym quite regularly to try and keep fit. He would come and collect me in his little yellow car, which he called Caprice. He had moved with his family, earlier that year, a few miles up the road and I could no longer walk along to his house or even get there on my scooter. If I wanted to go to his house he would have to come down and get me or someone would have to take me. His family moved to a house in the countryside, quite a large house with three bedrooms two toilets, a living room and another room, which was used as a computer room. It had quite a large garden and a barn as well. A house warming was held that summer and quite a few people came along. It was a lovely evening so most of the party was held outside in the garden. Phill had some of his family from Edinburgh and some of his own friends, and his sister had some of her friends. The house was quite full that night and most of them stayed overnight. I had quite a lot to drink and got up to be sick. As I got up I woke one of Phills other friends and he helped me to the toilet. As it happened, I was a little sick half-way there but I managed to reach the toilet for the main event.

Phill and I started up our own pool competition in the pub; it was me against him. Each time we would play the first one to win five games and the loser would buy all the drinks the next time we were in the pub. We didn't just play this through the summer; it went on for weeks. I often won, but as my sight deteriorated further, I started to lose more. I started drinking at my cousin Eck's house too and we had some wild parties. Eck shared a house with his friend and the parties were quite regular as he was one of the only cousins that had their own place. I wasn't into their kind of music at first; rock and heavy metal, but I soon got to like it. Phill was never invited, as Michael, John and Eck didn't like him. This was when I really started getting into the drink and we would often play drinking games. I was never much good at it; I was always sick.

Once I had raised the money to buy all of the computer equipment, I asked one of the technicians from the Blind Society to help pick the right computer for me and as I had the money now for the Supernova software, I asked him to help me send for that as well. He went with my Mum and me to a computer shop and looked at all of the computers that would be suitable. He knew a lot about computers so he didn't take very long till he found what I needed. I also bought a scanner so that I could scan documents into the computer then get the Supernova software to read it on the computer screen. Once I had my computer I also wanted to be on the Internet so I thought that it would be a good idea to have a separate phone line installed in my bedroom. This would keep my Mum's telephone line free. I phoned to arrange for an engineer to come out and install a separate line and this meant I also had my own number. The bill would be itemised so we knew whose calls were whose. Once the line had been put in I asked Phill down to help me connect to the Internet. Phill inserted the system disk and set my account up. He knew how to do it as his family had just gone online. That was me - I was now online too. I gave some people my phone number, but asked not to have it in the phone book. Trouble was, nobody could ever get through – I had an anytime package and I was online all the time. People that did have my number knew to phone my parents if my number was engaged. I originally had my phone beside the computer but later I had my Dad move it to my bedside cabinet for easiness when I was in my bed - or laziness.

Dad left the fishing and got a job on the stand-by boats. These are the big ships that lie alongside oil rigs to prevent any other boats going too close to the rig. They're found all around Britain and the boat he was put on was just out of Liverpool, in Liverpool Bay. Instead of Dad being away for about ten days at a time and home for roughly three while at the fishing, he was now away for a month and home for a month with this new job. I phoned him most nights, when he was away. As he wasn't far offshore, he always got a signal. I was always up anyway and he started his shift at midnight so I would phone him about quarter past twelve. My Mum was often in her bed when I phoned so he would phone her on his afternoon shift or before he went to sleep.

That year my granddad fell ill with leukaemia. Nobody who knew him expected a solid man like my granddad to go down with leukaemia. This was my dad's Dad, a very strong man and very lovable. I never did see much of Granddad but we were still very close. I was always closer to Dae, my mum's Dad and he did the rounds every teatime, visiting his children. One night it would be my Mum's turn and other nights it would be my aunties and uncles. He would always come in just as we were sitting down to our tea. My granddad was taken to hospital for tests and things before being diagnosed with leukaemia. He was given treatment for it – and endless amounts of blood to try and save him. After a few weeks of treatment he was allowed to go home but the doctors told us that it was only a matter of time before he died - they didn't know how long. They said that it could be two years or it could be twenty years. They said he was a strong man and if anyone could fight it, he could.

Chapter 13

BLACKPOOL

During the summer break from College I was tidying up my room one night, listening to the Radio, and I heard about a competition that was running for three nights. The prize was a weekend trip for two. This meant two nights and two days in Blackpool. All the travel was paid for and so was the accommodation. All you had to do to win this trip was to listen out for a song and when it came on we had to ring in and leave our name and number. As soon as I heard the song I was straight on the phone. I left my name and number and was just pottering about my room tidying up and I heard my name being read out to say that I had won. Shortly afterwards the phone rang, it was the Radio presenter phoning me for my details. I was so excited I rang my mum to tell her. She was over the moon that I had won. All I had to do now was think of someone to go with me, and I decided to take Phill. I rang him straight after I had told Mum. He was ecstatic and without hesitation said, "Yes."

We had quite a while to prepare as the trip was about a month away. When the day arrived, we had to be at the departure point by 9:00am so that we could sign a form and register that we had arrived and then we were off. I made sure that I had plenty money with me. I took £160 but was shocked to hear how much Phill had with him; only £20. What was he going to do with £20 in Blackpool, I thought? I tried not to let it bother me and took out a bottle of gin that I had brought for the journey. I had left my lemonade in the baggage area of the bus and Phill only had tins of Coke so we made do. I was half drunk by the time we got there and Phill was worse than me. We had quite a bit to carry and it wasn't easy - me being on crutches – so Phill was trying to carry the bags himself. He started to struggle; so another person in the party helped us. His name was Reg. After we dumped our bags, we went straight out again into the town. We ended up in a karaoke bar where a few of us got up to sing. I didn't. I took my wheelchair on the trip, as I didn't know what to expect. While I was sitting in my chair drinking bottles of beer, I noticed Phill getting extremely drunk. He actually came up to me and bit me on the ear. I shouted at him and said, "What did you do that for?" and he immediately apologised. We left the bar soon after that and headed back to the hotel. Phill was pushing me in my chair, and I didn't feel very secure with him drunk and sure enough, he fell and nearly tipped me over. Reg caught me and then took over pushing me. After a while we got split up. Reg was pushing me around Blackpool looking for the hotel and Phill was nowhere to be seen. I didn't know how to feel with a complete stranger pushing me, but as long as I got back to the hotel I wasn't too bothered. I started to trust him and we did get back eventually. We went straight into the bar and Reg bought me a pint. We sat for a while having a chat then I started to get worried about Phill. Reg went to our room to see if he was there. He soon came back and told me that our room door was wide open and Phill was sleeping in the bath. He had been sick in the sink and fell, trying to hold onto the sink. He had pulled it away from the wall, fallen into the bath and fallen asleep. A short time later, he came out and joined us.

We went back to our room and I let him sober up for a while and then we went for something to eat. Phill said he had spent fifteen pounds already and he needed to keep five pounds for emergences so I had to lend him money for the rest of the weekend. My £160 would have been plenty for me but by the end of the weekend I had nothing left as I'd given Phill half. Even at that, he took money from me. When I discovered that there was money missing, I blamed one of the cleaners, but it was Phill all along. We went out the first night to see what there was to do and we spotted a Lap Dancing Club – heaven. We went in. I'd never been to such a place before and it was a first experience of boobies in my face. A lot of women came up and asked us if we wanted them to dance for us. How could we refuse? I had three and Phill had two - I wasn't lending him any more money that night. It was great. I would have loved to have been there forever but I would've had no money left at all, if I'd done that! We left there about one in the morning and went back to our hotel room. Shortly after we got back, Reg came in. He'd fallen out with his mates, so he came in to our room and talked with us until about three in the morning.

In the morning, we went for a cooked breakfast - just what we needed after a night on the town. Phill had to take the fat off of my bacon for me as I can't see well enough to do it myself. When he'd finished I dived into my breakfast and what a lovely breakfast it was too - I ate the whole lot. We had a whole day ahead of us and we were going to go on the Pepsi Max Roller coaster and look around Blackpool. When we went on the Pepsi Max everyone was screaming and terrified. I wasn't because I couldn't see what was going on but the experience was good. We got a photo of Phill and me on the Pepsi Max to prove to everyone that we were on it. After that we walked back and forth along the pier. Well - I got pushed back and forth. We must have walked back and forth about five times and that pier isn't small. Phill's arms must have been aching the next day. Along the way, we went into a joke shop and I bought a fake poop. When we got back at night I kept leaving the fake poo all over the hotel. It was really funny.

I don't know what was wrong with Phill but he decided to go for a walk on his own. I didn't want him to go because I was worried about him, but I let him go, anyway. He wasn't gone long. In fact he arrived back after about ten minutes. He had met some girls in the games room so he dragged me through there and we spent the rest of the night with them. When we were sleeping we were woken by a knock on our door at three in the morning. We thought it was Reg. I went to the door to let him in, but there was no one there. I never thought any more about it until the morning when I opened the door and kicked something. He had bought a fake poo too and knocked on our door and left it there. Before breakfast Phill went upstairs to return Reg's poo to his door.

We were all shattered on the Sunday morning. We were tired, it was really hot and we had a long journey ahead of us. We wanted to stay but also were glad to be going home. Mum and her friend were waiting for us when we got back. I gave her a big hug and told her I was so glad to get home. Phill said he would pay me back fifty pounds as soon as he could but I never saw that until seven months later. Still, it had been a great weekend. Reg and I swapped email addresses and kept in touch for a while. I bought the album that had the prize-winning song on it, on the way home. The Song was 'Angel' by Shaggy. The atmosphere on the way home in the car was very quiet. Mum was furious when she found out how much I had lent Phill in Blackpool and what I had bought for him but that's what mates do - they look out for each other.

Chapter 14

TENERIFE

I was sitting in my bedroom one afternoon, in summer 2000, watching Wimbledon on television while my parents were at my auntie's having drinks and a laugh. Later on, when they came home, they told my brother and me that we were going to Tenerife, the following week. They had booked the holiday that afternoon so that they could surprise my mum's friends, Helen and Ali, who were already in Tenerife. I didn't really want to go because I felt that it was going abroad the last time that caused my sight to go - with the heat. I went anyway, as I didn't want to stay at home while the rest of them were on holiday. Nine of us went altogether - Mum, Dad, Michael, Auntie Julie, Uncle Eck and their three daughters – Arlene, Ainsley, Anya and me. We flew from Newcastle Airport. As I was disabled and took my wheelchair, the whole nine of us were allowed to sit together at the front of the plane and I got preferential treatment. I was taken on the plane first, with Dad and my wheelchair. On the flight across, Michael, like he did the last time, fell asleep and missed most of the journey. Dad also fell asleep but I was awake again, all the way. When we landed I didn't feel as sick as I had that last time but it was just as hot, if not hotter, than the last time. Once we were through Customs, we were taken to our hotel by coach. Our hotel happened to be right next to Mum's friends' hotel, so, on the coach, we all covered our faces to avoid being seen, as if they would be looking out for us - they didn't even know we were coming. Once we arrived we all went to our rooms to dump our luggage and get changed. Mum and Dad's room was next to Auntie and Uncle's room while Michael and I had our own room down the hall, a short distance. Once we were all ready, we all went to surprise Mum's friends.

I thought that I would be seen first as I was in my wheelchair but again they weren't looking out for us. Uncle Eck had the video camera on to get their reaction. Well, we spotted Marc, Helen and Ali's son, first. Uncle Eck walked up to Marc with the camera and said, "Surprise!" Marc turned round and said, "Holy Fuck, how did *you* get here". Marc would only be eleven years old at the time! He went into the Games Room and told his mum and dad to close their eyes. We all walked in together and they were shocked when they opened their eyes to see all nine of us standing in front of them. We spent the day by their poolside - the young ones playing in the pool while the 'oldies' sunbathed on the side. Ali thought that he would be smart and jump in the pool but he slipped and cracked his ribs on the side of the pool.

It must have been something to do with the Spanish beer because every time I drank it, I felt like I only had half a head and I was never drunk. The holiday was quite boring for me as I sat in my chair for most of the holiday and wasn't able to join in many things. We all went to the water park one day. There was plenty for the rest of them to do there, but not for me. I had a little swim in the pool and Dad had a look around to see if there were any water rides that I could go on, but there weren't any.

One night Michael went out with a few guys that he met on holiday, fell asleep in a toilet and was mugged. He had his room key, his watch, his jewellery and his wallet all stolen. He came banging on our room door at daft o'clock in the morning so I had to get out of bed and let him in. The next day there was someone at the door changing the lock. After that, I stayed in my parents room for a couple of nights as I didn't feel safe.

Most of the things we did on holiday, we did together. One night we would stay in and go to the hotel entertainment and the next night we'd go next door to Helen and Ali's hotel for the entertainment there. Helen was a pool person. She would laze only beside the pool while the rest of us liked the beach as well as the pool. I think we were actually at the beach more than the pool. I was always okay in the water whether it was the pool or the sea, as long as I stayed close. If I lost sight of my family, I quickly panicked. I'd often have someone swim alongside me so that I wouldn't get lost. Times were getting tough with my eyesight and I wasn't enjoying myself very much on this holiday because I was bored with nothing to do. Michael was off doing his own thing all the time, all the adults were a lot older than me and my cousins were a lot younger so, most of the time, I had to stick with the adults. We did have plenty of laughs on holiday, like Ali getting a single braid in his hair and he was half bald! Still, it wasn't a great holiday for me. Although the weather was great, with no rain at all, I was bored, with very little to do and just wanted to go home.

Chapter 15

BACK TO COLLEGE

I was looking forward to going back to college this time. I had quite a good summer - had a great tan, was getting fit by going to the gym most days and was having a good drink with my brother and cousins. But when I got back to college there was Yvonne - and Claire. This time I tried to avoid getting too close to either of them and tried to enjoy my course at College. I went back to do HNC Office Management - a two year course. I didn't have Chic, to take me to College, after the summer. A local taxi firm got the contract to do that. That was okay, as I knew them already. Although I was on a course that was more advanced than Kendal's or Neil's, I still saw them a lot. And I had a change of Auxiliary - her name was Ann. One of the first things she said to me was "Do you go to the gym?" I must have gotten much bigger over the summer for her to say that. I had two days off the College each week and on these days I continued going to the gym. If I couldn't go with Phill, I'd go on my own. Afterwards, I would lie down and rest on my bed and listen to music. I'd often lie there for ten or fifteen minutes and fall asleep. The gym work was really tiring. Ann and I had some great times at the College. I would never do any work with her. We would just sit and have a laugh and go to the canteen for most of the day. I was still having problems with Christine pestering me and I was getting closer to Tasha. There was one day I was so annoyed with Christine when she phoned me at my Auntie Julie's that I stood up and swore down the phone at her. Mum was shocked, as she wasn't used to hearing me swear, and wondered why. I explained to her about Christine and when we got home I phoned Christine and this time Mum had a word with her and told her politely to leave me alone. Even that didn't stop Christine so I told her that I had given my phone away to my Dae - had a new phone and a new number. Providing Neil wouldn't tell her that I still had the same phone - and the same number, I reckoned that would do the trick.

During the summer I had thought about asking Yvonne and Claire's friend out. She was Susan - quite a small girl with ginger hair, but like the others, she said no. She often said that she should go out with me because the guys she did go out with were not nice to her - but she never did go out with me. I had a lot of feelings for her but not as much as Yvonne and Claire. She told me where she stayed and Phill and I decided to visit her one night. We sat in her house with her Mum and told a lot of jokes and I think Phill was getting flirty with Susan's Mum, smoking cigarettes, while Susan and I were sitting talking to each other. I found out that Phill had gone along on his own, to see Susan and her Mum, which pissed me off a little.

I was still never getting any work done with Ann, but I was getting on with other subjects, with another Auxiliary, called Daniel. As I was really good with English at School, and at my old college, I had no problems with Communications here. Communications was a six-month course, which I finished in six weeks, with Daniel's help. Subjects like Accounts and Information Technology took a little longer. I struggled more with IT so on days that the classroom was empty, Daniel and I would go in and do extra course work. Tasha would come too, and sit behind us.

Claire started coming over to my house a few times. She came on Christmas Day to go to the Christmas

Night Disco at the Craw's Nest with me, and then stayed overnight. The Craw's Nest is quite big and a lot of people go to that Disco. I don't usually go, as it gets very busy. We sat together for a little while, and then she started getting up, mingling and dancing with other people, leaving me alone, so I wanted to go home. Eck was there that night so I asked him to walk us home. After he got us home, he went back to the Disco, leaving Claire and me alone. Claire was staying in my brother's room so that she could get a bed to herself but she made sure that I was okay first. She got into her pyjamas and came through to see me. She got in beside me and we talked for a while. After a short time I got an erection and she jumped out of bed, saying, "I can't have sex with you - it wouldn't be right." She gave me a kiss and went back to my brother's room. Sometime later, I heard Michael come home and go into his room. He must have forgotten she was there. I didn't hear any more after that, as I fell asleep.

I invited some friends to my twentieth birthday party in The Sally, one of my local pubs. Claire was there – and Tasha, Craig, and my cousins Eck and John and my brother. A few of Eck's friends were there too. Phill didn't come because John and Eck were there. It was a superb night in the pub. We had a play fight and Eck put his foot through a wall and then covered it up with a poster. By this time Craig was driving so he came down in the car and drank soft drinks while the rest of us got pissed. I went outside with Claire and told her that I fancied a cigarette so we went round the corner and she lit one for me. I tried dragging on it but she said, "You're not smoking it right!" I had another go and this time I started to cough. She said, "That's better!" After I'd finished the whole cigarette, I went back inside, feeling light-headed. Craig was still outside, wondering where I'd gone. Nobody knew what

I had done. At the end of the night, Tasha and Claire decided to stay overnight, so we set off together, the three of us, heading for my house. On the way home I tried to be smart and said, "Watch this." I tried to jump, with my crutches, onto a kerb and fell flat on my backside. Claire and Tasha burst out laughing. We got home and went up stairs to get into our pyjamas. Of course, Tasha didn't have any with her so she had to borrow a T-shirt and a pair of shorts and she undressed in front of me knowing that I wouldn't see her. We then went downstairs and sat at the kitchen table and talked for a while and Claire offered us a cigarette. We took one each but I was surprised that Tasha took one. The three of us slept in the living room, Tasha and me on the floor and Claire on the couch. I was just messing around, feeling Tasha's bum for a laugh and this started to annoy Claire. In the morning Mum came downstairs quite early and when Claire heard her she went through to the kitchen to join her. Mum wasn't a talkative person in the morning but Claire was. On top of that, Mum wasn't very keen on Claire and never had been. Yet when Tasha came through that morning, Mum took to her instantly. It was a Sunday so Mum cooked us a Sunday Breakfast. Claire often said that she didn't like red meat but she always ate it. I asked her to leave some cigarettes for me but that didn't happen as her dad arrived for her earlier than expected and she forgot. Tasha went home with Claire as they stayed in the same area. Mum and I had a long talk that day and she said she didn't think Claire was right for me – too overpowering. I agreed with some of what she said but I broke down in tears because I still believed that Claire *was* right. That night I knew Claire would phone. She phoned my number first but I ignored it and said to Mum, "If your house phone rings, it might be Claire. Just tell her I'm not available." The phone did ring – it was Claire and Mum put her off. I ignored her for a few days until I thought that I had to speak to her, eventually. When I finally did speak to her, I told her what I was feeling but told her that it was over and I couldn't see her again. She didn't take that too well and cried for weeks. I really didn't want it to end that way. Then she reminded me about a text message that I once sent her. I had said, "Claire, we will always be friends and we will never lose each other." I felt a bit guilty then and started to be friends with her again but we weren't in touch as often. It was tough when we went back to college and had to face each other again. I did tell her about Louise, the girl that had fancied me at school. I told her what she was like and that I was thinking about her. A little while later she came back with Louise - she was at the college too. She was very different – taller, with spikey hair. We were really happy to see each other again but it turned out that Louise was a lesbian. I didn't have a problem with her being a lesbian, but she decided that we should go our separate ways and we never saw each other again after that.

Phill started to stay sometimes; on college nights and he would transport me so that I didn't have to go by taxi. He just wanted to check out my girl friends and the talent. This was early March. Although it had snowed quite a bit overnight, we went in to college anyway. I didn't stay long at the college that day, as I was frightened for not getting home, so we left early. Phill was driving out of the car park quite slowly when a car reversed out in front of him. Phill couldn't stop in time and went in to the back of the car. We didn't get away as soon as we would like to because the drivers had to swap insurance details and quite a few people came out of the college to see what was going on. A few of the staff were out defending Phill as they saw from the front office what had happened and said that it was the other driver's fault. He disagreed, as he would, but gave in eventually and said that he would pay for the damages. We got home eventually but Phill didn't stay when he dropped me off, as he wanted to get his car home as soon as possible. A few of my friends got a bit friendlier with Phill after that incident. Yvonne started to fancy Phill and then Claire did too. This started to piss me off as they were fancying my friend, instead of me – but what could I do? We both went to see Claire quite a lot though and Phill started getting intimate with her. One time, she claimed that Phill tried it on with her but that was nonsense. It certainly didn't ever stop her hanging around with us. Phill would often take me to visit Claire at home but I suspect he only took me because he wanted to see her, too.

It was May of 2002 and my grandad was more frequently in and out of hospital because of his leukaemia. He caught a virus and was rushed in to hospital and the news wasn't good - he didn't have long to live. He was only given a few days and my dad was away at sea. Granddad was asking for Dad, wondering where he was, so my mum phoned the ship rather than his mobile to tell him to come home. Dad was taken to the rig and then was air lifted off the rig and got the train home. For all of the time Granddad was in hospital I always went with my mum to see him and when my dad arrived home he went with us every day. We were the only family that did visit every day. Granny was there every day as well and it got to the stage that she was shattered and I don't blame her. The night before my granddad died, most of the family were there. Dad told my granny to go home and get some rest and he would sit with Granddad through the night. With a bit of persuasion she decided to go home and get some rest. Everyone else left that night, apart from my Dad. He was the only one that stayed. He sat most of the night reading a book, while we all went home and I got the phone call in the morning to tell me that Granddad had passed away. Again, it was like when my mum was the only one by Granny's side when she died – Dad was the only one by my granddad's bedside when he died. After being diagnosed with leukaemia, my granddad lived for about a year - a lot longer than we all thought he would last.

His funeral was a few days later and with me being the second oldest grandchild, I was asked to take a cord. I thought it would be very difficult, with my crutches and my poor eyesight, but I wanted to do it for my granddad - I was taking one. Michael stood beside me in case I needed a hand. I was one of eight that had a chord. It needed eight strong men to lower my granddad into the ground, as he was a really strong, heavy man. Granddad died in May 2002, which left only two grand parents, my mum's dad and my dad's mum. I didn't shed a tear the day my granddad died although deep down inside I was on the verge of it. I wanted to cry but nothing happened. It wasn't until that night; I woke up from my sleep thinking about him. That's when it hit me - and that's when I let everything go and had a right long cry to myself.

I had to give up my scooter at some point while I was at the college, as I just couldn't see well enough to ride it anymore. One night I was driving it down the road from the Waid, following the double yellow lines on the road to see where I was going, looking up now and again to check ahead. Suddenly there was a loud BANG, as I ran right into the back of a Land Rover. The car was parked at the kerb while the driver was in a shop. When she came out she found me lying at the back of her car, with my leg stuck under the back bumper. She said she would take the car forward a little so that I could get my leg free but I was frightened in case the car rolled back and crushed my leg so I wrestled my leg free. I just hadn't seen it in time. The driver, and a man that was with her, put my scooter in the back of her car and gave me a lift home. That happened at night, but there were a few scary incidents during the daytime as well. I almost went into the back of a parked lorry in broad daylight and another time I almost went right up the ramp of a removal van. Just as well I stopped in time or who knows where I could have landed up that day – and with someone else's furniture! Enough was enough – for my own safety, I decided to give up my precious scooter.

After my granddad died and with everything going on at college, I started to think of where I could be in a few years time. I realised that my eyes were not getting any better and neither were my legs. As I was struggling with a couple of my college subjects I decided I wanted to cut short my two year course and go to the Royal National College for the Blind (RNC) to do a course there. I finished off the subjects that I could and pulled out of the one that I was having real trouble with, as I would still get rewarded for the topics I had completed. Ann and I really had to knuckle down and finish Admin as we skived most of it, however with the help of Yvonne and a few other auxiliaries we finally got it finished.

I called the RNC for a prospectus to see what I wanted to study and this time it was completely my decision. I chose Music Technology, something different. I had to go to the RNC for an assessment so Mum and I went down on the train to Hereford, all expenses paid. Michael drove us up to the station, early in the morning, to catch the train. It was due to leave at about nine-o-clock. However, there had been an accident on the way and we had to be diverted. Mum was getting nervous as she thought we would miss the train but Michael knew a short cut. He put the foot down and got us to the station with minutes to spare. I took my wheelchair for convenience, as I didn't have a clue what the college was like. Mum and I were both anxious about travelling all the way to Hereford without Dad, who was away at sea. We managed to get there all right though, but there was a bit of a mix up when we got to Waverley Station in Edinburgh. Mum thought we had to change trains there so she got off. Then she tried to get my wheelchair off. After a good bit of difficulty she finally got it off and we got on another train. We discovered later that we were supposed to stay on the train at Edinburgh and that's why Mum had so much trouble getting permission to get the wheelchair off! Anyway, this time we definitely didn't have to change until we got to Crewe Station. Eventually, we got to Hereford, a little stressed, a little late, but we made it.

A taxi was supposed to pick us up at Hereford Station but as we were very late, it had gone away. No big problem, though – as one of the station stewards put us into another taxi and off we went. When we reached the college, we retrieved our luggage, including my wheelchair and went in through the main entrance. There were three steps to the front door. Mum carried the wheelchair up for me, and then I sat in it and rolled over to the reception desk. I let the lady know who I was and she called for another woman to come and meet me. When she arrived she introduced herself as Pat. Pat took my Mum and me through part of the college to a room where other people were sitting. They were also blind. Some of them had guide canes and one or two had guide dogs. This was our assessment group and these people would be with me for part of the assessment. After we had introduced ourselves to each other, we had some coffee and then Pat showed us to our accommodation. On the way I met Tony – from the Rehab Centre, back in 1999. He was really pleased to see me and we agreed to meet up again, that night, for a drink. Pat wheeled me across the road to the Halls of Residence where Mum and I were going to be staying but when we got inside we found that the lift was out of order. Without asking if I could use the stairs Pat wheeled me straight outside again and had a bit of a search for more suitable accommodation. I wasn't too happy about that. Pat had assumed that I was wheelchair-bound and didn't think to ask if I could walk at all. She arranged for us to stay in the sick bay of Gardner Hall which was all on the one level but there I would have to stay in the same room as my mum. I didn't make too much of a fuss about it as we were only staying for a couple of days and I was afraid that if I complained they might not have invited me back, to do a course.

The first day at the college was really just fitting in - getting to know the college and meeting some of the lecturers and other staff. We went for tea that night which most of the people down there called supper, which neither Mum nor myself enjoyed too much as we were used to our own kind of foods. During tea I met Tony again and we arranged a time and place to meet for a drink. I told him where I was staying so that he could come and 'collect' me. Mum came to the Student Bar with us, for a drink but Tony and I had a lot to catch up on so she spent most of the night talking to the staff. We didn't stay too long in the bar that night as I had my assessment the next day.

The purpose of Assessment Day was to see what skills we had. Mum didn't have to be around for this so Pat told her that she could go away for a while, maybe into town, so she wandered off, on her own. I had numeracy and literature tests to find out what my general ability was with numbers and words. I managed all right with the literature side but I struggled a bit with numeracy - I never was good at Maths. I also had interviews with a number of college people, people from Management and Rehabilitation as well as Music Technology Tutors. It was quite a long and tiring afternoon, doing so much and meeting so many people, but it was nice to get acquainted before starting the college – that was of course, if I was going to be accepted. I met up with Mum again when she came back from the shops, but she had only got as far as the local Co-op and brought back a bottle of wine. Maybe I should have left my wheelchair at home so that I could get a real feel for the college as I couldn't really find my way about well, while I was in my chair. I went out with Tony that night again to the Student Bar, but Mum decided to stay behind with her bottle of wine and let me go on my own with Tony. He brought someone with him this time – a female friend. I left my wheelchair behind this time and followed them to the bar. This time at the bar was much better. As my mum wasn't there we had a great laugh and I met some of Tony's mates who were nutters - some of them anyway. I had a little more drink than the previous night. I had met lots of people during Assessment Day and now I was enjoying myself. The Student Bar didn't stay open late – just till eleven, so when it closed Tony walked me back to my room. When I got back Mum was standing outside having a cigarette and by the sound of her she'd had quite a bit of her wine too!

The next day was leaving day but before we went home we were invited to the canteen for some lunch - just a few sandwiches and some tea before heading off. The taxi that took us to the station was the one that was supposed to collect us when we arrived. It stopped right outside Gardner Hall so we didn't have to walk any distance. The train arrived on time and we settled in for the long journey home. On the journey we got stuck with a lady that liked to talk a lot. Mum was never a talkative person but I didn't mind too much and just sat in my wheelchair, listening to her. I think Mum was glad when the lady got off at Crewe. Fortunately, we didn't have to change there, this time. Our first change was Manchester and then our next one wasn't until we got to Edinburgh. From Manchester to Edinburgh was very boring as we were on seats side by side, with not much room to move. I was glad Michael was waiting on the platform when we reached the station. Never mind jet lag, I'm sure I had train lag for a few days, after that journey.

Once I was home again, I just had to sit and wait to see if I was offered a place or not. While I was waiting, I was thinking about what to take down with me if I was offered a place. My Disability Employment person 'Ann' had said that not everyone was offered a place at the RNC and not to be too disappointed if I wasn't accepted. However, I waited patiently for a few weeks to hear if I was to be offered a place or not. The news finally arrived, by post, to say that I had been successful. It wasn't exactly the course I was looking for, but I thought that it would be a great opportunity, so I decided to accept. I was offered a year's course in Customer Service at NVQ level Two. I assumed that it was something different from general office work so I wanted to give it a go. The main reason I wanted to attend the blind college was to develop my independence and living skills so that I could eventually live on my own and take care of myself. So as much as it was office related again, I didn't care, I was going to the blind college. I was offered a place on the RTU course, which meant Residential Training

Unit and having to stay on campus but I was allowed to travel home every second weekend - if I wanted to.

I didn't want to go away without saying goodbye to all my friends. Even though I intended coming home every second weekend or so I still wouldn't see them very often. I decided to throw a going-away party although I knew I would eventually be coming back home to stay. This going-away party had to be special. By this stage in my life I knew a large amount of people and I wanted to make sure that the people that mattered most to me were there. I invited the usual, like my family and close friends, like Craig and Phill. I also arranged a mini-bus to bring some of my college mates and support workers along which included Yvonne, Daniel and a few other friends and college staff. There were about eight people from the college and about eighty altogether. It was a great night for everyone - knowing that I was going away to a very good place for me, but my Mum was getting very nervous about letting me go. I arranged to present Mum with a big bunch of flowers that night, just to show my appreciation to her and for sticking by me through all the trouble I'd had with my legs and the loss of my eyesight. Mum hadn't eaten properly for three years, through worrying about my eyes and I wanted to give her something in return for being there for me. When the time came for the presentation, I stood up and gave a speech to thank everyone for coming and then I said, "Mum, come up here a minute, please!" When she came up, I got someone to bring the flowers out and I presented them to her. I said "Mum, these are for you, for being there for me every step of the way during my sight loss." She said, "You didn't have to do this son, this is your night not mine." Then she gave me a kiss and a cuddle and told me to enjoy the rest of the night.

Before going to the college I still needed to meet up

with some other friends that couldn't make it to the party. One of these people was Aileen, from my old school, Waid. Aileen still stayed in the same place as she had when we were at The Waid so I looked her number up in the book, hoping that I could phone her and then visit. She wasn't in when I phoned so I gave her mum my mobile number and asked if she would call me. I was out shopping with my mum when Aileen phoned. We arranged for her to come to my place and then we would go to St Andrews for an ice cream. It had been so long since I'd seen Aileen I had almost forgotten what she looked like. When she turned up at the door, I was surprised to see how much she had changed. She was still fairly small but she was a lot more blonde than I remembered her. She was very nice but I had no intentions of taking things any further - I just wanted to say goodbye to all my good friends.

Chapter 16

THE BLIND COLLEGE

Settling Inn

The day was fast approaching for me to go to the Blind College. My mum decided that the best way of getting most of my clothes to the college was to post them in a large box and they would probably arrive around the same time as I did. Mum started to cry when she was helping me pack, as she couldn't believe that I was going so far away from home. She couldn't face taking me to the train station on her own so our next door neighbour offered to go with us to give her a little support. All my travel assistance was already booked and I had my tickets so it was just a case of turning up at the station where the 'travel assistance' person helped me on to the train. This time my wheelchair wasn't coming; it was just my crutches and me.

The Train arrived on time and off I went, leaving home behind. My mum watched me get to my seat and then the train trundled off. First stop was to be Birmingham New Street Station and I would transfer there, for Hereford. I carried a rucksack with me on the train, with some clothes, a packed lunch and some music to listen to on the way. A man, who had got on at Dundee, was sitting in front of me, so I had some company all the way to Birmingham. I must have gone through a few CD's on my Compact CD player and I don't know how many times I went to the toilet, as I was so nervous travelling on my own. I was also thinking about all the friends and family that I was leaving behind but I didn't want to think about that *too* much or I would be home sick before I even *got* to the Blind College. The man from Dundee was quite quiet and kept falling asleep. But not realising he was sleeping, I kept asking him to help me to the toilet. One time I couldn't wake him so I had to attempt going to the toilet on my own. While I was away, he woke up, wondered where I was and came to see if I was managing okay. He turned out to be very helpful again when we eventually got to Birmingham and I started to worry in case my 'travel assistance' wasn't there to help me. 'Mr Dundee' helped me off the train just in case they didn't turn up. When I stepped off the train the 'travel assistance team' was waiting for me, with a wheelchair, but - they were really supposed to come onto the train and collect me. I thanked 'Mr Dundee' for all his help and wished him good luck for wherever he was going and the travel assistance person whisked me away. He wheeled me to the platform for the Hereford train, parked my chair, told me the train would be a while coming, and said he'd come back for me. This made me quite anxious, in case he forgot about me, and I got stranded but a short while later he did come back and I got safely on board the Hereford train. This time I was completely surrounded with people but I didn't talk to anyone during the entire journey. No matter, it wasn't very far and when I finally reached Hereford a helper came onto the train for me. Then he wheeled me all the way along the platform and across the tracks to my taxi that was already waiting, to take me to the college.

When I arrived at the college, the taxi driver helped me in with my rucksack, and Pat came to meet me. She was surprised to see me without my wheelchair and so I told her, "I don't need my chair Pat. I only brought it before as I didn't know what to expect of the college, but now I'm going to learn how to get around the college without it". She took me to a room in Gardner Hall where other people had congregated, and explained what was going to happen. As I wasn't familiar with the layout of the college and its surroundings she said someone from the rehabilitation team would come and show me around. When I asked if a large box had arrived for me, she went to check and came back with my box of clothes. She then took me to the halls of residence - to the same hall that I was supposed to be staying in on assessment, but this time, on the ground floor. The hall was called Dowdell Hall. The others were Armitage, Campbell, Orchard and Gardner Hall. Once she was sure I was settled, she went to fetch one of the Residential Support Workers (RSWs), to show me round the kitchen and the Common Room. The RSW introduced herself as Mandy - a large, dark haired woman with dark clothes. Once I'd been shown around I went back into my room and phoned my mum to say that I had arrived safe and well. I made my room a little bit more homely by putting my clothes away, plugging in my CD player and organising some of my CD's. The room still looked a little bare though, as I didn't have a television or computer. It was a Friday when most of us arrived and there was no college at the weekend so I had to try and occupy myself for the weekend. I did meet some of the students on the Friday night. The guy next door and a girl on the same floor both came to introduce themselves but it had been a very long day for me so I decided to have an early night.

When I woke in the morning, I had a shower. My room had an en-suite and the shower was a wet room so I was able to walk in, and out of it, without having to step up or down. After I'd had my shower, and dressed, I began to wonder how I was going to do my own washing and where it was done. I'd never done my own washing before. Just at that someone knocked on my door. It was Gareth, to help me with my mobility training. We spoke for a while and then I told him about my washing worries. He asked if I had any washing powder or tablets. I said, "No, I didn't realise I had to provide such things." Gareth went and found some washing tablets and then showed me where the laundry room was on my floor and how to use the washing machine. He was supposed to give me mobility training but taught me some living skills instead. We only had a half hour slot so didn't have time to do the mobility training. He said he would come back the following day to do that. Vince, one of the RSWs on duty came to see if I needed help to get to the Refectory for lunch. Of course the answer was, "Yes" and so he walked me across to the Refectory and back again when I was finished. After lunch I was sitting in my room again when someone else knocked on the door. It was my Key Worker, Mark. He came to help me do a bit of shopping - Gareth had obviously told him about the tablet situation. Mark took me in his car to the local Safeway store in Hereford. I didn't buy a lot - just washing tablets and a case of Coca Cola. We were just about ready to go back to Dowdell Hall when Mark noticed a bunch of guys playing football and asked me if I wanted to see if Tony was there, knowing that I was friends with Tony. Turned out, Tony wasn't there so I just went back to my room with my tablets and listened to some music until it was time to go for tea. Vince had asked if I wanted him to come back for me again at teatime so I was waiting for him to knock on the door. The RSWs were walking me across the road because I wasn't familiar with the campus and they continued to help me until I was confident to manage alone. I wasn't too keen on the food in the Refectory and most of the time I finished up taking a sandwich for my lunch or tea, which wasn't enough. I met up with Tony that night in the Refectory and he offered to come and collect me to go up to the Student Bar that night. Later, when we went to the bar, it didn't have anything I really liked so I settled for a bottle of Budweiser, not something I'd usually drink but I had a few. We caught up on a lot of gossip that Saturday night – stuff about back home and the clients that went to the Rehabilitation Centre. Tony asked if I kept in touch with anyone else from the Centre. I told him that I called Craig a lot but not many other people. When I was ready to go back to Dowdell Hall, Tony arranged for someone to walk me across. The person he asked was a Student Support Worker (SSW) and he was foreign. He walked in front and I followed on behind. Once back in my room, he asked me if I wanted locked in. I was suddenly frightened. "No," I said, "I'm okay," not realising that I could lock and unlock the door from the inside. I was a little bit unsure of myself after only one night and a day on campus, and decided to go straight to bed.

When I woke the next morning, I felt like I was coming down with a cold, so I had a little lie in, after all it was Sunday morning and I had nothing else to do. When I finally surfaced, I got myself showered and dressed, ready for Vince taking me for my lunch again. I was getting used to the route to the Refectory, so I knew it wouldn't be long before I could go by myself. Gareth came in the afternoon to give me the bit of mobility training that I was supposed to get the day before. This is when I really started getting to know my own way around the college. I was amazed to find out the ways for a blind person getting around, especially when Gareth was my Rehabilitation Officer. He was great. He would walk me from Dowdell Hall to the Refectory and round the outside of the college. He talked about shorelines, something I would never have thought of. What he meant by shorelines were grass verges and raised kerbstones and things. He showed me the one-way system in the Refectory where there was a metal strip along the middle of the floor for people to follow, and was especially helpful for people that were totally blind and used long canes. They could feel their way with their canes - what a clever idea. Another thing I thought was very clever was that there was a carpet or rug at every external door of the college to let a blind person know that they were at a door. Some of the cane users were quite lethal with them. They were so used to using their cane and were so fast at feeling their way about that I literally had to jump out the way to avoid them. It didn't take me long to get familiar with the college thanks to Gareth and by the Monday morning I was almost doing it on my own.

When I woke up on the Monday morning my cold arrived with a vengeance. I could hardly breathe and I was completely bunged up, on induction day. I tried my best to keep myself together for Induction but I had to eventually give in and go back to my room, where one of the nurses came to see me. I was given some cough sweets and some medicine and was laid up for a few days in my bed. I couldn't think what could have caused my cold apart from the climate change from a quiet fishing village in Anstruther to a City in Hereford. So I started college a few days later than planned and while I was off I got to know the Independence Worker on the ground floor of Dowdell. The Independence Workers came in Monday to Friday mornings to clean and help students with their breakfast and things. We often called them cleaners as that's what they mainly did, cleaning up people's rooms and each Hall, but they preferred being called Independence workers, or better still, by their first name. There were three Independence Workers in each Hall and they each had their own floor to look after - A floor, B Floor and C Floor. As I didn't have a television in my room I eventually ventured out of my room and mixed with some of the other students in the Common Room. Everyone used their room key to get into the building and also into the Common Room. There weren't many people about for the first few days in the Common Room, so I sat and watched the tele on my own. But when people started coming in I began to interact with them. As I started to feel better, I decided it was time to start College and meet some of the Students that were on the course. My Course Tutor was on holiday for the first two weeks, so we had a stand-in Tutor for that time. She showed me around and got me settled in. She showed me the classes that I would most likely be in and all of them were upstairs on the top floor. I was given a tape and a Dictaphone. On the tape was a timetable to let me know what classes to go to on certain days. This was very helpful but I had never had a Dictaphone before so I wasn't very sure how to use it. However, I played around with it in my room and it didn't take me very long to figure it out. I noticed little gaps in my timetable - free periods to do what I wanted. Well, I couldn't really explore the college, as I couldn't see, so Gareth filled a couple of these free periods with mobility training. He also got a hold of my timetable so that he could show me how to navigate through the college to get to the classes. The College had a lift so I was able to use that, with Gareth's help, and I was racing round the college in no time. Gareth also showed me how to get to College Green, a place outside the campus with a chip shop, a hairdresser and a grocer's. College Green was quite a bit further away from the college so we needed a little bit more than half-an-hour. Gareth met me in my room and as he walked me to

College Green, he pointed out everything on the way. There were a couple of ways to get there but he took me on the safest route. This took us across a pedestrian crossing. The crossing beeped when the green man appeared and it had little white squares along each side, which were quite visible and easy to follow. After the crossing, we went along, beside the road for quite a bit. The road was quite busy and I was concerned in case my crutches slipped off the pavement – I could land up on the road. Gareth, however, showed me a grass verge on my left side and said, " Run your left crutch along the grass verge and you can't go wrong." I did as he said until my feet hit one of those tactile pavement things and I stopped. He said, "Do you feel that?" I said, "Yes I do, what is it?" He said, "That's telling you, you're at a crossing." At this point there was a black iron fence to follow and when I got to the end of it I had to turn to get ready to cross the road. This was a red man, green man crossing with cars coming from all directions. I thought, "How on earth am I going to manage this, I can't see the coloured men." But, just at that, Gareth said, "Now - you have a box with a button on it here. The green man will appear when it's time to cross, but you won't be able to see him and this crossing doesn't beep to tell you when to cross. But if you put your hand underneath the box you will feel a cone shaped object. When that starts to spin, that's when the green man appears and that's when you cross the road." Amazing! Once across the road we had to go through a lane which was pretty straight forward as it had a grass verge on both sides and was quite wide. Once I got to the end of the lane, there was another road to cross. This was a quiet road. It had a drop down kerb at both sides with a drain next to it so that was easy enough to follow. I then went left and followed the kerb all the way round and then I was there. I had reached College Green. Before I got to the shop though, I had one final crossing which had a grass island in the middle and was a one-way system and wasn't busy. So - it was, across the road, across the grass, across the other road and I had made it. While I was there Gareth told me how to get to the bus stop which was just a few feet away and he would teach me how to get into town from there another day. The trip to College Green took quite a while but I knew that the more I did it, the quicker I would get the hang of it.

Pat approached me on the first week of college to explain how, and when, I was allowed to go home for the weekend. She said I could go home every second weekend if I wanted to. When I did decide to go home I would leave on the Friday afternoon and travel back on the Sunday evening. She also told me that flying home was an option rather than travelling on the train. Flying sounded good. As I stayed so far away, by the time I got home, using the train, it would almost be time to go back again, so I decided to take the flying option. This meant that I would get a taxi to Birmingham Airport on Friday afternoon and I would be home by eight o'clock. If I got a taxi from Edinburgh Airport or someone came for me there, my travel expenses would be refunded when I got back to the college. I decided that I'd stay for three weeks and then go home for my auntie Heather and uncle Alex's Silver Wedding. I had to get special clearance from Pat to go early on that Friday as the Silver Wedding celebration was on the Friday night. I also got Pat to make it a one-way ticket as I wanted to bring my computer and television back with me, which meant Mum and Dad bringing me back by car.

I wanted to get a few things sorted before I took the weekend break and one of these was to get enrolled in the college gym. As I had been going to the gym on a regular basis, back home, I didn't want to undo all the work I had gone through to get fit so I arranged an induction appointment with the Sport and Recreation Department. A member of staff gave me a tour of the gym and showed me the equipment. Most of it was the same as I had been using back home but the layout was very different. I quickly got to grips with this, though, and was soon back pumping up my muscles again. Tony, one of the Sport and Rec team, said he was quite impressed with me in the gym. He was especially impressed with the way I handled the weights, despite my disability, and asked if I would like to play football on Monday and Thursday nights. I didn't need asking twice! They had different levels that they called B1 and B2. The players in B1 were totally blind while people in B2 and upwards had partial sight. I turned up, expecting to play with the B2s and above but Tony suggested that I should join the B1s. I said, "No, I'd like to try out with these guys. I've had a knock-about with them already!" Tony relented and that was me - playing football with 'the big boys'. It was only a five-a-side pitch so you can play anywhere. I liked to play on the right wing but sometimes Tony and Dixie, the other Sport and Rec person, would move me around and put me in different positions and eventually I ended up playing in defence, at right back. It was great! I thought my football days were over, but actually, they had just begun.

The fire alarm went off quite a few times during the first three weeks at college and kept freaking me out. Apparently, insects kept tripping the sensor and setting the alarm off. One night, I was standing outside Dowdell Hall after the alarm had gone off, when suddenly, I was aware of someone speaking to me. It was dark and he was a black man though I didn't know that at the time. And – I didn't know that he had been boxing and hadn't had time to put his clothes on. His boxing shorts were white, and with my limited vision, I was able to see them – but not him. Talk about freaked out!

Chapter 17

ON THE MOVE

It was getting close to the day that I would travel home for the weekend. I was so looking forward to be going home to see my family again as I had never been away from them for this long before. I'd enjoyed my first three weeks at the Blind College but it was nice to be going home for a while. The taxi for Birmingham Airport picked me up about lunchtime. There were three students in the taxi – two heading for Edinburgh, the other, to Glasgow. The drive to Birmingham took about an hour and a half. When we got to the airport, the driver made sure we got ourselves booked in and settled down for the travel assistance people to come and collect us, to help us onto the plane. I hadn't flown since we had been to Tenerife and I'd never travelled on a plane on my own so I was crapping myself. The cabin crew were excellent - they made sure I was comfortable and settled. As it was a British Airways flight we were offered a complimentary drink, so I took a whisky with some Coke. The flight only lasted about forty-five minutes and I really enjoyed it - my first flight on my own. As Mum and Dad had to prepare themselves for the Silver Wedding they thought it would be best if I booked a Taxi to bring me home, so I booked a local taxi firm prior to my flight. I booked them because I knew them really well and I would have some company on the way home rather than booking an Edinburgh firm that I didn't know and risk being bored on the way home. I couldn't wait to get home and give all my family a big hug.

    I got home in good time for the Silver Wedding

celebrations, hugged my mum, my dad and Michael, had my tea and then got dressed up for 'the do'. I think a lot of my relatives and friends had misunderstood me when I told them that I was going down south. They seemed to think that I was gone for good so when I arrived with my family at the Silver Wedding, everyone said, "It's good to see you back." My uncle Alex thanked me personally for coming back to attend his Anniversary and I made it clear to everybody that night, that I had every intention of coming home again when I had finished my course and wasn't staying on any longer than I had to. The night was great - mingling with my family, drinking large amounts of whisky and Coke and having a laugh with John, Kev, Eck and the rest of them. A lot of whisky was consumed that night! I only really started to drink whisky as it was the favourite tipple of another uncle and he introduced me to the stuff. A great night was had by all. Then it was back to my Arsenal bedroom to enjoy my sleep in my own bed.

On the Saturday morning, I got thinking about what to take back down to the Blind College with me. I knew my computer equipment was going, but I thought my television was way too big to take with me. Mum suggested that I should buy a portable and take that with me, so that afternoon we went to the shops to buy a portable tele. I wasn't after anything special, just a small '14 – 16 inch' and not too expensive, as I wouldn't be using it for long. As it happened, I picked a nice one up for just under fifty pounds. I packed a few CDs and some more clothes and that was me ready for the return journey. What I wore to come home with on the Friday was washed and put back on again on the Sunday. Once I was packed, I arranged to go to The Sally on Saturday, with John and Eck. We had a few drinks and a few games of pool. I didn't stay late though as I had a long car journey ahead of me on Sunday. Dad loaded the car while I was out with my two cousins. When Sunday morning came, the three of us got ready for the long journey to Hereford in the car. We showered and changed, had a bite to eat and set off. I don't know how many times the radio changed stations that day, with all the different places we passed through - and we passed through a lot of places. It was a scorching day – so hot that Mum had her feet out the window for a bit. I was so bored sitting in the back doing nothing. I couldn't exactly look out the window at the scenery, as I couldn't see anyway. After a number of pee and food breaks, we eventually reached Hereford, after eight long hours. Mum and Dad booked themselves into a hotel for the night. I didn't realise that I could have put them up for the night in a room at the college – for a lot less. However, they came in to see where I stayed and had a look at my room and then headed back to the hotel for their tea – and a much-needed sleep. They said they'd bring my things in the morning.

That night, there was an earthquake - in Hereford of all places. A small tremor, apparently, I didn't feel it but my parents said they did. No harm was done so I went off for my regular Monday morning meeting with my Course Tutor, telling Mum and Dad that I would see them when I came back. When I got back they were waiting for me outside Dowdell Hall. The car was parked outside the front door, something you shouldn't really do, but it was only for a few minutes while Dad unloaded my things. He then moved the car into the car park out of the way. Next thing I knew, Mandy came down from the office (to be nosey, I think) so I introduced her to my parents and she offered them tea and coffee. They appreciated the offer but thought it was best to get going as they had a long journey ahead of them. I would never have thought to offer them anything, but that's just me. When they left, they said they would see me in a couple of weeks. So that was me - back at college and ready to continue my course.

The only contact I had with the outside world was through my mobile phone, as we had no telephones in our rooms – small wonder as that would probably have landed the college with massive bills. So I used my mobile to call my family and friends. I didn't have a clue how to set up my computer equipment so Vince kindly offered to help me. While I was out playing football with the boys Vince was in my room setting up my computer. Once the computer was set up I asked the IT manager about getting Internet access in my room. During our discussion he explained that he was thinking about getting Internet access in the Hall but said they had an asbestos problem. He was hopeful that the problem could be solved but said it might take sometime. Another building in the college, called Queens Building, had a learning centre which already had internet but that was some distance away and I could never be bothered to walk there. Once I was back from my weekend at home I started to mix with the people on my floor and that's when I realised that there was another side to the hall. I found this out as some of the students on my floor came through the other side of the Common Room. As Tony already had some other mates I started to hang around with some of the students on my floor and go to the Student Bar with them. I got friendly with a man called Peter, who was very quiet and never talked much. Well - I didn't *think* he talked much but it turned out, he did – he just always whispered instead of speaking out loud. There was also another guy that always wore shorts and T-shirts even through the winter. Most Saturdays that I stayed at the college I ordered a Chinese takeaway and ate it with him. Most of the students on A Floor of Dowdell Hall were younger than me and I hadn't known I was going to be around them. I did get on with them fairly well, though. I liked to spend most of my time in my own room, watching my television and using my computer. Peter didn't last very long at the college - he didn't think he fitted in very well. I tried to change his mind but he left a couple of weeks later. One night I was sitting in my room bored, with nothing to do, so I decided to walk to College Green. I'd had plenty of practice with Gareth so I decided to try it on my own. I was determined to start smoking regularly, after trying it a few times before and I thought to myself, 'My family are miles away, they're not going to know.' It was a horrible night, the rain was pouring down, but I went anyway. I put my Arsenal jacket on and put my rucksack on my back and headed off. I took the bag in case I decided to buy some lager. It didn't take me very long to walk to College Green and when I got to the shop I thought about turning back but I went in as, otherwise, it would have been a wasted journey. I nervously walked up to the counter and asked for ten Regal and a lighter. I also bought some cans of Fosters Lager while I was there. Into my bag they all went and I headed back again in the pouring rain. On the way back to Dowdell my mobile rang. It was Kendal. She was phoning to see how I was getting on. I told her I was heading back to my room, that it was pouring rain and I'd phone her when I got back. I was soaked when I did get back and it took some time to dry off and get changed – then I called Kendal back. Once I finished my conversation with Kendal, I decided it was time to try my new bought cigarettes. I took one out of the packet, went through to the bathroom, opened the bathroom window and lit up. I coughed a couple of times with the first few draws and flicked the ash out the window. When I finished the ciggie, I dropped it into the toilet and flushed it away to hide the evidence then I went back to my room to watch the tele. I thought I was stinking of cigarette smoke and decided that I better not have anymore but a short time later I was off to have another one, before I went to bed. I didn't really enjoy smoking that night, it just felt wrong, but I did it anyway. The next day when I came back from classes for a coffee, I met the independence worker in the kitchen. She made coffee for both of us and as we drank it, she had a cigarette. She asked me if I smoked and I said, "No!" She said, "I found a cigarette in your toilet bowl!" I denied that it was mine and left it at that. After that I was too shy and embarrassed to tell anyone what I had done.

Every morning as I walked across the road to the college I kept hearing music blaring from an upstairs window and always wondered who's it was. I later found out that it was from a tall black man that stayed on B floor of Dowdell Hall. I never did like the kind of music that he played but I liked the sound I heard when I walked out the front door. That was his alarm. It was really loud but somehow he still managed to sleep through it! I was getting on really well with some of my tutors and my classes. The tutors were lovely people and never left you stuck with anything. If I ever needed a hand with anything they were always willing to help. Most of my class work was in what they called the model office. Before seeing it, I thought it was going to be a model of an office, but it turned out to be a classroom in the style of an office. It was one of the few classrooms that had an outside telephone line. The aim of my course was to build up a portfolio with all the work that I had done throughout the course. A lot of this work was made up of personal statements that we had to write up if we had done anything different. My supervisor and I signed it. If there was anything around the college that you weren't sure about you could always go and ask Barry at Student Services. Barry was extremely helpful and Student Services was also where most of the SSW's congregated. If I had any training to do with Gareth, this is mostly the place I had to meet him as well. I became quite familiar with Student Services and spent most of my time there when I had nothing else to do. Student Services was also the place where you collected any mail and was home to the Sport and Rec team, the SSW's manager and Mark's office. They all had their own little offices within Student Services. I spent most of my time here as I was beginning to drift away from my mates on A floor of Dowdell and I didn't really have anyone else that I hung around with. I did however start meeting up with people that stayed on B floor of Dowdell. I met Andrew in the Gym when I needed a hand with the weights, and his mate on the same floor, who was Jason. Both Andrew and Jason were very well built and round about the same height and age. Andrew had blonde hair and Jason had dark hair, I think. Sometimes I would pass a man a few years older than me with long dark hair and a baseball cap. He was called Ray and always said hello when we passed each other. I wasn't being rude when I didn't answer back; it was just that I didn't know him. One night, in the bar, Ray came across and asked if I would like to sit with him and his mates - so I did. He was planning a Quiz Night and asked me if I had a computer in my room. I told him that I did and that he could use it if he wanted. So Ray came and used my computer for his Quiz. He suggested that I should think about moving digs up onto B Floor with the rest of his mates. It was all men on B Floor. I said I would think about it and that I would talk to Vince and Mandy first. All the men on B floor were a few years older than me but I was used to being around older people. When I talked to Vince and Mandy, Vince thought it would be a great idea but Mandy wasn't so sure. There was no wet-floor shower room available on B Floor, but Vince said "Ah, don't worry about it, we'll move someone." I think Vince was more aware that I wasn't too happy where I was and I had more friends on B floor. It took a lot of persuading for the man to move out of his room down to A floor as he had a nice large room with a large bed - he was about seven feet tall! It turned out he was the tall black man whose loud music was supposed to wake him up every morning. I was going in to his room and he was moving down stairs - not into my room but another room on A floor. He got on a lot better with the people on A floor, than I did. Vince took me up to have a look at the room and the bathroom on B floor to see if I would manage the shower. The room was perfect but I said that I might need a grab rail in the shower cubical. I was going home for the weekend, so Vince and Mandy said that if I packed my things they would do the removal for me while I was at home. Before I moved though I had to let the people on A Floor know. I had only smoked about four of the cigarettes that I bought and I didn't enjoy them so I gave them to the guy next door on A Floor. So that was me, when I came back from the weekend I had a new home and was a member of B Floor.

Chapter 18

ONE OF THE BOYS

When I returned to the College, I went to the Dowdell office to pick up my key for B floor. One of the office staff took me through the Common Room, where a few of the guys were sitting, and then on to my new room. I was shown in by one of the RSW's and then was left to it. All of my things had been moved, as promised, and were lying on the floor ready for me to unpack and put away. Again, my computer was dismantled and I would have to ask Vince to set it up for me again, but thought I would leave that for a few days. After I'd unpacked everything I turned my attention to my television. It was easy enough to set up - I just had to plug it in and put the co-axial lead in the wall and that was that. Once I was settled in, I went through to the Common Room and joined a couple of other students there. One of them got me a coffee and we had a little chat. Most of the people on B floor smoked. That was another reason why Mandy thought it would be a bad idea to move rooms. It was a Sunday night and most of the guys on B floor had gone home for the weekend. When I got back to my room I heard most of them coming in but decided to stay put for the night, and meet them in the morning.

The next morning, I had a shower – much better than in my previous room. Although it was a cubicle instead of a wet-floor shower, I enjoyed it better as it was more powerful - and the water didn't go everywhere. The wet-floor shower on A floor always flooded and often soaked the clothes that I'd left at the side. After my shower, I went through to the kitchen to make myself a cup of coffee. There were a few people there, having breakfast before heading out. I was never really a breakfast person but Sandie, the Independence Worker on our floor, insisted that I should always have breakfast, and she made me a couple of slices of toast. Some people were smoking at the table – something I hated when I was eating. I didn't say anything about it that morning - I thought I should wait a few days; after all it was my first day on B floor.

After my breakfast I headed across to the college to meet with my tutor, Val. As I was now on the same floor as Ray, he walked across with me, something that nobody on A floor ever did. My tutor asked if there was anything in particular I wanted to discuss. When I said that I was originally interested in doing Music Technology rather than Customer Services, she suggested I did a couple of periods a week on the subject. I said, "Yes, I'd love to." Val went off for a discussion with the music department and later informed me that she had registered me for an introductory course on a Thursday morning, before lunch. So my timetable was starting to build up.

On my breaks I would often go to student services and chat to Barry, go back across to Dowdell for a coffee with Sandie or go to the Gym for a while. If I ever went back to my room at break times I had a habit of lying on my bed and falling asleep. Sometimes I'd wake up to discover that I'd missed half of my class, so I'd have to run across the road on my crutches and apologise for being late. Some of the tutors would be okay with it but you always had one that would come down on you like a ton of bricks.

Most nights, after tea, the B floor Common Room was full and as much as I had stayed in my room on A floor, I was hardly in my room on B floor. I liked to sit in the Common Room with the lads. Mandy often joined us in the Common Room, as she liked being in our company a lot. When Mandy or Vince left for the evening there were two other RSW's that came on duty after Ten, to do the night shift. They were called Terry and Gary. I didn't really know them because I hadn't yet seen them while I was at the college. Terry took over from Mandy, and Gary from Vince. Gary wasn't really one for venturing out of the office at night although all the others did, and Terry would often come through and sit with us when he was on. Terry often helped himself to some toast and tea and would often make some for me. Sometimes I'd chat with Terry right up till midnight, and then head off to bed.

When I got round to it, I finally asked Vince to set my computer up again, as I was fed up looking at it, dismantled in the corner. Once he'd assembled it all again, I was able to do some work in my room which saved me from walking all the way across to the Queens Building. I started to use my computer more for a CD player and used my small CD player for listening to the radio. I had everything laid out the way I wanted. I had all of my CD's assembled on the shelf above my head where I slept, my computer in the corner with my CD player to the left and my television on the end of the desk, by the door. The local radio station I listened to at Hereford was called Wyvern FM - quite a good radio station. I set the radio up to wake me in the morning and play until I left for college and to switch itself off at night after midnight. I often listened to Wyvern FM in the afternoon if I was having a rest on my bed. My dad would often bring home a bundle of mp3 disks from the boat for me, which were top 40 albums. I'd feed these into my computer and choose the album I wanted to listen to. I used to think a lot while I was listening to my music. One of the things I'd think about was my eating problem. As it happened, the college had a meeting one-day to talk about eating arrangements and see if they could make any improvements in this for the students in the Refectory. A member from each Hall had to volunteer to attend the meeting, so I attended from Dowdell Hall. Les, who was also on my floor, came along with me, to give a bit of moral support. Les was quite a big man from London, very big, in fact. Sometimes he would lie across one of the settees in the Common Room, on his stomach, and watch television. If nobody else was in the room he'd turn the television and stand around so that it was facing him. As everyone had been at the college for a couple of months by this time, the meeting was to get our views and opinions on the type of food that was on offer in the Refectory. As I was struggling to eat from the Refectory I suggested that there should be more British style food available instead of all of the foreign meals. I didn't really need Les's help for this but Mandy suggested that he should come with me, as I was quite shy. After the meeting it was agreed that I should meet with the Refectory manager at the start of each week to have a look at the week's menu and see what I liked and didn't like. This was really helpful as the manager often asked me to try some of the other things that I wouldn't otherwise have chosen. When I tried her suggestions, I often found, much to my surprise, that I enjoyed them. Sometimes, I even went back for seconds. From then on, I started to eat a lot better in the Refectory and I would sit with Ray, Les and some others from our floor. Ray seldom stayed at the weekend as his home was in Worcestershire, not far from Hereford. It was the same for most of the guys on our floor. They usually went home at the weekend too, apart from Anthony who said that the journey was too awkward for him. Although you could go home every second weekend, expenses paid, these people went home every weekend as they had a rail card and paid for their own way home. So it was usually just Anthony and me most weekends. Every Sunday morning the Refectory did a cooked breakfast and if Terry was on duty on Saturday night, I would ask him to give me a knock, to go across for breakfast in the morning - if I wasn't too hung over from the night before in the bar. There wasn't much to do at the weekends when I didn't go home, so I would just laze around in my room most of the day listening to the radio or my own music on my computer or go through to the Common Room beside Anthony. I would go to the Student Bar at night and see who was around but Anthony was not much of a drinker so I often had to go on my own. I didn't mind this, as there was often someone else there to talk to. Tony was sometimes there, so I would go and sit with him. I didn't see a lot of Tony, as Orchard Hall, where he used to stay, had been demolished and now he was living in one of the college's outside houses. He'd often turn up for football on a Monday or Thursday night though.

It was coming up to Jason's birthday so we decided to hold a party for him. Everyone from B floor, and a couple of Ray's friends, came along. Someone from our floor brought their CD player through to the Common Room so that we could have some music and Ray and his friend brought some beer. We all chipped in and they brought back loads of beer – a whole lot - we were never going to run out, anyway. The evening went really well and a lot of drink was consumed. A lot of games were played as well. One of the games was the Word Association game. You probably know that this means that each person, in turn, has to say a word that's associated with the word that was said by the previous person. If you hesitate for too long or say a word that isn't associated at all, you have to down a drink. It was very funny - especially when it came to one particular guy. He was so slow and didn't have a clue what was going on. He downed the most drinks that night – didn't surface till *very* late, the next day! Jason got so drunk that night that he mistakenly tried to snog me. I didn't fancy that at all. It was a hilarious night, though. Although there was a lot of drink consumed, there was no hassle. There were a lot of drinks left lying around and a couple of students fell asleep on the settee. If I remember rightly, this was a college night and there were a few sore heads in the morning. I was okay. I got up on time and went to classes as normal in the morning. That weekend, I headed home to see my family and meet Michael's girlfriend, Lecia, she was a lovely young girl, I say young as she was only Fifteen. She was very nice and my parents thoroughly approved of her. When she looked at me, I looked back and although I couldn't see her clearly, she sounded good and as long as my brother was happy, so was I.

I started to get quite friendly with some of the Student Support Workers at the college, especially Santiago and Paulo, Paul for short. I was friendlier with Santiago than with Paul. After I found out that there were a couple of MacDonalds in Hereford, Santiago would often borrow a college car and take me there. He would sometimes take another SSW with him – a girl called Danita; Dana for short. Santiago preferred his name shortened too – to Santi. All three of these SSW's were from Ecuador. Santi would sometimes visit me in my room and watch some films with me on my computer. Paul was a pain in the ass when we played football. He would run rings around us at five-a-sides. He wasn't such a great football player – but he could see - and the rest of us were all just partially sighted!

During another visit home, I was sitting in Michael's bedroom, having a drink with him and one of his mates, when he started talking about Claire, from college. He told me, that the Christmas before, when she came to see me, he had slept with her. At first, I couldn't believe what he was saying but then it suddenly hit me. I remembered the night she stayed in his room and him coming home and going in to his room and then, I fell asleep. Then I thought about my twentieth birthday when I had invited Claire and Tasha through. Claire had been trying to fool around with Michael all night and I was none the wiser. I had an idea that Claire liked my brother but I had no idea that she had already slept with him. I was furious with Michael and told him how I felt. He said he thought that I wouldn't mind, but I did - she was a friend and a good one at that. I phoned Claire when I got back to the college and confronted her about it. She told me that she hadn't planned on it happening - that Michael had come on quite strong towards her. She then said, "What was I supposed to do?" I replied, "You could have said, NO." It seemed to me that Claire had been after Michael from the beginning and she used me to get to him. I just left it at that and didn't speak to Claire much afterwards. I really felt she had let me down.

I started to drift away from Tony while I was at the college. He had his mates and I had mine. Sometimes I would see him in the college or on the football field, and we would meet up from time to time for a drink. One night, playing football, I was standing in defence and our goalkeeper rolled the ball out to me, just outside his penalty box. I ran with it a few paces, chipped it in to the middle of the pitch where someone passed it to Tony and he stuck it in the net. That goal came from my foot as I started the move off. As I said earlier, Tony was moved to an outside house because Orchard Hall got demolished. This house was about a mile from the college and so I began to see less and less of him. Sometimes he came to my room, to change for football but that was about it. With him staying so far from the college, he started not turning up for football or college through the day. He stayed in the outside house with two of his mates. I didn't bother too much as I had my own mates in Dowdell Hall.

It was approaching December - already three months into my course and I loved my time at the RNC. Ray had a birthday coming up in December so it was time for another party. We did the same as the last time by bringing a CD player through to the Common Room and all chipping in for the beers, which again we weren't going to run out of. I would say this party was better than the first one. The Common Room was packed and we had all ordered Chinese Takeaways. The bill for the food was quite big as there were a lot of us. After the food, we started on the beer. As it was Ray's birthday he was quite drunk – while the party was still quite young. We played the Word Association game again and some people drank so much that they could barely walk – or talk. I *think* I eventually crawled back to my room. I was one of the lucky ones – my room was right next to the Common Room. When I went through to the Common Room in the morning, I was expecting to find it in a mess, but someone must have cleared everything up before they went to bed. I suspected Ray was one of them. Everybody was sitting in the kitchen having their breakfast and, as usual, Sandie still tried to get me to eat something. It was a good night but there were a few sore heads in the morning – just like the last party. As it was December the Performing Arts students put on a play for Christmas. I wasn't in the play but because I was doing Customer Services at college, I got involved in most of the college events. On the night of the performance, I sat outside the hall, with a few other students, giving out programmes to the students and staff and making them feel welcome. Once everyone was seated, we all went inside and watched the performance. The play was beautiful and the students that were performing it were excellent. One of the songs was 'A Spaceman Came Travelling,' by Chris DeBurgh and I remember a girl from Australia saying that she had never seen snow back home.

I also phoned Aynsley at the start of December. She was the girl that I had bought drink for when I worked at the Waid Centre and I liked her a lot. She was far too young for me at the time - I was about to leave school and she was only in Second Year. I phoned a few times and mentioned that I quite liked her friend. She said she would try to set something up. She never did. After a while, I gave up playing the mind games and told her straight, "It's you I really like Aynsley, not your friend!" She said she really liked me too, so I asked her out and she said, "Yes." I had just landed myself a cracker, a lovely person with long blonde hair - and she was *my* girlfriend. Okay, she was a few years younger than me but I was more than happy to give it a shot. Christmas was near and it was time to go home. I left most of my things at the college – just taking a few clothes home with me. Christmas was so close when Aynsley and I started going out together that we didn't even buy each other a present.

Chapter 19

MY TWENTY-FIRST

I was getting on really well with my mates on B floor and my twenty-first birthday was coming up in January. I planned a party back home and another one for the college when I returned. As I rarely saw Tony now, I asked him to spend the weekend at my parents' and go to my party back home so instead of travelling to Glasgow, he would travel to Edinburgh with me. I had to ask Pat if this would be okay and she said it would be fine. Tony was in two minds whether to come or not but in the end he did come with me. As I wanted to have a really long weekend at home, Tony and I planned to travel back on the Monday morning instead of Sunday, as was usual. Pam arranged the taxi to take us to Birmingham on the Friday afternoon and my parents were to meet us at Edinburgh Airport. While we were in the departure lounge Tony disappeared and while he was away our travel assistance arrived to get us on the plane. As he could see quite a bit better than I could, Tony spotted the woman and came right back. The flight didn't take long and soon we were in Edinburgh – and ready for a great weekend. On the way home in the car, we stopped for a Chinese Takeaway and ate it the moment we got home.

   I wanted Tony to see a bit of Anstruther so I took him to the harbour on the Friday night. After that we went to The Sally. Tony liked the Sally - he thought it was a nice friendly pub. We played a few games of pool, had a few drinks and he met a few of my cousins. When The Sally closed we started heading home. It was January. It was very cold and windy – and it was late. Mum had laid out a mattress on the floor next to my bed and Tony slept on that. When Mum found that out in the morning, she went ballistic. Tony was a lot taller than me and Mum had intended for me to sleep on the mattress and our guest to have my bed – but we didn't know! Anyway, I gave him my bed for the rest of the weekend.

I wanted an entertainment system for my twenty-first - more for the sound than the vision so Mum and Dad got me a 25-inch television with a DVD player and surround-sound speakers. There were seven speakers altogether, dotted around in a very small room. Dad had set it all up while I was at college so it was ready for me when I got home. There wasn't much for us to do on the Saturday so Tony and I played a football computer game most of the day until it was time to go to the party at night. I had invited most of my family and friends, including Kendal and Neil from Glenrothes College. I didn't think Kendal or Neil would turn up as they were both in wheelchairs but they did – both of them. I had invited Phill too, although we weren't getting along very well. He didn't appear but my other good friend, Craig, and his sister, came. I always invited his sister to my parties. She was the same age as me and we'd always got on well. Craig and his sister brought Colin from the Rehabilitation Centre with them so I had all these good friends at my party – and Tony as well. Tony spent a long time talking to Craig and Colin as they hadn't seen each other for years and I noticed Neil with them quite a lot, too. I sat and got pissed with my friends and enjoyed myself. I had arranged a disco and a buffet and everyone seemed to be having a great time, including me. Unfortunately, when I got up to go to the toilet, I tripped and fell flat on my face. There was a lot of 'ooing' and 'aaaing' and a lot of people crowded around me but Craig shouted,

"It's okay. He'll get up in a minute with a big grin on his face!" And that's exactly what happened. Towards the end of the night, everyone was looking forward to my speech. They knew I enjoyed this part. My speeches are usually quite long-winded but I like to think, funny at the same time. I started off by thanking everyone for coming, especially my dad and my uncle. I don't think they'd ever managed to one of my parties together, because there was always one of them at sea but they were both there that night. I had a photo taken of me cutting the cake – or, at least, trying to cut the cake. It was a great night and – I was well blootered.

I planned to go and see Aynsley on the Sunday before I went back to college, as I hadn't seen her since we had started going out. I phoned her to say that we would be coming to visit but she said that she wouldn't be in, so that put an end to that. I didn't even know where she lived. I had a rough idea but wasn't certain. Tony and I played football all day and went for a couple of drinks at The Sally again on the Sunday night. I slept in my brother's bed on the Sunday night, as Tony and I were to be up early on the Monday morning and we both needed a good night's sleep. That didn't happen, though. We were both up, most of the night. I couldn't sleep for Tony talking on his phone. Eventually, I had to go through and tell him to go to sleep.

It was up early and back to college on the Monday morning, back to college for another birthday party, for me. When we got back to Hereford, Tony was dropped off at his 'digs' and I was dropped off at Dowdell Hall. I had a quick shower, freshened up after the long journey and headed off to my classes. I knew I looked shattered, as it had been quite an eventful weekend. My first tutor quickly spotted my condition and, as she knew I was having another party for my birthday that night, she advised me to go back to my room and have a sleep. So - I managed to get a few hours kip before the celebrations started again!

I wanted to have plenty to eat before the party so we went across to the Refectory for tea and I ate as much as possible, before drinking anything, that night. I had another shower before the party and changed into my best clothes, clothes that people had bought me for my twenty-first back home. As I was sitting in my room, I knew there was something going on when I heard a lot of footsteps going back and forward past my door. Eventually Ray came to take me into the Common Room. The place was full. The guys had asked people from upstairs and downstairs to come and join in the celebrations. We were all having a quiet drink and a chat when Jason and Anthony started clearing the tables away from the middle of the floor. I thought, 'What are *they* up to?' Then they put a chair in the middle of the floor. What were they going to do to me? They came and asked me to sit in the chair then Jason and Anthony disappeared. I was sitting there in the middle of the floor in front of everyone, wondering what was going to happen. Then a bell rang and in trots a gorgeous young woman, dressed as a nurse. A Stripagram! Was I surprised! I knew they had something up their sleeve but I didn't expect that! I sat there in the chair while she played a couple of games with me. One of the games was, that I had to put a big false nose on and then try to take the girl's outfit off with my teeth. If my nose fell off, I had to do a forfeit. The nose didn't stay on long so I had to do the forfeit. She asked me what my favourite kind of pet was. I think she must have been disappointed when I said, "A fish," because she put a dog's lead around my neck and tried to take me for a walk. After this, she opened a bottle of wine and put some of the wine on her breasts and I had to lick the wine off. That was great! At the end of her turn I had my photo taken with her on my knee. By this time she was down to her bra and knickers. Mandy stayed out of the way until the stripper was gone and then she joined us. Some of the blind students weren't too pleased. They hadn't seen anything that happened but had to contribute for the Stripagram along with the rest. I found out after the stripper was gone that Jason and Mandy had been planning this for weeks. The photo was scanned and put on my computer as my screen saver. It was a really enjoyable night for most of us and we fired into the drinks afterwards. We went up to the Student Bar to celebrate then came back to finish the night off in the Common Room with my mates from B Floor. I got really drunk that night – again. And why not, it was my twenty-first – and I still made it to college the next morning! I had bought myself a bottle of Jack Daniels for my birthday and most of it was consumed that night. In the morning, Sandie made sure that I was sorted for breakfast, with cereal, toast and coffee, before heading off to college as she always did. I popped back across to Dowdell after my first class for another cup of coffee and Ray and Ed were in the kitchen. They wondered if we might finish off the Jack Daniels between us. There was only enough in the bottle for one shot each and we had it straight. After that, I went back across for my next class - half pissed. Everyone was asking how my birthday had gone. Great!

Chapter 20

A JOKE TOO FAR

It was sometime in January that I was interested in taking up the guitar, so I enquired about it through my Course Tutor. She booked me in for a lesson with a man who gave guitar lessons for students at the college. He came into the college to provide these lessons and charged eight pounds for half an hour. Gareth walked me up to the room for my first lesson. I turned up without a guitar, not realising that you had to bring one, so I borrowed the man's guitar until I got my own. The Guitar Tutor was good enough to drive me to a music shop in Leominster where I bought a second-hand electric guitar and a practice amp. I got the lot, and a case for £105. Now I had my own guitar to practice on. For the next step, I needed some help from the mobility team. Two of them placed little stickers on every second fret on the neck of my guitar so that I could easily and quickly find the finger positions. There was a band performance in April and Dave, the Guitar Tutor, was determined to teach me enough so that I could join in on the night. He taught me some basic chords and blues, such as Johnny Be Good, just to get me started.

    I went home again in the middle of February, as I wanted to try and see Aynsley. It was approaching Valentine's Day so I wanted to buy a card and some gifts for her. Mum was going out on one of the nights I was home but before she went, she poured a couple of whiskies for me, knowing that I couldn't pour them myself. I sat in my room having a drink and watching the tele for a while and then I decided to go for a wander. I thought I'd try to find out where Aynsley lived. As I said before, I had a rough idea where she lived - in a flat on the other side of Anstruther. It was a cold but calm evening so I started out walking – to the other side of Anstruther. It took me quite a while and as it was dark, with my limited sight, I kept bumping into lampposts and things on the way. I didn't have far left to go when a taxi pulled up alongside me. The driver was the one that often brought me back from Edinburgh Airport and he stopped to give me a lift. Although he was able to identify Aynsley's flat for me when he dropped me off, I discovered that the main entry door was locked and to get in, visitors had to key in the number of the flat they wanted to visit. I didn't know this so I couldn't get in. Luckily, while I was wondering what to do, a pizza delivery man arrived and the next minute – I was inside. Aynsley stayed on the top level - two flights up - so I walked up and knocked on her door. There was no answer. I rang her mobile and her house phone, together. Standing at the door, I could hear them both ringing, but still no answer. I decided to settle down on the floor and wait. After a while it seemed that I was probably wasting my time so I decided to give up, and phoned for a taxi. I got home long before Mum and went up to bed. By this time, the ice that Mum had left for my drinks had melted in the bowl. So - a couple of months going out with Aynsley, and I still hadn't seen her.

I phoned her the following day and she said that she was sorry that she hadn't been in after me walking all that way. On the Sunday before travelling back to Hereford I asked Mum to pick a Valentine Card for Aynsley. She wasn't very keen. She didn't really approve of us seeing each other because of the age difference but she got one anyway. I took it with me when I went back to college and asked a Support

Worker there, to take me into town to buy Aynsley a CD. I knew she liked Pink so I bought her the latest album. I got Terry, the night warden, to write the card for me so that it would be neat and tidy writing and then sent the card and the CD to Aynsley, from the College Green post office the next day. I also arranged for a florist back home to deliver a big bunch of flowers to her. Aynsley was delighted with the presents and I was delighted for her - but I didn't even get a card. The relationship didn't last long after that. I finished it between us - finished what hadn't really started!

It was around the same time that my brother and Lecia picked me up from Edinburgh Airport. They had some news and wanted me to be the first to know. Lecia stayed in the car while Michael came into the Airport to collect me. Once we were settled in the car, Michael said, "How do you feel about being an uncle, Billy?" Well! I was shocked but happy at the same time and congratulated them. However, they were terrified to tell our parents. Although Lecia would be sixteen by the time the baby was born, in October, right then, she was only fifteen! When we got home, Michael came in the house with me and Lecia stayed in the car, she was too scared to come in. At first, Mum was dumbstruck but soon became quite delirious at the prospect of being a granny. She asked Michael to fetch Lecia from the car and she gave her a big cuddle. Then we went across to Auntie Julie's to give her the news and she was over the moon as well. However, I had serious doubts about the whole thing. Although I would be delighted to be an uncle, Michael was only nineteen and Lecia, fifteen, and I thought they were a little young to be starting a family.

My Customer Service and Music Technology courses were going fine and part of my NVQ was a placement period in a working environment. My tutor asked if I wanted to work in Student Services for my work experience. I accepted her suggestion, but like any job, you had to apply for it first and go for an interview. My interview was with Mark and Barry and I got the job. I was to be working alongside Barry and the Student Support Workers. I knew I was going to enjoy it and by working there I would be able to meet lots of people coming in and out. The work experience started in April, for six weeks and during that time I would be dealing with internal student enquiries as well as taking external calls from members of the public. The work wasn't easy. I had to do a personal statement for every task I carried out and get Barry to counter-sign each one. Sometimes it was a bit tricky but I enjoyed it.

About this time, I decided to contact my local council, back home, and apply for my own house. I got the application form sent to the college, filled it in and sent it back. I thought, after all that I was learning at the college, it was time to move into a house of my own. I knew that if I went home after finishing the college, Mum would do everything for me and I didn't want that - it would have undone all the independent living skills I had learned - the main reason I had for going to the blind college.

Come April, I was looking forward to playing in the band, up in the Dog and Cane, which was the Student Bar. I hadn't practiced very long but Dave had taught me a fair bit. I was never too great with the guitar, as my left hand has always been quite stiff. It doesn't turn very well and I have trouble arching it, but I tried my best. I only played along with two songs that night. I remember Dave turning round to adjust my fingers on the strings but with him being a professional he still managed to keep playing while helping me. It was a great night. I really enjoyed being part of the show, especially hearing everyone cheering for us, in the bar.

My days at college were becoming quite hectic. As well as my course work, I was also working in Student Services and I was still involved with Music Technology in the taster course. I didn't attend so many classes though, when I was in Student Services and Barry was great to work with. He tried to get me involved as much as possible. The task I enjoyed most was phoning the mobiles of the various halls, to relay messages to them. He also sent me to the General Office with messages and asked me to help with the student enquiries whenever I could. I became so familiar with the work that I often covered for Barry when he was off. But - I was never allowed to sit at his desk in his seat, no - that was his desk.

I wasn't really enjoying the Music Technology course as I wasn't really into mixing music and that's basically what it was - operating a mixing desk. I really wanted to do a Radio Broadcast. It just so happened that a new member of staff came in round about April and thought about doing that very thing and made me the front man, the presenter - something I had always dreamed about. We called the Radio station Radio NCB, like the Royal National College for the Blind without the R at the beginning. It wasn't named after the college though, it was named after the students that were on the taster course – the letters were our first initials. There was still going to be mixing involved but there was also going to be recording, playing music, talking and recording jingles for the station as well. I was allowed to choose the music, as I was the presenter so I gathered up some songs, which I thought would fit with the show. We had a weather reporter, a news reporter, a traffic reporter, a sports reporter and me, the presenter. The news reporter and travel reporter were both blind. It was quite funny presenting the travel report as if it was being done from a helicopter - which we did the sound effects for. The Radio Show was a lot of hard work and would take a long time to get it right. The show was never going to be broadcast - it was just for fun and teaching us how everything worked.

I fell out with Anthony and Jason round about April. We liked to play tricks on each other, or rather; they liked to play tricks on me. One of their 'tricks' was to pick me up, take me up in the lift to the top floor and dump me there, on the floor. Then they'd ring someone's bell, and run away with my crutches. I tried to give as good as I got but it wasn't easy - they were a lot bigger than me. It was more Jason than Anthony, really. One night, I foolishly told them about a problem I was having, 'down below' and that I was going to the hospital for an investigation. As it turned out, the doctor told me that too much caffeine caused my problem and that there was nothing to worry about. However, he said I would need to have a minor operation. Jason and Anthony thought they would have a laugh in front of the Common Room crowd. They got a banana and a pot of yoghurt from the kitchen and followed me into the Common Room. In front of all the guys in the Common Room, they pinned me to the floor and pulled my trousers down. One of them forced the banana up my arse and the other one put my dick in the yoghurt. While they were doing this, I couldn't move and the boys in the Common Room were pissing themselves laughing at me. Jason told me (and everybody else) that it would help with my problem. I wasn't happy that night and was about sick with the smell of the yoghurt. How I hate yoghurt! I took a shower, to wash the stuff off but it was still all over my clothes. In my eyes, this meant war.

I knew that Jason always left his room door unlocked. And – I knew that he always went to the toilet right after lunch. From my room, I heard him and Anthony coming back from lunch. They went into the Common Room across the hall, for a chit-chat and a coffee, a regular occurrence before Jason went to the toilet. Once they were inside, I left my room, with a tube of toothpaste. I walked to Jason's room without my crutches, so I wouldn't make any noise. I opened his door quietly and went inside. I crept cautiously to his bathroom, with my legs shaking like a leaf, and I rimmed the toilet seat with Sensodine toothpaste, not realising that it would sting. Once 'the trick' was done, I quickly made my exit and went back to my own room. I didn't want to hang around so I gathered up some washing and went downstairs to the washroom, out of sight. Just as I was putting my washing in, I heard a mighty roar. Jason was bawling my name! I heard him charging about upstairs, searching for me and banging on my door. I thought he would find me wherever I was so I just let him look. A few minutes later Jason and Anthony came downstairs and - walked right past me and out the door. I was safe - they were gone. With my 'friends' out of the way, I strolled back upstairs, into the Common Room, and made myself a coffee before going back to Student Services.

That night, in the Refectory, I was sitting at the table when Jason and Anthony came in. They sat right down next to me and Jason said, "This means war!" I wasn't too concerned. However, later that night, I was sitting in my room watching the tele when there was a knock on the door. It was Jason. He invited me next door for a coffee and some chocolate, so I stupidly, went along. Jason loved it. Although I didn't know it at the time, the chocolate he was feeding me was laxative! Actually, it was quite nice and Jason tried to encourage me to have some more. Anthony was subtler. He said, "Leave him alone, Jason. Do you want him to be sick?"

I should have known but they were eating chocolate too. The difference, of course, was that theirs was the genuine stuff. I was hardly in bed when I had to get up to the toilet. After that, I hardly slept a wink - I was up most of the night, with the runs! It was dire – and disgusting, but it didn't dawn on me until the following day what must have caused it. It was Saturday and I struggled to get out of bed. Eventually, I managed to have a shower and go for tea. Again, Jason and Anthony came and sat beside me. When I questioned them about the chocolate, they just laughed and said, "And it's taken you all this time to figure that out!"

I was mad! They were supposed to be my mates. I decided to get revenge on them. First, I tried fixing sticky sweets on their door handles. Then I tried lacing their coffees with tons of sugar. I was persistent. I tried putting an egg in Jason's bed, hoping it would burst when he lay on it. He found out! I didn't know that. He knocked on my door and asked me if I wanted to come to the Common Room for coffee. Yes – I should have known, especially after the last time. When I got settled in the Common Room, he came up behind me and cracked the egg over my head. My 'trick' had backfired! I wasn't finished, though. One night, I don't know what came over me, but I was so mad, I picked up the fire bucket in the Common Room and tried to empty it over Anthony's head. As I swung the bucket, I slipped and accidentally hit him on the head, instead. Anthony, big Anthony, picked me up and threw me and my head struck Jason on the knee. I lay motionless on the Common Room floor - the jokes had gone too far. I was wheeled to the nurse's room to be checked out. It turned out that I was okay but that wasn't the end of the story. I went to Mark the next day and told him what had been happening. I just went to get it off my chest but Mark started taking notes and told me that this was serious bullying, and possibly a police matter. I didn't really want it to go that far. I just wanted the capers to stop. I didn't want Mark to speak to Jason or Anthony but he did and it only made things worse. After that, they didn't speak to me for months.

Chapter 21

AMY

I tried to get away from Jason and Anthony for a while. At every opportunity I was out on the football field playing football with the other boys or sometimes I borrowed a ball and went outside on my own and had a kick around against the advertising boards. When I tired of that, I would kick shots into the empty goal. I didn't enjoy that much, as I had to go and fetch the ball every time I scored! Football wasn't the only activity available, though. There was swimming in the local pool and I played in the Blind Bowling League, every second Tuesday. Although the Swimming was also on a Tuesday night, it was *every* Tuesday so I got to each of them, alternate weeks. Nobody else from Dowdell Hall went bowling but a few from B floor went swimming, including Ray, Les, Les's brother, who had joined us in January, and Ed. Wherever we went, we always started out from Gardner Hall. The Swimming pool wasn't open to the public, only to people like us, and it was free of charge. Another couple of students also went swimming. One of them was called Gavin; the other was a female, called Cari. She was a bit of a tomboy, always wearing boy's clothes. I think she may have been a lesbian. I got to know Gavin and Cari a bit better, through the swimming, and it got me away from Jason and Anthony.

I became really good mates with Gavin as we both had the same condition and we had an understanding between us. I also became quite attached to Cari and began to hang around with her a lot. She was quite small with short, blonde hair. I tried to convert her from being gay, without success. She often came to my room to talk and listen to music, and sometimes she would stay over. Sometimes I would go to another one of the colleges outside houses that she shared with two guys, where she had a bed sit with a cooker and a fridge. One night, when I stayed over, I left my bag in the taxi and we had to phone for another taxi to bring the bag back!

I learned that Cari wasn't very reliable about money; good at borrowing, not good at paying back. There was one time when I did lend her some money - and never saw it again. She also borrowed some clothes and some CDs but didn't return them either. When she left the college without telling anyone I didn't think she was coming back, so I asked Mark and Barry to go to her house to retrieve my things. They went along and found a single CD case but no CD. I didn't get anything back.

Gavin and I used to spend a lot of time just talking – either in his room, in Campbell Hall, or in mine. Sometimes we would talk for hours. Although we didn't do much else together, apart from swimming, it was good to talk to someone else that had cerebral palsy. Gavin's palsy wasn't as severe as mine. He could walk without the aid of sticks, and had better balance than I had. There might have been slight differences between us but I thought of us as being the same.

It was approaching summer so all of the YTS students were going home, including Gavin. This meant new students after the holidays. My Course Tutor told me that the Braille Transcription Unit was looking for someone to help out during the summer and she thought I would be perfect for the job. This meant doing another work placement but something totally different. I would have to apply again but that turned out okay because, just like the previous interview, I was the man for the job. In the BTU I would have to wear a fresh shirt and tie everyday and since I wanted to be independent when I left the college, I asked Gareth to teach me some domestic skills. He started off by teaching me to iron my shirts. He taught me how to iron without steam, as it would be difficult for a blind person to fill an iron with water. He was a really good teacher and taught me the safest way to iron without burning myself. He also taught me how to hoover, use a dustpan and a mop, and clean the toilet, sink and shower cubical. I also learned to cook for myself. Before Gareth was finished with me, I could fry, grill, bake and use the microwave. As I learned, he was constantly challenging me with questions as to how I would do each task.

As I really enjoyed listening to the local radio station, Wyvern FM, my tutor arranged for me to go to the station in Worcester with a view to a possible work placement. I was really looking forward to this and an added bonus was that I was to be driven there by one of the most gorgeous girls that I had ever seen. She was blonde - and she was stunning. We arrived shortly before the mid morning presenter was going on-air. This presenter was the boss of the station. The breakfast presenters met us when we arrived and showed us around one of the studios before taking us through to the main studio to sit with the boss during his show. He was a lovely man and guided us through everything that he did during the show, explaining about the choice of music and a clock system that helped him to fit everything in. It was a great day out and it was great to get real-life experience of a radio station. Although I didn't get a work placement, he did send me some programmes to help me with my own radio presentation.

At the end of term, the Summer Ball was held in the college. The Beat, a band from the Eighties, was providing the music. I managed to persuade Ray to stay on for the Ball - initially he hadn't been too keen. I found out that Hereford had a shop that hired kilts so I arranged for an SSW to take me there in a college car. I was fitted for what they called 'Highland Wear' - they never once called it a kilt. I hired the Scottish National Tartan, which I had worn before. On the night of the Ball, Sandie helped me get into my kilt and the rest of my gear. Once I was fully kitted out Sandie said I looked so smart, she just had to take a photo. The photo later finished up in a very prominent position on the wall of the Common Room, providing a fine 'worm's eye view of a scotsman in 'Highland Wear'!

When I got dressed I wore boxer shorts under my kilt but when I got across to the college I immediately went into the toilets and took them off - I wanted to be a true Scotsman. Once the Ball got underway, it wasn't long before some curious female just had to put her hand up my kilt to check what I had underneath. Surprise, surprise! A buffet meal was laid out in the Refectory and soft piano music was playing there for the benefit of anyone who couldn't take the full whack of the stuff that The Beat were belting out in the Assembly Hall. Ray and I were happy to spend most of the night in the Hall, with the Beat. I did a lot of sitting while Ray did a lot of dancing and jumping about to the music. It was a great night. Even Ray thoroughly enjoyed himself even though he hadn't really wanted to go in the first place.

Finally, it was summer and the YTS students had gone home. The college was almost deserted. It turned out to be one of the hottest summers on record and I was constantly taking showers to freshen up. Although the YTS students had left, the RTU students were still there and that meant everyone on my floor, including Ray and Les, who kept me company throughout the summer. I was really bored in the Braille Transcription Unit. I think that was partly because I'd rather have spent the summer at home with my family and partly because of what happened previously with Jason and Anthony. I did get to run the BTU at times when the boss wasn't there and this meant phoning clients who had left messages on the answer-machine. While I was in classes in the model office I was also in charge of taking bookings for the Remedial Therapy Department where Jason and Anthony were. I liked this part of my course. It was really satisfying, dealing with the public. I was doing well with my course but my tutor didn't think I was going to be finished by September so she applied for an extension until Christmas. I got the extension. We had finished the radio presentation, apart from editing it and putting it all together. Ray helped me finish it as the Music Tech tutors seemed to have given up. Ray stayed a lot during the summer to keep me company and I always went for meals with him and Les, and Les's brother.

I was a little bored one day so I decided to walk up to College Green and buy some cigarettes, thinking I'd give them another try. Because I didn't want anyone to know, I brought an ashtray through from the kitchen and kept it in my room. This time I smoked the full packet, not just a couple. Soon, I was making regular visits to College Green. I'd buy packets of forty to save me going too often – and before long I was getting hooked on them. I hid the ashtray in a drawer so that there would be little chance of anyone finding it while I was in college. When the ashtray was full, I would dump the contents into an old pizza box and put it in the bin in our small snack bar kitchen. I didn't want to smoke in front of anyone or have anyone find out so I'd pop back to my room during breaks, have a quick puff and then spray myself with deodorant and aftershave to hide the smell. I could have smoked in front of anyone on our floor as they were all smokers but I felt a little embarrassed.

I think it was Geoff's Birthday celebration during the summer, when he got really drunk and started verbally abusing people in the Common Room. He had a go at everyone individually and when he got around to me he said, "Billy Stix, the world does not revolve around you!" I just laughed. Actually, it was a great night with *lots* of laughs but a girl student came down from the top floor to complain about the racket. She was from Scotland but she was a pain in the arse. We turned her around and sent her on her way. On the way out, she tried to slam the door behind her but the door had a damper device on it and closed very slowly, much to our alcohol-fuelled amusement.

The appointment for my latest surgery finally came through. As I got on really well with Terry, the duty night warden, I asked him if he would take me into hospital on the day of the op. The hospital was only a few minutes walk from the college but Terry took me in a taxi to make it easier for me. When we arrived at the hospital I was checked in and asked to change into a theatre gown. I wasn't so nervous about this operation but I was a bit anxious that Mum couldn't be with me this time. I was sitting on my bed, with Terry beside me, when his mobile suddenly rang and he answered it. One of the nurses immediately took off at a rate of knots - I think to report Terry for having the mobile on in the hospital. Terry, on the other hand, didn't seem to be aware that he had done anything wrong and long before the nurse reappeared he had finished his call and gone back to college. Before he left, he told me that Vince would come and collect me, later - just to phone for him when I was ready. While I relaxed on my bed, waiting for the next move, I made a call home, using the hospital phone beside my bed. I was still on the phone when a nurse came to collect me for Theatre. On the operating table, I was trying my best to relax, as a number of staff milled around me, preparing me for the op, when something suddenly went wrong. As they started to inject the anaesthetic, the needle popped out and a searing pain shot up my left arm. The last I remember of that is screaming in agony - and then I passed out!

When I woke again, there was only silence. I didn't have much pain but was still a bit drowsy when a nurse finally appeared by my bed. After she checked that I was okay, she told me that I would have to pass urine before I would be allowed to go home. I soon passed that test - with flying colours - and the nurse phoned for Vince to collect me. Back in college, I had to spend a few days in the Sick Bay, gathering my strength, before I could return to my own room. I was due to go home the following weekend and had to make sure I was fit to travel.

When I went home that weekend, I was at a bit of a loose end so I called The Phone Bar. This was a chat-line service that I had got into when I was at Glenrothes College. Men have to pay for the service; women get to use it for free. I got talking to two girls from Durham, one of whom was very reluctant to say very much but eventually we got into a good conversation. She introduced herself as 'Nicky' and sounded really nice. After a long discussion about our backgrounds, interests and what we looked like - I made sure I told her about my disabilities - we swapped mobile numbers and promised to speak again.

When I got back to college I called Nicky again, and discovered - that she had been less than honest with me. Her name was in fact; Amy and she had a boyfriend in Durham. However, she was fed up with him and wanted to break up. I talked to her for weeks on my mobile. She'd often phone me late at night and we'd speak for hours. This meant I was often shattered when I had to get up for college, the next morning, but it was worth it – I really liked her.

Knowing I had the BTU to go to, I made sure I did my laundry each Sunday. I brought the ironing board into my room and ironed while I listened to The Sunday Surgery on Radio One. It was nice and relaxing that way. Amy would often phone when I was in the Common Room with the boys so I'd leave the room to take her call. I'd also take that opportunity to have a smoke in my room, while we chatted. Amy smoked too so I told her that I smoked. I'd never told anyone else at this point. Our conversations were getting quite serious and she wanted to come and see me at the college. I booked her a room across from mine for a Saturday night but she was coming to stay Friday and Saturday night – and planning on staying in my room with me.

As Amy was coming to see me I realised that I would be in the Common Room quite a lot with her and that the boys there would be smoking. When it was just me and Ray staying one weekend, and he had left to go to College Green, I lit up a cigarette and when he got back, he asked who had been smoking. When I said, "Me," he said, "You don't smoke, Billy Stix." When I showed him my packet of cigarettes, he still didn't believe me so I had to smoke one just to prove the point.

Now that Ray knew, all of B floor found out and I was able to have one in the Common Room without causing a fuss. Still, it felt really strange, smoking in front of people. Some of them already had an idea – the ones that had a sniff each time they passed my door! The one person that was really disappointed was Sandie. Sandie was like my second mother at the college; she looked after me, made my breakfast each morning and chatted with me when I came across from the college. I'd always had trouble putting the duvet cover on my bed because my balance was so poor, so Sandie did that for me too. So, we were very close and she was – very disappointed.

When I knew for sure, that Amy was coming, I tried to dress to impress. When Sandie saw what I was wearing she came into my room and found me something better to wear! I was hanging around with Santi quite a lot by this stage and being such a good friend, he offered to pick Amy up from the station. On the day, he collected a college car and I went along with him. Everyone on B floor knew she was coming and one of them tried to find a condom machine for me - just in case. When he finally located one I went along with him and bought a packet – no harm in being prepared. Unfortunately, my stitches still hadn't healed by this time. If I was going to do the business I would have to go through a little pain as well.

I was extremely nervous when we went to pick Amy up. I had only heard her voice on the phone and only knew her by how she had described herself - fairly tall, with strawberry blonde hair. I was meeting her with my mohican hairstyle, bleached blonde. I had a lot of daft hair styles back then. After we picked her up, we hardly spoke a word all the way back to the college. Although Vince saw her get out of the car and wondered who she was, he didn't ask, just stayed out of the way. Amy'd had a long journey and was shattered so she lay down on my bed and had a snooze. This was a first for me - a girl lying on my bed. I let her rest while I watched the tele in my room. When she woke again, I took her through to the Common Room to meet some of the boys. I got her a soft drink and tried to make her as welcome as possible, still hoping to make a good impression.

I took her out that night, to a popular steak house. Turned out she was a vegetarian. Still, she seemed to enjoy her vegiburger and chips. As it was a nice, warm evening we sat for a while afterwards, in the beer garden, drinking, talking and having a smoke. On our way back to Dowdell Hall, we stopped at Tesco's and bought a bottle of wine for Amy, and a Coke to go with the whisky that I had back in my room. We sat in my room for a while before going through to the Common Room, where I spent most of the night drinking whisky and cuddling Amy. I can't remember how it happened but we ended up back in my room. She was looking for music on my computer while I was sitting in front of the tele. On an impulse, I said, "Amy, you haven't told me what you think of me! Are we going to kiss?" She hesitated a moment and then said, "I really like you, Billy, and it's a pity you asked me about a kiss . . . I was just going to spring it on you!" I sat quiet for a while after that, as Amy carried on her music search and then suddenly she turned round and planted a great big passionate kiss on my lips. It was a beautiful snog, much better than I'd ever had with Yvonne or Claire. We kissed again a few minutes later and I thought it was going to lead somewhere – and it did, but only back to the Common Room. I got quite drunk after that, spilled some whisky and went back to my room to be sick.

I told Amy that I was going to bed and she said she would be through in a minute. The next thing I knew it was morning and she wasn't beside me. I panicked and thought she had gone home but her bag was still at the bottom of my bed. My mind started to race and I remembered Ed getting quite friendly with her. I jumped out of bed and charged through to the Common Room where I spotted two guys, sound asleep. I couldn't see who they were so I shook one of them – hard. It was Ed. I asked him where Amy was but he was half asleep and just mumbled so I went to his room and walked straight in. Sure enough, Amy was there, lying in Ed's bed. I tried to wake her but she seemed sound asleep. I was so upset, I started to sob – and that woke her. We went through to my room then, and lay in bed together for most of the morning, just lying - not doing or saying anything. Some time, mid-morning, my dad phoned from the boat to have a chat. Amy tried not to make a sound, but she coughed and Dad asked who was with me. When I explained, he said he didn't want to hear that I was lying next to a woman, and left me to it.

It was a lovely day outside but all I wanted to do was lie beside Amy. She said she wanted to leave that day because she had called in sick too many times before and didn't want to get fired from her job. It was already in the back of my mind that she didn't really like me. She'd found the condoms in my drawer when she was looking for some cigarettes, the night before. She didn't seem too pleased and asked if I'd been planning on having sex with her. I told her, only if it was what we both wanted - that I wasn't looking for it to happen. She didn't say much after that – just had a shower and dressed to go home. She didn't have enough money for the train home so she borrowed some from me. I knew I'd never see her, or the money, again. She gathered up her things, gave me a kiss and walked out the door. I let her go on her own. It would have been too hard for me to see her off at the station.

I didn't want to face anyone that day so I didn't go for lunch and I didn't really fancy going for tea, either. I was upset, hungover and disappointed that I had crashed out. That was the last day I wore my glasses. They weren't making any difference to my sight so I took them off and haven't worn them since. Amy phoned me that night to let me know she was home safe and sound. I was glad to hear her voice. I had thought I would never hear from her again but she still kept in touch. I took a lot of my frustration out on my floor mates, especially Ed. I accused him of sleeping with Amy and then sleeping in the Common Room to look like he hadn't been with her. He always denied it and was adamant that he only gave her a bed for the night because I was legless and had flaked out on mine.

Chapter 22

I'M GOING HOME

After Amy left, I didn't feel happy in the Braille Transcription Unit. I decided that I wanted to go home in September and not stay on for my extension. Although we weren't allowed home for the whole summer, we did get to go home for two weeks, in August. I was bored at home, although I was still in touch with Amy. I decided to call the Phone Bar again and I got talking to a lovely girl from Dundee. She left me her number and I called her back – several times. After a few days of phone calls, we decided to meet up. At first, just like Amy, she gave me a false name. She called herself Rachel, not Carrie, which was in fact her real name.

The day she came to Anstruther on the bus, I stood at the bus stop, nervously waiting for her to arrive. Eventually, two buses pulled in at the same time and I watched for her getting off. After a few minutes, both buses pulled away again – and she hadn't got off. I rang her mobile. It turned out that she *was* on one of the buses but didn't realise that she should have got off at that stop. I ran towards the next bus stop as quickly as I could, still talking to her on the phone – and Carrie got off at the next stop and ran back to meet me. When we met, she gave me a little kiss and I started walking home with her. About halfway home, my Auntie Julie came along in her car, and gave us a lift the rest of the way. Once we got in the house, we went upstairs and lay down on my single bed, listening to the radio. Carrie was quite small, with black hair and lovely green eyes. She also had very large breasts but I wasn't interested in how big her breasts were, I was just interested in her. We hadn't been lying there long when she started to kiss me. She snogged me quite passionately with a very long, lingering kiss, the longest I'd ever had. A short time later, Mum came in and came straight upstairs. I had a lock on my bedroom door but rarely locked it. Mum walked in and was taken aback to find the two of us lying there. She didn't really approve but she left us to it and we continued kissing. I remember this being a Thursday as Craig's sister had invited me to her 'Twenty-First' in Cupar on the Saturday night. Carrie was staying over Thursday and Friday and going home on Saturday lunchtime so that Dad and I could go together to watch East Fife in the afternoon. On Thursday night we had sex for the first time - not for her, but for me. As I'd never had sex before, I didn't produce anything and Carrie thought it was her fault. She perked up a bit when I said it was more likely my fault because it was my first time and I didn't know what to expect. Even so, I was still able to satisfy her with a variety of different sexual pleasures. There wasn't much room for both of us to sleep in my single bed. Neither of us was exactly skinny, but we managed, somehow.

I took Carrie out to The Sally for her tea on Friday night. After our meal, we had a slow romantic walk back home. Everyone was out so we had the place to ourselves. Carrie wanted us to have a bath together. I thought she was trying to warm me up for something and I instantly agreed. After our bath we went through to my room and watched a film but we didn't see much of the film, for kissing. One thing led to another and we tried to have sex again. This time it was different. It had been such a good night - I was really fired up. This time everything that should happen, happened, and I was no longer a virgin. Carrie didn't want to leave me on the

Saturday but I had already promised to go to the football with my dad and then to Craig's sister's birthday party at night. Carrie wasn't happy but I walked her to the bus, after lunch, gave her a kiss and waved her off as the bus pulled out.

My mum, my dad, Auntie Julie, Uncle Eck, Helen and Ali were all going to another birthday party, not too far from where I was going in Cupar, so I shared their taxi. On the way, Mum talked about Carrie and asked if I'd done the business. I told the truth and Mum asked if I was protected. I said no, because she was on the pill. Mum was horrified, not because I had sex but because I hadn't used a condom. She said she was happy for me that I had found someone to have a relationship with and she thought that Carrie was a lovely girl. She said she was just looking out for her wee boy.

Because the party was held in a hall, we had to bring our own drink so I brought a bottle of whisky and a bottle of Coke. I sat most of the night with Craig and his mates and Craig's family came over from time to time, to talk to me. It was good to see them all again. I hadn't seen them since I went up to Craig's in early January of 2000. One of Craig's mates was pouring my drinks for me and they were pretty large ones at that. Instead of pouring singles his measures were more like trebles. I was quite steaming by the end of the night. Towards the end of the night, I needed the toilet and Craig's mum kindly took me. She was about to leave me to it but then I fell and she went to get Craig and his dad to help me up. It was a bit embarrassing because, as they were helping me up, my willie was still hanging out. After that incident, Craig's mum put me in a wheelchair, for safety's sake so I sat in that for the rest of the night. Partway through the celebrations, my mobile rang and it was Amy. I could barely hear her for the music in the hall so I hung up. I had arranged for a taxi to pick me up but it didn't appear. He had gone to pick the others up from their party, told them he had come for me and I wasn't there and he said he wouldn't go back for me. He was going to leave me stranded in Cupar but Mum told him, "You go back for Billy – right now!" - and he did. Craig's Mum and Dad waited with me until the taxi arrived. When it did, I thanked them for a great night. They were still waving as we drove out of sight.

I phoned Amy the next day to apologise and explain why I had hung up on her. Then I phoned Carrie. I felt a bit awkward because although I was now in a relationship with Carrie, I still had strong feelings for Amy. Amy had phoned me one night when I was lying next to Carrie and I had to tell her that I was busy. I think Amy had feelings for me too because she wasn't very pleased and complained that we didn't speak to each other as often. Later, when I got back to the college, I came clean with her and told her about Carrie. We were still friends but we drifted away from each other a bit after that.

Carrie came through again before I went back to the college and we went out for a meal, but this time four of us went; Carrie, Michael, Lecia and me. Carrie and Lecia got on well together, hence the reason for the foursome. After the meal, we went to The Sally for a drink, and Carrie met my cousins, John and Eck, and Eck's girlfriend, Laura. As Lecia was pregnant, she stayed on the soft drinks. We had a good night but after that, Carrie and I spent the rest of the weekend on our own, enjoying the short time together before I had to go back to college.

My relationship with Carrie made me more determined to finish my course before Christmas. I wanted to go home and spend time with her. I talked to my Course Tutor but she didn't want me to go home until Christmas. She suggested that I have another spell in Student Services until I left. I agreed to give it another try but I said I wasn't staying until Christmas. I told her I was going home on the seventeenth of October, come rain or come shine, whether my course was finished or not.

I started in Student Services again in September, ready for all the students, new and 'old' returning. There were also some new SSWs starting. Most of the old SSWs, including Santi, Dana and Paul had all left to go back to Ecuador; Santi being the last of my friends to leave. Santi and I spent a lot of time together before he left. He used to visit me regularly, in my room and I would visit him in the various halls, when he was on Warden duty. He didn't speak much English when he arrived at the RNC but by the time he left he spoke it well. I was sad to see him go but we swapped phone numbers and email addresses so that we could keep in touch.

When I started back in Student Services for the second time I didn't have to wear a shirt and tie like I did in the Braille Transcription Unit. After sleeping with Carrie, I got myself checked out to make sure that I hadn't picked up any transmittable diseases. If I wanted my relationship with Carrie to work I wanted to make sure she and I were both clean. During my appointment at the clinic, the doctor noticed a lump above my right testicle. He was quite concerned and sent for another doctor to get a second opinion. It seemed that I had a hernia and as I was going home soon, the doctor suggested that I have it checked out by my own GP whenever I got home. A few days later, the clinic reported that my tests were clear. That was excellent news and I was now looking forward to spending more time with Carrie.

Having a Hernia meant that I had to stay out of the

gym and not do any heavy lifting. I had made up with Jason and Anthony by this time and they said that although I would have to give up the leg weights, I could continue with some arm weights and other less strenuous exercises. They were both due to leave the college soon so I was pleased to have made up with them. It was a bit harder to make up with Jason – he seemed quite reluctant at first but Anthony was fine about it and gave me a big hug before he left the college. I really liked them both and despite the hassles we had, I new I was really going to miss them.

I hadn't heard from Phill for a long time and I started wondering how he was getting on so I phoned him. It took a few calls before I eventually got him. He seemed to be confused and kept asking, "Billy who?" I already knew he had a problem but I hadn't thought it was so bad that he wouldn't know who I was. I tried telling him that I was Billy Horsburgh, his best mate but he didn't seem to understand. I loved Phill as a mate - we did almost everything together and now he didn't even know who I was.

I'd had a number of hospital investigations on my throat while I was at college. Sometimes it was quite painful and I tended to choke a lot. It became quite worrying. At the hospital, the doctors passed cameras up my nose and down my throat to find the root of the problem but without much success. Eventually, one of these camera investigations discovered that I had a lot of excess acid in my stomach so I was given tablets, to be taken daily, to neutralise this excess acid. At least they got to the bottom of that problem. I wasn't very keen to take the tablets but in the end I had to, as the pain sometimes got unbearable.

I was really looking forward to Student Services again. I got the same desk as I had the last time I was there. I think some of the existing SSWs were a bit jealous of me sitting where they usually sat but that was now my seat until I left the college. Barry asked me to provide guidance for the new students and SSWs and I was able to point quite a few people in the right direction now that I had been at the college for a full year. As quite a few students were blind, I often had to walk them to the departments they wanted and I was also getting to know the new SSWs, well. One of them was Santi's cousin from Ecuador. I got on quite well with him but, like Santi, he struggled with his English, to begin with. Apart from a couple, I got on well with most of the new SSWs. Santi's cousin had three SSW friends, one being an Italian woman. She was very nice – and very nice looking. Her English was extremely good because, although she was Italian, she had been living in London for a number of years. Her name was Fiamma. She called me Billy Bhoo and I called her Fiamma Bhoo. She had a boyfriend at the college who was also an SSW. He was from Ecuador; a big tall man. His English was good, too. Not surprising, as he was a Canadian citizen. I had now made four new SSW friends but I still had a really good 'old' SSW friend. That was Jacob and he was Polish. I had always been friendly with Jacob but I started hanging around with him more when Santi left. Jacob wanted to stay on at the college to do a course in Music Technology.

Some of the new SSWs played football with us on Monday and Thursday nights. Towards the end of the summer, I was asked to play in the Hereford United Disabled League. Most of the players were from the college. I went along, with the rest of the boys, to Hereford United's football ground where we had our photo taken wearing the Hereford United kit. I had already started training for the Disabled League when the coach got back from holiday and declared that crutches weren't allowed in the Disabled League . . . so

I couldn't play! I was still allowed to train with them but not allowed to play. I was gutted. I so wanted to play football. I don't think the coach liked me anyway - I injured his son playing football one night. He tried to run in front of me and he clipped my crutches and fell on the ground, rolling around like he had broken his leg. When he stopped writhing about we discovered that he had only cut his leg on my crutches. Anyway, I took my subs back and I didn't train again with the Disabled Team. I still played on Monday and Thursday nights though, and I was determined to score a goal before I left the college. One night, I slowly drifted from defence into the midfield and onwards to the penalty box when the ball was passed to me. I controlled it with my left foot and struck it hard with my right. I struck the ball with a lot of curve and although it started wide of goal, it bounced just in front of the far post and the curve took it into the net. The keeper didn't even move as he thought it was going well wide. My cousin, Eck, once said that scoring a goal was better than sex. I'm not so sure!

It was nearing the end of my time in college and my Course Tutor was still trying to change my mind about leaving. I was having none of it - I was still going in October. I had already arranged for my dad to drive down and collect me. I started working really hard in Students Services and in the Model Office so that I would be finished in October. Barry helped a lot by thinking of different tasks for me to do so that I could get the evidence I needed for my portfolio. I was running out of time fast and still had a lot to do but with the help of Barry and my tutors, I finally managed to finish in time to go home.

I couldn't go home without saying goodbye to a few people. People like Gareth, Barry, Mark and the SSWs. Should I throw a party? Vince suggested that he, Barry,

Mark and I should all go for a drink before I left. Good idea. Vince made all the arrangements and I was to take a taxi and meet up with the rest of them in town. On the night, Barry and Mark were late, and Vince didn't even turn up . . . and it was his idea. The three of us sat and had a few pints and spoke about the college and how much I enjoyed it. It was nice to talk to them outside of work and we had a great night.

I also asked Gareth out for a drink, to thank him for everything he had done for me; my mobility training and all my Living Skills. We decided to go for a drink together, just after college had finished for the day. First, I went to the Refectory for a sandwich, as I didn't want to drink on an empty stomach. Gareth's girlfriend, an ex-SSW, drove us to a pub near the college. Once we got settled in the pub, Gareth asked me if I smoked. I said, "Yes, but not a lot of people know - why?" He said, "It's just that I like a cigarette when I have a drink!" I gave him a cigarette. We sat and had a couple of drinks and a smoke and I thanked him for all of his help. Gareth's girlfriend drove us back to the college when we had finished and Gareth told me how much he liked me and how much he thought I was a great student. That felt good. I got out of the car and headed up to my room for a good night's sleep.

I arranged a party for the Thursday night before I left, on the Saturday. During my last week I often heard a lot of movement outside my room door, a lot of people going back and forward, but I had no idea what was going on. On the Thursday night, a few of us went up to the bar for a going away drink and then went back to Dowdell for the full-on party. While I was in the bar I was talking to a girl called Naomi, from my Music Tech taster course. Naomi wasn't the brightest of girls but I had a crush on her all through college. I took her into the bathroom that night and taught her how to kiss, as she didn't know how to kiss properly. I sat on the edge of the bath and started to kiss her and showed her how to snog. After that, she kissed me several times that night. I was still very much in love with Carrie, back home, but wanted to kiss Naomi before I went home. I had no intentions of taking it any further. We left the bar early to go to the party back at Dowdell. Terry had told us that there were to be no parties that night because other floors, especially C floor, had began to complain. We had a party anyway; B floor wanted to give me a good send off. When we got back to Dowdell the guys on B floor brought out a surprise for me. That's when I finally realised what all the movement outside my door had been. Instead of a card with everyone's messages on it, Ed had been getting everyone to record their messages onto a CD. There were messages from Sandie, Mandy, Terry, Ed, Ray, Les, Geoff and a few others on B floor.

We didn't make much noise that night but a staff member from the main college building was on call to come in, if anything got out of hand. It was her birthday that day and we didn't really want to spoil her birthday but we were having a drink and a really good time and Terry had already been through a few times so the inevitable happened. Terry called her in to deal with the trouble and break up the party. It was a real pity. My friend, Tony, had gone home in September but had come back for my going away party. I was disappointed to have to tell him that he couldn't get in because Terry wasn't letting anyone in, who wasn't on B floor. I was so upset with Terry that night, I protested by lying outside the Warden's office until another member of B floor came and dragged me back to the Common Room. The party was a disaster! I went outside and sat on one of the picnic benches on my own, to have a cigarette. I knew Terry was watching me from the window. Tony came along and sat with me for a while and then Terry came down to see if I was all right. I hardly said a word to him. Eventually, I went back upstairs and had a quiet drink with some of the students still in the Common Room - and then I went to bed.

My dad was travelling down to Hereford on the Friday, staying overnight and taking me home on the Saturday. Dad wasn't due to arrive until teatime so I had plenty of time to say goodbye. As it was my last day at the college I was smoking in front of anyone and everyone – and Fiamma was offering me cigarettes from time to time. I said my goodbyes to Sandie – a very special person in my life. She looked after me like a mother, always making sure I was ok. Another special person for me was Mark. He came to see me in my room on Friday afternoon and spoke about the party. I told him that there had been no real trouble – we were just having a good time. I said I just wanted to leave on a high, but now I felt I was leaving on a low. He said everything would be okay, and not to worry – no one would hold a grudge. He said I was a much-loved person at the college and that I would be badly missed. I felt a lot better after Mark's comforting words and I did leave on a high after all. I shook Mark's hand and he wished me the best of luck.

I ordered a Chinese Takeaway for Dad and me and after we'd finished that we went to the bar for a drink. Although Dad had needed a smoke when he arrived, he waited until we got to the Common Room – he said he didn't want to spoil my room with the smell of cigarettes. Little did he know! While we were having a drink, in the bar, Fiamma came across and offered me a cigarette. She gave me a funny look when I said I didn't smoke but she didn't say anything. Dad didn't say anything, either, but by his expression I thought he was beginning to wonder.

Dad and I went to bed as we had a very long drive ahead of us Saturday. Dad had already fallen asleep when I heard footsteps outside, in the hall, followed by a very faint knock on the door. I jumped out of bed and ran to the door in my pyjamas. Fiamma, Santi's cousin and the other two SSWs had come to say goodbye. We went through to the Common Room where we had a chat – and a smoke. Dad was still sound when I got back, about twenty minutes later. Another few minutes and I was sound, too. Although Dad had packed the car on Friday, we got up early on Saturday morning and handed my room key in to the Duty Warden, who turned out to be Terry. After one final goodbye, we set off, leaving the RNC behind. Some of the staff and students had said I'd be back in a couple of months to do another course – I didn't think so.

On the way home, I thought about the time I'd spent at the college. It was one of the best experiences of my life - meeting so many other people with sight problems, learning how to live on my own so far away from home, and learning a new college course 'the blind way'. I loved the college and the guys - and Sandie. And I especially loved room 16, B Floor, Dowdell Hall.

Chapter 23

RIGHT AT HOME

I slept most of the journey home from the Blind College – only waking from time to time when Dad spoke to me. We stopped a couple of times, at service stations, for something to eat but didn't put off much time there. When we got home, Dad carried my bags and stuff upstairs and I started unpacking straight away.

Carrie didn't come through on the weekend I came home so I spent most of the weekend on my own, sitting in my bedroom, listening to the radio and playing football on the computer. I tried to help Mum in the house when I got back from the college but she wasn't keen on that. She said as long as I was at home it was her job to look after me. I didn't want that because I felt that all the living skills I had learned would be going to waste. I couldn't wait for a letter from the council to offer me a flat.

Carrie came through now and then and stayed for a few days each time. We would just lie there on my bed watching films or go out for a drink. One night, when she wanted to sleep head to toe, I had a visual hallucination. I didn't have many of these when I was at the college but I had one that night. I had already warned her about these visions so she was prepared when I suddenly screamed in the middle of the night. I was half awake when it happened. I was looking at Carrie, standing next to my bed, telling me not to move, when a rat suddenly ran across the bed covers. That's when I screamed. Actually, Carrie wasn't really standing next to my bed at all, she was in it – and there was no rat. When I screamed, Carrie was so startled that she leaped out of bed. She comforted me for a long while, until I calmed down and stopped shaking.

Carrie stayed in Dundee, with her mum. Her mum and dad had split up. I went to her house in early November, to meet her mum and her brother. I also met one of Carrie's best friends that day. The three of us went out in the afternoon to where Carrie worked, to have a couple of drinks. I've never been an afternoon drinker and I was getting quite drunk very quickly. Carrie noticed this and suggested we go back to her place. We stopped on the way to pick up a fish supper. The three of us were watching the tele, upstairs in Carrie's room, when I fell asleep on her bed. When her friend left, Carrie and I lay on her bed, kissing and cuddling. Staying at Carrie's was different from staying at my mum's. Carrie's mum didn't let us sleep in the same bed. She was very religious and 'wouldn't allow that under her roof.' Carrie slept on the couch and let me have her bed. I did offer to sleep on the couch but she wouldn't hear of it. The next day, she said she wanted to slow things down a little and not see each other so often. Where did that come from? I wasn't expecting that. I didn't want to lose her altogether so I didn't argue – I said that would be okay. She was pleased at that and gave me a long, lingering kiss. When my dad came up for me that night, he asked how things had gone at Carrie's. I said it had been really nice.

Carrie broke up with me, only a few days after the visit. She said she thought I was cheating on her. I would never have cheated on her – I loved her too much. But I had my suspicions that she might be cheating on me. Several times, I was aware of secret incoming calls to her mobile. Although it was set on silent, the incoming call would interfere with the radio. She once told me, while I was at the college, that she was going through to Glasgow to look after her friends' cat. She didn't even like cats! I never did say that I thought she was cheating on me, but I thought it, just the same.

I spent a lot of time with Lecia, during the last few months when she was pregnant with my niece. All the family were out working so it was often just Lecia and me in the house on our own. Lecia slept a lot during her pregnancy but when she wasn't sleeping I would spend time with her in Michael's room. Carrie had often told me to let my parents know that I smoked - get it out in the open. Lecia didn't know that I smoked but one day she lit one for me and said that she wouldn't tell anyone. When Michael came home, I was sitting in his room with Lecia and he said, "You two look cosy." I told him that I was smoking now. He wasn't surprised. He had a cigarette with me in my room, later that night, and said that he wouldn't tell Mum and Dad - but he did. Mum and Dad just burst out laughing. I was the last person they thought would smoke because I used to hate people smoking around me when I was young. I still don't like people smoking when I'm eating. I only started smoking in front of my parents after I was caught having a cigarette in my room.

Now that Carrie and I were finished, I went on the Phone Bar for someone to talk to. I spoke to a woman called Maxine, from Newcastle, but who was now living in Shetland. I'd skipped past her a few times to see who else was on and kept hearing Maxine's voice sounding like she had a cold. I talked to her a few times that night and swapped numbers so that we could talk offline – that was cheaper. I quickly learned that Maxine was older than my mum. I didn't know how to handle that. We continued to talk to each other despite this. Maxine kept on asking me what the weather was like in Anstruther, knowing that I couldn't see. I used to have a laugh with her and say, "I don't know, I'll stick my head out my window and find out!" Maxine and I could have a laugh about anything.

Michael and Lecia were staying with us until they got a place of their own. That turned out to be a whole seven weeks after Mya was born, in October. After Lecia had her baby I was bored sitting around my room all day. I often lay on the floor of my room talking to her through my bedroom door, while she did her hair. I needed Michael and Lecia to move out - I was getting far too attached to her. I was really anxious to move out into my own house, too. Mum was still doing everything for me. I did clean the bathroom from time to time but that was about it. Someone from the Blind Society came out to put raised dots on the cooker, microwave, washing machine and iron. Mum had a bacon tray for the microwave and decided to teach me how to cook with it. This didn't go too well. It took me about forty-five minutes to cook bacon that day and Mum was losing patience with me. Straightaway, I was struggling, trying to peel the bacon rashers apart. Once that was done, I had difficulty placing the bacon on the tray as the rashers kept folding over instead of lying flat. Then, I couldn't understand how to work Mum's microwave, although she had told me a hundred times. I didn't realise that the knob had a little arrow on it and this had to be lined up properly. However, I persevered and eventually managed to make a bacon roll for myself. My very frustrated mum did the other one for me. I couldn't blame her! After that, I never touched any of Mum's appliances, again.

I was getting bored at home so I contacted my Disability Employment adviser 'Ann', to see what she could come up with and she suggested that I go, for a few months, to Momentum Fife, a training unit like the one I had attended in Buckhaven. I got a call from

'Momentum', soon afterwards, to go along for an assessment. Dad took me along and I spoke to a lovely man called Eddie. I talked to Eddie for about an hour and he was quite amazed at what I had achieved. He was also amazed that I could talk so well as he had dealt with people with cerebral palsy before, and their speech wasn't nearly as good as mine. Eddie talked to me about my life and asked what I would like to do. This was something different. People usually just told me what I should be doing - not Eddie. I said I was interested in radio, counselling or telesales. Eddie thought I meant I *wanted* counselling – not that I was interested in being a counsellor. We had a good chat and I left, feeling that I had been treated as a normal person, for a change. Eddie said they would contact me early in 2004.

Michael and his mate had set up a karaoke business in the area. I met Rachel at one of them, in Pittenweem. She hadn't realised that I was home from college – now I was back in touch with her again. I spoke to Michael's mate one day, about getting my own house and he told me that there were a few empty flats up where he lived, on the east side of Anstruther. Apparently, they were all on the ground floor so I phoned the Council and asked if I could put my name forward for one of them. A man at the Council said that my qualifying points had increased and that they would get back to me as soon as possible. Michael, Lecia and Mya moved out of Mum's house just before Christmas and I was going to be next. I got a call from the local Council office in early January, offering me a flat. When I went to view the flat, I took Mum, Auntie Julie and a lady from the Blind Society with me. I wanted to get the opinions of some people with experience. I didn't want to move into just any old flat. As it happened, it turned out to be the block of flats that

Aynsley lived in. The Area Officer showed me round. The flat had only one bedroom but that was okay with me. I had a walk round on my own just so that I could get a feel for the place and familiarise myself with the surroundings. The main thing that concerned me was that, although the bathroom had a bath, it had no shower. Otherwise, it seemed okay. Mum and Auntie Julie thought the flat was ideal for me and that I should accept it right away but I needed a little time to think about it.

After a few days of careful consideration I decided to take the flat. Mum and Auntie Julie said they would paper the walls for me and Dad said he would do the painting. I had to think hard about which colours would be best, considering my failing eyesight. I had to consider which colours would be most helpful for seeing things clearly in each room of the house. I talked to Craig and Maxine about this and they said that I was the only one that could make the decision; no one else knew exactly the impression different colours made on me.

Before I was handed the keys for the flat, I had another birthday to celebrate; my twenty-second birthday. This might not seem special to most people but I see every birthday as a special birthday - a special birthday for each year I still have some of my sight. We decided to go to St Andrews, for a change. I usually spent my birthdays in Anstruther so it was time to go somewhere different. I went to St. Andrews with Michael, my cousins Kevin, Eck and John, and a few other mates. We did a pub-crawl there and ended up in the Gin House, at the end of the night. Poor Kevin wasn't allowed in; he had been spotted by the bouncer, being sick just round the corner, and was refused entry. Kevin went home. The rest of us had a real good time in the Gin house. I got talking to a girl, a few years older than me. We chatted for ages and I told her we were up for my birthday. I didn't want to leave the Gin House that night - I was having such a great time talking to this girl. Michael kept falling asleep and eventually we had to leave before he was thrown out. On our way out, the girl I had been talking to took off her Gin House T-shirt and handed it to me. I was chuffed at that. When we got outside, everyone else had disappeared and left us on our own so we had to find our own way home. Michael went across the road and bought a Pizza, which we ate on the way home in a taxi. It was a great night and I really enjoyed myself.

I had to fill out a few forms and sign some papers before I could get the keys for my flat. Eventually, I got the keys on the second of February 2004, a week after my twenty-second birthday. The Council gave me a grant to help with the cost of decorating the flat. It wasn't a lot but I did manage to buy most of the wallpaper and paint that I needed. However, there were other things that I was going to need, like a cooker and a microwave. Luckily, the Blind Society helped me with those. I was told that the government would reimburse me for all the essential stuff I had to buy for my flat but I never got a penny. I wanted to paper my living room, bedroom and kitchen with light and dark contrasting colours so that I could see where I was going in the flat. I decided to use green and cream for the living room. I planned to get a dark green carpet and two different colours of wallpaper, with dark green at the bottom and green and cream stripes for the top. A black painted dado rail would separate these colours. The skirting board was to be painted white, to distinguish the walls from the floor. My bedroom would be decorated in a similar way but with dark blue wallpaper on the bottom of the walls and plain cream for the top, with a paper border. The carpet would be cream and it, too, would be separated from the walls by white painted skirting boards. I wanted dark blue covers for my bed so that it would be easy to distinguish from the floor. I thought I'd paint the kitchen dark blue as that would make a good contrast with the white appliances. The worktops were already light coloured so that would be okay. The hallway would be cream with laminate flooring and I would leave the bathroom just as it was.

I applied to go back to Glenrothes College in January to do an 'Introduction to Counselling' course. I wanted to help others like myself who had gone through countless problems so I thought a counselling course would be ideal. The course was an evening class, one night a week and started at six o'clock on a Monday night. This meant that I would have to get the bus from Anstruther around four o'clock. Once I arrived at the bus station in Glenrothes I would have to get a taxi to the college and Dad would come for me when I finished. I'd only been at my course a week, before we started work on the flat. Mum, Julie, Eck and Dad stripped the old wallpaper off the walls. I helped a little with this but once the wallpaper was off, I sat back and watched Mum and Julie hang the new wallpaper. I couldn't do an awful lot to help but I did manage to sit there and dictate. As the bottom part of the green wallpaper went up I was able to see the wall of my living room quite easily. Mum and Julie had papered for years so they were a dab hand at it. They had both bottom and top done in no time; my living room was beginning to look the part. The Dado Rail had to be painted on the floor before Michael put it up, as I didn't want the black paint to run. Once the Dado Rail was up, Dad painted the skirting boards, windowsills and ceiling, while Mum and Julie started on my bedroom. The bedroom was slightly smaller than the living room and the wallpapering there was finished in no time at all. I went across to my flat most days that Mum and Julie were decorating. It was boring but I still wanted to be there. I used the type of wallpaper that you can paint on, for my hall and kitchen. Dad did the painting. He did most of it at night, as he was busy during the day. In between painting and papering we went shopping for carpets, a suite and a bed. I wanted a cream leather suite so that it would stand out against my wallpaper and carpet in my living room. I bought a three-piece, cream leather suite, and a green carpet, for my living room, and a cream carpet for my bedroom. I also looked for a double bed; if I was going to be living on my own I wanted to sleep in my own double bed. Everything was arranged to arrive on the same day. I was just hoping it would all come in the right order; carpet first, then my bed and then the Suite. The carpets arrived first in the morning and the carpet fitters laid them. My bed arrived at lunchtime and then my suite came in the afternoon. Everything was going as planned. We struggled to get the suite in the house, as it was quite big and bulky. We finally had to take the front door off to get it in. As everything came on the same day, I was able to move in. I had my bed to sleep in and my suite to sit on; I felt right at home. I brought everything from my bedroom at Mum's - like my bedside cabinet, drawers and computer desk. I also brought my tele and surround-sound entertainment system, and my CD player. I also brought my television that I had used at the Blind College. Dad dismantled my computer, writing down where each lead went so that he could set it up again, in my flat. Everything was now in place and strategically suited to where I wanted it to be. It had taken two weeks to get the flat ready and I was now about to spend my first night in my new home. I had a bath that night, got into my pyjamas, phoned Mum, said goodnight and went to bed. It felt really strange sleeping in my own home for the first time. It was so quiet and lonely but it was what I wanted. The only sound I heard that night was a woman's high heels coming up the stairs to her flat. That was me settled in. I was now living on my own but Mum and Dad were never far away - if I needed them. I didn't have a washing machine for the first few weeks so Mum still did my washing for me.

I had already planned a house warming but as I only moved in a few days prior to the house warming party I only invited family - and Craig. I didn't want to invite people that would make a mess of my flat. The house warming went really well and there was no trouble. I asked people to bring their own drink, as I couldn't afford to buy enough drink for everyone. Michael was the first to spill a drink on my lovely new carpet. Surprise, surprise! Still, it was easy enough to clean up as it just lay on the surface and didn't soak in. I was a little worried about the noise level and tried to keep it to a minimum. I didn't want to upset my new neighbours, after only living there for a few days. When the party finished, I wasn't left to tidy everything up - my family did that – and that was great. Don't get me wrong. I would clean up but it would be very difficult for me with my poor sight so it was easier for people to clean up after themselves. I directed all smokers, myself included, to the kitchen, that night. I didn't want a burnt carpet on my first week in my new home. After everyone left to go home, I watched some tele and had a nightcap. Sitting there, in front of the tele with a whisky and Coke in my hand, I felt right at home.

Chapter 24

VISITORS

Now that I was settled in my new flat, I went to Mum's for lunch, the next day, a Sunday. Although I was living on my own I still needed to make sure that I was eating properly! Dad came to collect me in the car. When I returned to my flat, I hesitated at my door before turning to go next door and introduce myself. Dad always thought it was a young woman that stayed next door and thought she had a small child. The woman who opened the door seemed to be in her late twenties and had long dark hair. She invited me in for a coffee and a chat. I discovered that she didn't have a baby after all; she was a single woman living on her own. I asked her about the night before - had she heard any noise? She said, she did but it didn't really bother her.

Living on my own, I was often at a loose end and got into the habit of taking regular walks down to the harbour and into the Ship Tavern for a Coke, before wandering home again. A mobility officer had been to see me prior to moving into the flat, to help me familiarise myself with the immediate surroundings. I'd played in the area when I was younger but I didn't have the same amount of sight now, that I had back then. I also needed a little mobility training to the bus stop and back. I still struggled a little to find my way back to my flat but I knew, the more I did it, the easier it would become. About this time I got into another habit – I'd often lie down on my settee for an afternoon rest. I didn't really get much rest though, as a family had just moved in above me and they had two children that seemed to be training for the Olympics all day long. The only time I was doing anything really worthwhile was Monday nights at my counselling course. The class was full of women except for another guy, who kept turning up drunk. He was asked not to come back. I think his reason for going was to *get* counselling but it didn't work that way. I started off sitting with a lovely young girl, younger than myself. She decided to sit with me, as we were the youngest in the class but this didn't last for long, a week later she was sitting with somebody else. That didn't bother me, as I was there to learn about counselling, and it was a lot harder than I thought it would be. There were a lot of new ideas to learn, like empathy, reflection, repression and a whole lot of words that I'd never heard of before. The Monday night class soon changed to a Wednesday night as our tutor had other commitments and could no longer take the class on a Monday. That worked better for me as Mum went to the Bingo on a Wednesday night and was able to pick me up. It was a while before I started going outside at break for a cigarette because the idea still embarrassed me. My Auxiliary smoked though, so I finally decided to light up and smoke with the rest of them.

Early on in the flat, Dad often came in to help me with the cooking. I'd been taught to boil potatoes at the Blind College but he gave me a few refresher sessions, just to get my confidence back. I used a George Foreman Grill to cook steaks, sausages and things and would put them in the oven while I was waiting on the potatoes. With Dad's help, I was cooking on my own again, in no time. I used the oven more than anything else as I felt that it was the safest way for me to cook and I wasn't keen on frying at all.

As Dae made his rounds, visiting my mum and my aunties each night of the week, he decided to visit me on Tuesdays at teatime. He used to come when I was making the tea. We'd sit and have a yarn and watch The Weakest Link on the tele. It got to a stage when I was never getting the tea ready before he arrived so I started to have it after he left. Dae would always have a small cup of tea at everyone's house as he did his visits. I'd make the tea for us, using my liquid level indicator given to me by the Blind Society. The level indicator had to be placed over the edge of the cup and when the water reached the prongs, the indicator beeped. Very clever!

Mum rarely visited - she just left me to get on with it because that's what I wanted but Dae wasn't my only visitor. Rachel used to come along on the bus from Pittenweem and my cousins; John and Eck came round quite regularly. Rachel often came during the day and was sometimes still there when Dae arrived. John and Eck just came when they felt like it. I really liked staying on my own but it was also great to have visitors. Rachel often stayed over. I always offered her my bed, saying I would sleep on the settee but she always declined and *she* slept on the settee. We would just snuggle up together in front of the tele and watch a film - just as friends, of course. If we weren't watching a film we were on the computer, downloading music, or having a drink and playing cards. Sometimes, we'd play 'drinking games' with the cards but Rachel never did win and she couldn't handle a lot of drink so we stopped the drinking games. Nights that she didn't stay, I would walk her to the bus stop and then get a bus down to The Ship and have a drink before the night was out.

I started to meet lots of new people while I was drinking in the Ship, including the bar staff. At first, I would go into The Ship on my own, to see who was there. Michael and his mate ran a karaoke there most weekends and I often got up to sing, although I was never really good at singing. I'd often meet John and Eck in The Ship and we'd sometimes go back to my house for a drink. Once they'd got me home they would walk down to the bake house to buy some pies and sausage rolls. It was some walk back up to my house from The Ship. Apart from the steep hill called Chalmers Brae, there was still a distance to go along the bottom of the park before we reached my flat. Sometimes John would fling me over his shoulder and carry me part of the way home. Eck would curl up on my settee and fall asleep when I crawled into my bed. Sometimes John would climb in beside me. I didn't mind that – John was my big cousin. One thing was always certain – it was always a good night when my big cousins came back to my place for a party.

I got a letter from Momentum Fife in April, to say that I would start with them in May. My counselling course was coming to an end in June so this was something else to look forward to. I was offered three days a week, under sixteen hours so I wouldn't lose my benefits. Momentum wasn't a very big place. It operated out of a small Portacabin in Dysart, by Kirkcaldy. There was a small office, one longer room with about five computers and another smaller room, which was the break room. This room also had a couple of computers and that's where I worked. I told Eddie that I'd been going to the counselling classes and that I'd like to do the advanced course. He thought that was a good idea but unfortunately, I wasn't accepted for the advanced course. I was very disappointed. I thought I'd handled the course really well but my tutor said she didn't think the advanced course would be right for me. She said she thought I had struggled on the basic course and if she did put me through it would be only be an act of pity. She suggested that I try again, once I had more life skills. I thought I had plenty of life skills, after what I'd already been through.

On the days I went to Momentum, I was picked up by a disabled driver who had his own mobility car and got paid for carrying passengers to and from Momentum. He was a very nice man, called Alex, but he always came in and waited while I got ready and it felt like he was breathing down my neck all the time. I started off at Momentum doing voiceovers on the computer, using my Supernova software. Eddie had another kind of software installed but I couldn't get to grips with it after using my software for so long, so Eddie kindly installed my software on the computer. I was allowed to try a variety of things at Momentum. I did some voiceovers, some music editing and some radio broadcasting.

One night in May, John and Eck came up to my place after the pub, with Eck's girlfriend, Laura. As usual, John and Eck went down to the baker's for some munchies and Laura went with them. I had a smoke while they were away as I still didn't feel comfortable smoking in front of anyone. They returned with the food and were in the kitchen preparing it while Laura and I were sitting in the living room. Laura glanced towards the kitchen and then suddenly turned round and started kissing me. I was amazed. I had gone out with her when I was younger but I didn't expect her to do that. When she did it a second time I decided it had to stop- she was Eck's girlfriend now. The three of them stayed the night. I could hardly sleep, thinking what had happened. Laura was quite pissed but I was worried about Eck finding out as both he and John had grown very close to me and I didn't want to lose them. However, I told Lecia. I had to tell someone - I didn't know what else to do. A few nights later, I was lying in bed watching the tele when I heard the intercom ring. I got out of bed and went to answer it but by the time I got there, there was nobody there as it only gives you a minute or two to answer it. I was heading back to bed when I heard a voice at my living room window. It was Eck. I let him in and asked, "What brings you round at this time of night?" Just at that, Laura walked in behind him, and said, "Actually, it's me that's here to see you. What have you been telling people about you and me?" Eck stood on one side, with his brows crossed! I told him the whole story – everything that had happened that night. When I had finished, Laura denied the whole thing. I looked straight at Eck. "I'm sorry it happened, Eck but I didn't start it – or want it," I said. I think Eck knew who was telling the truth but nothing more was said. Eck made a gesture to Laura, with his head, and they left. Who told Laura? I only told Lecia! I confronted Lecia. She was quite indignant and denied saying anything. I was fighting a losing battle.

Everything was going great back at Momentum but Eddie was finding it difficult to find me suitable work in the kind of fields I was looking for. It wasn't just me; it was getting difficult to find work for any of us.

I was hoping to get Sky TV in my new flat but the Sky Engineers said they couldn't fix a satellite dish because of the type of walls on the block – they said an independent company could do it. I mentioned this to Eddie and he gave me a number for a man who would put the dish up as a 'homer' and only charge about £50. Sure enough, I contacted the man, he came, did the job – and only charged £45. Then he arranged for his company to install the box for me. One of the reasons I wanted Sky was that they had an Audio Description Service for blind or partially sighted viewers. The service runs an audio soundtrack that doesn't interfere with the programme you're watching but tells you what's going on. I also wanted to watch Euro 2004, the

European Nations football competition. It was on normal terrestrial tele but the coverage on Sky was much better. I invited a mate from across the road to watch the France v England game and have a few beers. The girl from next door came in that day and we had a Chinese Takeaway before he arrived. She didn't know he was coming round and I hadn't had a chance to tell her, when he strolled in. My friend, Norma, had a problem with panic attacks and thought it would be best to go and leave us to watch the football. We had a great night – a few beers, good banter and a good score.

John, Eck, Michael and Lecia all did the Great Scottish Walk in Edinburgh, in June. It was a twelve-mile walk and afterwards we were all supposed to go to Legends, in Anstruther. They said they would phone me to let me know when they were back. They didn't. When I realised that they weren't going to call, I went for a bath then phoned Michael to say that I would be across in a while. I hated that night. When I got to the pub, Lecia and Laura were both there. I tried to keep out of their way, but it didn't happen. I was getting a bit drunk and started talking to Lecia about what happened with Laura and me but she still denied that she had 'grassed'. She started suggesting I had told other people and went running to Michael, so I left it at that. A row of Absinths was lined up on the bar for all of us to down. While the rest of them were arguing about who would go first, I picked mine up and downed it. Eck didn't see me do it so he filled up another one. After the rest of the pub customers had gone home, only our little group was left. We all crashed out on the floor, for the night. I slept in the entrance to the toilets. In the morning Laura and Lecia had to step over me to get to the toilets. After that night, and the Absinth, I was ill for a week.

My course at Momentum was coming to an end.

Eddie hadn't been able to find me work but, as I was really interested in radio, he arranged for me to visit Kirkcaldy Hospital Radio for some experience. This time I was able to talk to the listeners, on air. About the same time I was due to perform in my first Stars in their Eyes event for charity, at Legends. I was going to be performing as Rod Stewart singing Tonight's The Night, on my last day with Momentum. So I was able to go on air and tell people what I was going to be doing for charity. I didn't play any music or talk in between songs but I had an interview with the presenter and that was good enough for me. Eddie went with me to hire my Rod Stewart outfit. If I was going to play the great man, I wanted to look the part. I hired the white flannel shirt, leopard skin trousers and the wig to go with them. I was finished with Momentum but I really enjoyed my time there, not only with my colleagues but with Eddie too. I liked Eddie a lot and I still keep in touch with him.

The Stars in their Eyes night was a great success. Auntie Julie organised the event and Michael played the music. I was on stage third as I needed more time to dress up than anyone else. Michael and one of my cousins were singing too. Come to think about it, of the ten performers only three weren't relatives of mine. There was a problem with my music. The words didn't come up on the screen. It didn't matter I knew all the words. A lot of people thought I did well and that I should have won best-dressed act on the night. As it was, I didn't win anything. I wasn't too disappointed. It was a really good night and we raised a lot of money for charity. At the end of the night I was speaking to a woman who explained that her husband, Chris, worked in The Ship and that they lived across the road from me. Pretty soon, I started visiting them regularly.

Chapter 25

LEEDS

John and Eck had been to the Carling Weekend Festival in Leeds, twice. Guns 'n' Roses were the headliners the first time and the guys loved it. The Carling Weekend is held every year - Friday to Sunday, over the August Bank Holiday weekend. Hundreds of bands play there and most of them are rock and punk bands. In 2003, John and Eck noticed a Disabled Campsite on the map and Eck said, "We have to bring Billy here next year, he'll love this." Of course, when he told me, I immediately said, "Definitely!" The headliners in 2004 included Green Day, The Darkness and The White Stripes. I'd already seen Green Day but not the others. Everyone wanted to go this year, but there wasn't room for everyone. It was finally decided that Michael, Lecia, John, Eck, myself – and Eck's girlfriend Laura would go. That made six and then Graham, my Auxiliary from school, and his girlfriend made the numbers up to eight. Graham and his girlfriend would make their own way there. To get into the Disabled Campsite, which was next to the arena, the tickets had to go under my name, so John, who was arranging all the tickets, came round to my house to take a copy of my Disabled Badge. He then filled in the application form and posted it off.

We had a few months to prepare for the festival and I began to feel awkward about the girlfriends going with us because of what had happened with Laura . . . I tried not to think about it too much as I just wanted to enjoy myself in Leeds. When it was getting close to the Festival time, I asked John and Eck how much money they usually took with them. John said, "About two hundred pounds." I was a bit strapped for cash, with not working, so I took one hundred pounds out of my account and Mum gave me another hundred. John's dad was at sea so John got to take his mini-bus to Leeds. That way, we thought, we'd have plenty room for the six of us, all our luggage, including the tents and my wheelchair. We left early, on the Friday. I was the first to be picked up, with Eck and Laura, and then we picked up Michael and Lecia and off we went. I sat in the back with Laura for the first part of the journey but about an hour down the road I realised that I'd forgotten my sleeping bag. I said, very quietly, to Laura, "Shit - I've forgotten my sleeping bag. Don't say anything, I'll manage without it."

Immediately, Laura shouts to Eck, "Billy's forgotten his sleeping bag." And Eck, who was sitting in the front with John said, "You tit - we're not going back for it. We'll try and get something for you, on the way." When we stopped at a Safeway store in Berwick to get our drink for the weekend, Eck had a wander round and came back with a duvet, for six quid, and said, "This'll have to do." Once we'd paid for all our beer and bits and bobs, we headed back to the mini-bus and roared away again.

The back of the mini-bus was a bit cramped so I swapped seats with Eck and sat in the front. By the time we got close to Leeds the traffic on the motorway was at a standstill. Eck opened the letter with the tickets, while we opened a few cans! After a few minutes, Eck shouted, "John!! Have you read this letter?" In a much calmer tone, John said, "No. Why?" Eck then went on a rant, complaining that we were only allowed my carer, two friends and myself into the Disabled campsite. There was a deathly hush as we all took in this information. Then – we decided we had to figure out a way of getting us all into the campsite. We finally agreed that we would claim that we didn't get the letter – that we only received the tickets and the directions.

As we had nothing else to do while we were stuck in the traffic, Michael got out onto the motorway to have a cigarette. Big mistake. The traffic started to move and Michael was left running alongside the mini-bus shouting at John to stop – cigarette still in hand. I don't think Michael thought John was going to stop and we were all pissing ourselves laughing. Finally, John did stop and Michael got in. Michael was mad but John just said, "That's what you get for jumpin' out on the motorway, you erse." We were going nowhere fast so when John got the chance, he pulled off the motorway and took a different route. A few minutes later, he phoned Graham to see where he was and it turned out that he was only a few miles behind us so John suggested he should follow the same route as us. By this time it was getting dark and when we finally reached the campsite it was starting to rain. We were almost frantic as we pitched the tents, hoping to avoid too much of a soaking. Eck, Graham and Michael all had their girlfriends with them so they had a tent each. John had brought two tents - one for him and one for me but he only put one of them up. He said, "We'll both sleep in here."

Everyone else only had groundsheets in their tents but I had an inflatable double mattress for us to sleep on - while my wheelchair slept outside.

On the Friday morning, we all got ourselves ready to go to the ticket office, to check-in, knowing that it was going to be awkward. John agreed that he would do the talking. When he spoke to the man at the desk, the man asked for my surname and how many of us there were. John said, "There's eight of us." The man's eyebrows shot up. He seemed seriously dubious when John said we didn't get a letter – but he let us all in, anyway.

He asked, "Who's the Carer?" and Eck shouted, "Me!" so the man put a special wrist tag on him and said that he had to be with me at all times in the arena. Eck laughed and said, "No way - I was only kidding, I'm not his carer!" But it was too late, he was tagged and the man refused to change it. Once we were checked in, we headed for the arena to watch some bands.

The Friday afternoon was a scorcher. We sat on the grass all day, watching bands and drinking pints of Carling. Graham wanted to buy more rounds of drinks and Eck had to tell him to calm down, we had all weekend. The Rasmus, Placebo and Ash were just some of the bands we watched that afternoon. After a while, we gave up drinking Carling and started on the cans we had smuggled in, in rucksacks on the back of my wheelchair. It was much cheaper that way. Although Eck had the wrist tag, the stewards weren't too bothered as long as someone was sitting with me and, most of the time it was Laura. John and Eck wanted to jump around in the mosh pit and I didn't blame them, so would I if I was able. But this meant I had to try to get along with Laura. On the Friday night, John wheeled me around to find something to eat. There wasn't much to choose from – just a pizza stall and a burger stall, so I had a pizza. The pizza was just cheese and tomato, and was really good but it cost a fortune. After that, I opted for burgers! Green Day were the headliners on the Friday. They came on stage in their usual way - the lead singer wearing a rabbit suit, swigging beer and eating a carrot. After a quick introduction they exploded into action and were superb from start to finish. They sang all my favourites and by the time they finished, it was dark. We all headed back to the campsite and tried to squeeze everybody into John's tent. It was tight but with everybody sitting cross-legged, it seemed it would work – until I tried to sit amongst them.

Eck got annoyed as I struggled to lower myself onto the ground and he tried to help me along by giving me a push. Of course that didn't help and I fell over. It was insult to injury when the rest of the gang burst out laughing. Now it was my turn to get annoyed and I let rip at Eck – and reminded him that I wasn't as supple as everybody else. He just told me not to cry about it and fetched a deck chair for me to sit on. That was a whole lot better. Now I was able to sit down and drink with everyone else, and enjoy myself.

When I woke on the Saturday morning, John was already up and sitting, reading. After I got dressed, he took me to a canteen in the arena, where we got bacon rolls and coffee. He complained when I asked him to take the fat off my bacon. I can't stand fat on food. When we'd finished the rolls, we headed back to the campsite, but on the way I needed the toilet so John took me to one of the Portaloos. The inside of the Portaloo was disgusting and the confined space made the process very difficult for me. After that nauseating experience I tried to avoid the Portaloos as much as possible!

Back at the campsite we discussed our plans for the day. Graham and his girlfriend wanted to do their own thing and the rest of us mostly landed up hanging out together. The Wildhearts were playing on the Saturday afternoon. John, Eck and I reckoned them as one of our favourites so we weren't going to miss them. Michael wasn't so keen on them, so he sat on the Disabled Platform with me while John and Eck were in amongst the crowd jumping around and having a good time. I don't know where the girls were at this time; maybe back at the campsite talking about girly things. I thought The Wildhearts were by far the best band we'd seen up to that point but they bored Michael stiff. Just goes to show! Although there were a lot of other great bands there, I would have settled for listening to The Wildhearts and Offspring but I just went wherever John and Eck went. I had no choice, as they were doing the pushing!

Offspring were a huge attraction. When they were on, I had to sit in my wheelchair on the Disabled Platform again while John, Eck and Michael were in amongst the crowd. And this time, Laura sat with me. There was silence for a few moments before Offspring started their set and then they really kicked in – fabulous music - and then Laura started to talk - to me. She got into a deep discussion about the 'kissing incident' and said she wanted to put it behind us. I was fine with that, but then she went on and on about it the whole way through the Offspring's gig and I didn't get a minute's peace to enjoy one of my favourite bands. And then – when they finished, Laura immediately stopped talking about it. And she said, she thought Offspring were rubbish. How would she know? She wasn't listening to them. I, on the other hand, thought they were great - what I heard of them! The Darkness were on next and were the final band of the evening. We weren't too keen on them but watched anyway and as it turned out, they were quite good, for a rock/pop band. During their turn some people around us started a few small fires and the smoke began to hurt my eyes. Once the Darkness were finished, we all headed back to the campsite but on the way we stopped to buy a burger. Michael was pissed and fell out with the person behind the counter. This server wouldn't give him a burger because, he said, he didn't like Michael's tone.

John tried to resolve the situation by buying two burgers – one for Michael and one for me. No luck, though. Michael threw his burger on the ground in disgust and stormed away from us. John wheeled me, gorging my burger, back to the campsite. When we finally got back, some of us sat outside our tents, having a few drinks, while Michael went walkabout. When he eventually did get back, there was just Eck, Laura and me sitting outside, the rest having gone to bed. He was very drunk and mumbling abuse at us. We told him to shut up . . . then we all went to bed.

I woke in the middle of the night disorientated and needing a pee. As I was frantically fighting with the tent door, I woke John by accidentally slapping him on the back. He woke with a start and wasn't best pleased but he opened the flap for me. I didn't go too far from the tent in case I couldn't find my way back. When I started to pee, I heard loud splashing on someone's tent – didn't know whose but thought I'd better change direction - quick. After I went back into the tent, the rain started – and poured all night long so that when I got up in the morning, my wheelchair, which always slept outside, was absolutely saturated. By breakfast time, however, the rain had stopped and the sky had begun to brighten overhead.

Once I was on my feet, I discovered that I was all alone. John had disappeared, Eck wasn't in his tent and I wondered where everyone had gone. I called out to see if anyone would answer. Only Laura replied. "It's okay, Billy – I'm over here," she shouted, from her tent. John returned a short while later – he had been for a shower – and a good while later again, Eck turned up. Eck had got up very early to go and see some bands. I had hoped to see the same bands but it was too late now - he had been, and was back again. I couldn't use the showers in the campsite as they weren't very 'disabled friendly' so I used baby wipes all weekend. Once I was cleaned and changed Michael and Lecia wheeled me for something to eat. I had a couple of rolls on sliced sausage instead of bacon rolls this time and these were a lot better. When we returned to the campsite, Eck asked me if there were any bands I particularly wanted to see. I said, "I'm easy really, but I heard The Roots are quite good." Eck fancied seeing The Bronx, Goldfinger and the Bouncing Souls but they were on later so we all headed into the arena to watch The Roots. Unfortunately, The Roots were nothing like I had hoped. They were a bunch of Reggae singers and none of us enjoyed their turn. The rest of the gang slagged me off, as if it was my fault, and they still do. Shortly after The Roots finished, John and Eck took me to see Goldfinger and then The Bouncing Souls. These were Punk bands that Eck had never seen before but he wanted to check them out and they weren't too bad. When I suddenly needed the toilet, a couple of songs into the Bouncing Souls set, I wasn't too keen to speak up because Eck was really keen to hear this band. But – I was desperate - I had no choice. Eck wasn't too pleased but he tore himself away and wheeled me across to the toilet. It didn't take us that long, there and back, and he only missed a couple of songs, but he was raging. That Sunday I was desperate to buy a couple of T-shirts. I wanted a Green Day T-shirt and an Offspring one. We struggled to find the shirts but eventually tracked them down. We also went to a music stall on the Sunday, where I asked Michael to look for a HIM CD, for me. He found a live album and read out the songs to me. They sounded good, so I bought it.

When we took all our purchases back to our tents, Michael and Lecia stayed to have a little sleep, before the White Stripes came onstage. This was the only band Michael was keen to see so he wanted to be fresh when they came on. The rest of us were wandering around the site when John spotted Ginger, the lead singer of The Wildhearts and wheeled me over to see him. When Eck told him that I was their biggest fan, Ginger was more than happy to give me his autograph. In fact, I didn't really know who the guy was and the autograph wasn't for me, it was for Eck! Sunday night finally came and it was time to sit back, relax and enjoy the highlight of the weekend – The White Stripes. Eck went in the crowd and John sat with me on the platform. Where were Michael and Lecia? Who knows? Who cared - I wasn't missing them. The White Stripes were superb. John described to me, everything that was going on. Jack White, the lead singer was playing the guitar and the organ, and singing at the same time. According to John, he was amazing - and Michael missed it all! The one performance he and Lecia were looking forward to seeing the most, and they slept through it, in their tent – or so they said! On the way back to the campsite, all the burger stalls were practically giving the burgers away so we all had a couple each. When we got back to the tents, we found Michael and his girlfriend awake. Michael was gutted that they had missed the show. We just laughed. We all sat up late and had a drink, as it was the last night in Leeds. Eck and Michael outdid everyone else at the drinking until Eck was left drinking on his own.

In the morning it was a mad rush to get our things packed and get off the campsite as quickly as possible. We wanted to leave early so that we would be home at a decent time. We stopped a couple of times on the road and one of the stops was, again, Safeways in Berwick. The made-to-order Pizzas took a little while so we wandered around Safeways until they were ready and then set off for home. Michael was first to be dropped off and then Eck and then me. The first thing I did when I got home was dump my bags and run a bath. I should really have phoned Mum first but I was tired and a bit smelly so I just wanted a soak in the bath. While I was lying there I thought about the weekend's events, how we had such a great time and the fact that I had made up with Laura. And – that I would be delighted to go back and do it all again.

Chapter 26

MY NEW FRIENDS

After the weekend at Leeds, a few of us decided to go to the Old Bank House pub for a change. New owners had recently taken over from a Spanish couple. One night, when the Spanish couple were still there, I was asked to leave as soon as I got in. I had been carried in because that was easier for me, and the owner thought I was drunk. He said in his best English accent, "You cannot bring him in here, he is too drunk!" My brother was disgusted at him and said, "He's not drunk, he's disabled!" Michael showed him my crutches; he apologised, and never questioned me again. John, Eck and I went into the Old Bank that night to check out the new owners. They were Richard the owner, Manuela and Jeanette, the manageress. I sat at a table near the front door talking to Richard. He had seen me before in The Ship but I didn't really know him. Richard was nice; a tall friendly man, in his early thirties with short ginger hair. I sat with him for a while – until I needed a pee. The toilet was downstairs so Eck went with me, guiding me through the crowd of people to the stairs and down to the toilet. Suddenly, Jeanette appeared at the top of the stairs and told me that there was a disabled toilet, through the poolroom. Eck then guided me back through the crowd of people, through the poolroom, to a door on the other side. Jeanette held the door open into another room, which had a disabled toilet in it. I stood there trying to hold it in while Jeanette found the key to the toilet. When she couldn't find the key, she went off looking for it. I looked at Eck. He shrugged his shoulders. I said, "I would've been quicker going downstairs!" Jeanette finally arrived back, but without the key. She said, "You'll have to go downstairs after all, or upstairs to our flat." The stairs to their flat were right beside me so I decided to go up to the flat. After all this hassle, I eventually got a pee and when I returned to the table with Richard, I said, "I think I deserve a free drink after all that!" I was well pleased when he bought me a whisky, on the house. That night was a nice change from The Ship, and the staff were really friendly. Jeanette was especially nice. She was tall, with long brown hair and came from New Zealand. Manuella was also tall, with brown hair, and came from Italy. I later found out that they had known each other for a number of years and had worked together in Edinburgh. I now knew if anything happened at The Ship and I couldn't go back, there was always a place for me at the Old Bank House.

Word had come through in August, for my hernia operation. It was scheduled for October thirtieth. That was Mya's first Birthday, but I had been waiting for this operation for about a year, so I wasn't going to postpone it. In September, I phoned the Occupational Therapy Department to ask about a wet-floor shower to be put in my house as I was struggling to get in and out of the bath. Someone came out to do an assessment and suggested handrails in my hall. I said that it would be helpful. The wet-floor bathroom was approved but she said there was a waiting list and I might have to wait some time. In the meantime, she arranged for a bath board to help me get in and out of the bath.

Around this same time, I met Ian, in the Ship. He was quite tall and in his early forties. We were both regulars but it wasn't until that night that I offered to buy him a drink and that's when I really got to know him. He worked on the Oil Rigs so he was only home for two weeks at a time, but when he was home he was in The Ship most nights and I started doing the same. Another couple of guy's started drinking in our company. Bill was an older man in his early fifties and Morris was in his forties. I called Bill, Bill o' the Hill as he stayed on the hill behind The Ship.

One night I spoke to Maxine on the phone. She told me that she had been to Glasgow and met a man called Malky, who moved up to Shetland with her. Maxine let me talk to Malky that night. Malky was disabled but hadn't been that way all of his life. He woke one morning, went to stand up and fell on the floor. He thought that he was just tired and not ready to get up so he went back to bed for a while. He later found out that he had Guillain-Barre Syndrome. When I looked this up, I discovered that Guillain-Barre Syndrome is a neurological disorder in which the body's immune system attacks part of the peripheral nervous system (PNS), the nerve network outwith the brain and the spinal cord.

The PNS consists of 12 pairs of cranial nerves, which emerge from the brain, carrying messages to and from the head, including our sense organs. Thirty-one pairs of spinal nerves, branch off from the spinal cord and supply the rest of the body; organs and muscles. With the help of the PNS, we are able to carry out voluntary and involuntary actions. Picking up a spoon, clapping our hands or riding a bike are all voluntary actions. In contrast, our heartbeat and intestinal functions occur without our conscious control. These are called involuntary actions. Malky explained that he had no feeling from his knees downwards, but went through extensive physio to be able to walk again and wouldn't leave hospital until he could. He used two walking sticks to help him get around as he, like myself, had poor balance. Malky and I hit it off that night and after that we spoke regularly on the phone – sometimes for an hour or more at a time. I liked Malky.

In October of 2004, I started receiving support from the Blind Society to help me read my mail and deal with correspondence, general housekeeping and food preparation. My mail had been piling up over the summer. I was able to read my own mail under my CCTV, but it was getting a bit much for me. My support worker turned out to be Ann, who worked with me while I was at Glenrothes College. She was good and so I had requested her. It didn't take us long to get on top of things and with Ann's help I was able to keep all my affairs in much better order.

The day was fast approaching for my hernia operation and I wasn't looking forward to it, and, of course, I was going to miss little Mya's first birthday. I hadn't really bonded with Mya during the first year of her life. It was difficult – she was so small – and I couldn't see. I did hold her a few times and tried feeding her with her bottle, but I didn't really expect to bond with her until she was a bit older. She had a fearsome pair of lungs and with my acute hearing; I sometimes couldn't handle the deafening noise she was able to produce.

I was advised to stay at Mum's after the operation, while I recuperated, just so I was looked after properly. Fixing my hernia was supposed to be a Day Case operation; in and out the same day but because of my physical difficulties, they wanted to keep me overnight. This is why I was going to miss Mya's birthday. My talking watch needed a new battery, so I sent it away to have this fitted while I was in getting my operation. The operation turned out to be the most painful one I have ever experienced. Mum drove me to the Queen Margaret Hospital in Dunfermline in the morning. From previous experience, I knew that I shouldn't eat anything after midnight, but when the anaesthetist came round and asked if I'd had anything to eat, I said, "Yes - a full, cooked breakfast!" His chin about dropped to the floor I think, before I said, "I'm only joking!" This time, Mum didn't stay to go down to the theatre with me, after all I was a big boy now and she had a lot to do for the party. I was in the same room that I had been in for my gums and eye operations. Lying in that room brought back many memories, and they weren't good. I was taken down for my operation later on that day and don't remember a thing about it. I can't even remember what I had for my tea when I woke up, back on the ward. I missed my talking watch, that night. I was dozing on and off and kept wondering what time it was, and when they were going to bring me breakfast. As the reception desk was next to my room I could hear the night staff talking. I thought it must be morning so I buzzed for the nurse to ask about breakfast. The nurse told me it was only two in the morning but said that, if I was hungry, she would go and make some toast for me. I just said, "No, it's ok, I didn't realise that was the time!" I fell asleep a short time later.

I didn't experience much pain while I was in hospital, probably because of the painkillers I was on. Mum came to collect me late that morning and that's when I began to feel the full effects of the operation. When I stood up, I was in agony. I'd never felt pain like it since my hamstring operation, and this was worse. When I was thirteen I was a little suppler, so the pain wasn't so bad but it was a few years down the line now and I was really suffering. I was given some painkillers to take home but because of my glaucoma, I have to watch what I take so I was prescribed co-

codamol, about the only painkiller that doesn't react with my glaucoma - but it does make you quite constipated! I was wheeled to my mum's car in a wheelchair and then struggled to get into the car because of the pain. When we got to Mum's it took me ages to walk from the car to the house; every step was excruciatingly painful. When I finally made it to the house, it was straight upstairs for a lie down in my brother's old room; my old room had been made into a sitting room. I had to go up each step on my bum, as I couldn't lift my legs up the steps. Just like the hamstring operation all over again.

I slept most of that day, recovering from the effects of the anaesthetic. Michael's old room still had a television in it and Mum brought a CD player up from downstairs, so that I could listen to the radio. I had to be careful when I watched anything funny on the TV, as it was very painful whenever I laughed. Mum brought my lunch up to me most days but I still went downstairs for tea – a very painful experience. I was incredibly bored after the first week, lying in bed most of the time, trying to keep myself occupied with the radio and television. I enjoyed The Frank Skinner show, but it made me laugh so much my pain level shot through the roof. I also liked Offside, with Tam Cowan, on the tele. Same problem! After a week, I was managing the stairs better but still with real discomfort. Dae, couldn't manage up the stairs when he came to visit, so I went downstairs to see him. I still wasn't ready to go home after that first week so I stayed for another week and let Mum take care of me.

When I did eventually go home, I was soon wishing I was back at my mum's. From my first weeks in that flat, I'd had trouble with people leaving buggies in front of my door just because they couldn't be bothered taking them up the stairs. I had to navigate my way around them to get into my house. The bath was still in the flat and I was concerned as to how I was going to get in and out of it by myself. When it came to the bit, I managed to get in and out, using the bath board but with great difficulty and – by going through the pain barrier to do it. The bath board wasn't the safest thing in the world, considering my poor sense of balance, and I'd already been struggling with it, before the operation. It was late November by this time and I still had pain from the operation. I began to wonder if something was wrong. It didn't stop me from going out though; I still went down to The Ship most weekends, but hired a taxi for the journey. I wanted to sing on my brother's karaoke and drink with Ian, Bill and Morris. I remember hobbling through to sing a song one night, when Michael's mate was running the karaoke, and him telling me to hurry up. "What's up with *you* tonight?" he said, "You're usually through here like a shot!" I told him to give me a break; I was still in a lot of pain. Their karaoke business didn't last long after that.

It was approaching Christmas and another Stars in their Eyes had been organised so I decided to take part again. This time, I decided to go as Kristian Leontiou, a Cypriot singer that had released a song earlier in the year, called Shining. I had made a CD for one of the barmaids that worked in The Ship; Shining was one of the tracks and so the song meant something to me. I always listen carefully to the words of a song and try to relate them to something, so I made up the CD and asked her to listen just as carefully, to the words.

I went to Dundee with John and Eck to do a little Christmas shopping and I picked up some black hair dye while we were there. It wasn't going to be difficult to dress as Kristian Leontiou - all he really wore was jeans and a T-shirt. He did have a small tattoo and I planned to get someone to draw that on my arm. Eck came across to my house the day before the event, shaved my hair, giving me a number two all over and then Mum came across to apply the hair dye. On the big night, I introduced myself, wearing my own clothes, with a baseball hat to cover my shaved black hair. Like the last Stars in their Eyes contest, I said that one of my hobbies was long distance running - just to get the crowd going. I knew that a lot of people had never heard of Kristian Leontiou but Shining was what I wanted to sing, as it meant something special to me at the time. When I said who I was going to be, I heard a lot of mutterings - "Who?" I was shaking like a leaf when the host called me back on stage and I was still shaking when I took the microphone, but when the song came on, I let everything go and sang my heart out. It was a really hard song to sing but I got through and when I finished, everyone started to cheer. I didn't win - I knew I wouldn't but it was the taking part that counted - and I knew I was going to win sometime.

This Christmas was going to be my first Christmas in my own home. I thought about spending Christmas Eve at Mum's and she wanted me to, but I thought that I should spend it at my own house. Mum had bought me an Advent Calendar, like she did every year, but it was getting very difficult for me to find the door numbers and I knew quite soon that the calendars were going to stop. It wasn't fun anymore and I was nearly twenty-three! Christmas Eve came and Mum brought my presents round and asked me where was the best place to put them so that I could find them easily.

I thought I would start a new tradition and go to the pub and then come home before midnight. The Ship wasn't too busy but there were a few people in so I sat at a table for a change instead of at the bar and enjoyed my whisky and coke. When eleven-thirty came, I finished my drink and walked home, like I said I would

- before Santa came. I put 'Santa Claus the Movie' on and then went to bed when it finished. Dad was away over Christmas and New Year so Mum came across to my place on Christmas morning to have boiled eggs and toast. This is something we did every year on Christmas morning at my mum's, after opening our presents. Christmas and New Year were no different than any other; we still spent them with the family, by taking turns to visit each other. I wanted to bring in the New Year in my own house and then go to wherever, after the bells, but Mum insisted that I spent it with everyone else. After much discussion, I finally gave in, and spent New Year with the family.

Chapter 27

PREMIER CONTACT

After New Year, I decided that it was time to find myself a job. I always wanted a job but it was difficult knowing what I could and couldn't do. In the summer, Eck had suggested that a Call Centre might be a good place for me. I contacted Anne, from the Job Centre for help. She made a few phone calls for me and came up with the name of Premier Contact, in Markinch. She gave me a number so that I could phone them myself. I spoke to a lovely woman called Lynn who set up an interview for me. The interview was for the week before my twenty-third birthday and I was so looking forward to it that I phoned Eddie, at Momentum, in case I got the job, and he would have to help me settle in.

Just before the interview, I was asked if I wanted to take part in another Stars in Their Eyes, in January, at The Craw's Nest Hotel in Anstruther. This time, I decided to go as Jim Diamond as I had heard a good song of his on the radio a few times. The song was called, I Should Have Known Better. As the Craw's Nest is a lot bigger than Legends, a much bigger crowd was expected. There were fourteen acts in all and I was number eleven. We were given one of the hotel's upstairs rooms to change in and as Michael was act nine, Mum asked him to help me get ready and then help me onto the stage, after he came off. Michael went as the lead singer from the Red Hot Chilli Peppers, singing Under The Bridge. My costume was fairly simple again; jeans and a T-shirt, and I simulated Jim Diamond's ginger hair with some coloured mousse that would wash off in the shower. It took about an hour for us all to get ready and the crowd was getting agitated, waiting on us. Finally we got underway. The speakers blew a fuse during the second act and this delayed things for a while. After half-an-hour we got underway again. When it was almost time for my turn, Michael still hadn't come back and so I went downstairs halfway through act ten. He was nowhere to be seen and I started to panic. The organisers started calling for me so I tried to find my own way to the stage and bumped into Michael on the way. "Where've you been," I shouted. "You were supposed to come and help me on to the stage and they're calling me now!" It turned out that Michael had got drunk before he started to sing and then he bumped into some friends when he came off stage and forgot about me. When I finally arrived onstage a few moments later I was extremely nervous. Again, when I started to sing, the nerves disappeared but then the hairs on the back of my neck stood up when everyone started to cheer. I concentrated as hard as I could to stay in time and remember all of the words and there was a point in the song where I thought I was slightly ahead of myself but I carried on regardless. When I was finished the crowd roared and clapped, to show their appreciation and I walked off the stage with my legs like jelly. Michael was there to help me off this time and guide me back to sit with the Family. I had a lot of people come up to me that night and congratulate me, and some said, "I didn't know you could sing!" Again, I didn't win anything but I really enjoyed myself and couldn't wait for the next competition to come along.

When it came to the job interview, I was asked to take my CV with me so I made sure that it was up to date. Dad took me to Markinch in the car and we arrived about twenty minutes too early. Lynn met us at the door and when she said how long we would have to wait, Dad went off for a walk, to kill time and returned just as I finished.

When I showed Lynn my CV, she was surprised that I already had so many qualifications. She offered me the job and asked if I could attend a training session on the 26th of January. As that was my birthday, I had already organised a trip to Dundee with my cousins. When I explained this to Lynn, she said, "That's okay, I'll have a think about it and let you know when you can start. I was so excited that I had got the job, I phoned Eddie, at Momentum, straightaway, to let him know.

I had two celebrations planned for my 23rd birthday - one in Dundee on my actual birthday, on the Wednesday and one on the Friday at my house. I wanted to go further a-field than St Andrews this time and decided to go to Dundee, to a few pubs and then on to a nightclub. Nightclubs weren't really my kind of thing but I had been at a couple while I was in Hereford and they were ok so I thought I would give this one a go. Six of us went up to Dundee that night in S & S Taxis from St Monans. I had used them a few times before. Two men ran S & S Taxis, Stuart and Scott, hence the name. I didn't really know them but they seemed to know me, and it was Stuart that drove us to Dundee and back that night. I took my wheelchair with me as I didn't know what to expect and didn't know how far it would be from pub to pub. Most of the places we went to weren't very disabled-friendly and there were quite a lot of stairs to negotiate. I can't remember any of the pub names but I do remember dropping my glass in one of the pubs and the barmaid having to clean it up. I went to place my glass on the bar but didn't realise that the edge of the bar was on a slope and the glass slid off and smashed. Because it was my birthday, Eck tried to get a free drink for me but the barmaid wasn't up for that. After three or four pubs, we finally got to the nightclub. Wednesday night was Student Night so all the drinks were fairly cheap but the selection was poor and I had to settle for a beer that I didn't like very much. I sat in my wheelchair most of the night and while I was sitting there, this girl of about 18 or 19 came up to me and started to talk to me. She was a lovely girl, with long dark hair and massive breasts. She was from Manchester and was studying at Dundee University. We hit it off really well and talked for ages. Eck had asked the DJ to do a birthday request so I thought it was appropriate to get up on the dance floor. Eck and John lifted me, and my chair, on to the floor then I got up on my crutches and started to dance with the Manchester girl. I can't dance for very long, especially after a few drinks, so, after only a couple of songs, I had to sit down again. By the end of the night the girl wanted to go home with me but when I told her where I stayed, she changed her mind as she had Uni the next morning. We got separated after that and we left without any contact details - I was gutted. I was telling the guys about her on the way home and they thought I was crazy – they said I should have gone home with her instead. Well, it was too late by that time, and anyway, I couldn't stay in Dundee on my own with a complete stranger. On the way home I asked Stuart, the driver, about the possibility of a contract run, taking me to and from work. He said he'd love to do it but he'd have to talk to Scott first. It was a good night in Dundee. Next up was another birthday bash on the Friday.

    I made sure that I cleaned my flat thoroughly on the Friday and then settled down to play a football game on the Nintendo until my guests started to arrive. My granny arrived first. She was really early and just sat watching me play the Nintendo until the rest of the people came. I offered her a drink but she said she preferred to wait until everyone else arrived. I switched the game off when my mum and dad arrived, and helped them to put crisps and snacks out on the table and in the kitchen. Like at my house warming party, I invited mostly family and a couple of friends but this time I also invited Ian, Bill and Morris as well as Chris and his wife from across the road. There still weren't many people in when the phone rang. Gayle, from Premier Contact, was phoning to tell me when I was to start work and what my hours would be. I was to do three nights a week, starting on the 21st of February. Mum wasn't very happy about being offered nights instead of afternoon shifts but said it was better than nothing. We had a great night with everyone talking away and the music playing in the background. It wasn't really loud but my friend from next-door burst in several times, complaining about the noise. I didn't invite her because she said she didn't like crowds. Eventually, Mum couldn't take it anymore and said, "What do you think you're doing, marching into my son's house like that!" Then she turned her around and marched her straight back out the door. The rest of us had a little smile at that. It wasn't as if the party was out of hand, everybody was behaving and, as I said, the music wasn't really loud. However, I'd learned previously that the girl liked a good moan and enjoyed complaining about things. She was an attractive young woman but very hard to please. After her exit, the party carried on and by the end we all agreed we'd had a great time.

    I phoned Eddie on the Monday to let him know about my start date and my hours. He was a little concerned about the hours. The reason was, I wanted to come off benefit payments but I would have to work at least sixteen hours to be better off and I wasn't getting sixteen hours. Eddie phoned Premier Contact. He explained the situation and asked if they could offer me anything else. They suggested four afternoon shifts instead, which would give me sixteen hours a week. Eddie thought I should work my way in gradually. He wanted me to do a work placement of less than sixteen hours a week, for three months, before starting employment proper. He thought I should start this way to familiarise myself with the computer systems and with the building itself. He also wanted me to see if I could handle a working environment. He arranged for me to visit Premier Contact prior to starting to check out where I would be sitting and how my Supernova software would work with the computer and the phones. I felt strange that day as I went in wearing casual clothes and everyone else seemed to be smartly dressed. A few of the staff gave me some funny looks. Even so, it felt like a friendly environment and a good company to work for and I thought I was going to like working for Premier contact.

On the Monday that should have been my first day at work, I had a stinker of a cold and had to phone in sick. My shifts were to be Monday, Thursday and Friday so I had a couple of days to recover and by the time Thursday came I was feeling a lot better and was able to go in. As my hours were 1:30 – 5:30pm, and I lived a good distance away, I had to leave the house around 12.40 pm. When I got to Premier Contact's front door, a young woman ushered me in. Alex, my driver, went back to the car and the young woman took me through to Gayle who was my Team Manager. There were two Team Managers - Lynn, who had interviewed me - fairly young, small with dark hair, and Gayle, who was in her mid-twenties, with blonde hair - again quite small. Lynn was in charge of the Cash

Calling Team who were mainly in at night - what I was originally lined up to do - so I wouldn't be seeing much of them. However, some of them worked a full shift, 1:30 – 9:00pm so I did see some of the people on the Cash Campaigns. In Cash Campaigns, agents phoned existing donors who already donated to particular charities to ask if they were able to contribute a little bit more. My job, on the other hand, was to phone new donors to thank them for supporting a particular charity. Much easier! I sat with Gayle for a while talking about what my work would involve and we discussed the skills I would need, working on the phones. She arranged for me to listen in on some of her agents' calls – to get an idea of what I would need to say when I made my own calls. I didn't *make* any calls on the Thursday - just listened to others – but was raring to have a go, the following day. My first day was over and plenty more to look forward to.

When Friday came I didn't feel that I was quite ready to go straight in and make calls so I 'call listened' for the first half of my shift. Then I made my first Welcome call. My Supernova was already installed on my PC so I just had to put my headset on, log in and make my first call. I used Supernova to help me navigate around the screens and I listened to the speech in my headphones, telling me what I was doing. There was a 'make call' button situated on the screen, to click. This would then do the dialling for me, to save hand dialling. I had already rehearsed the Welcome script, which had been sent to me by email. I was the only agent with two headsets - one for talking with the donor and the other headset over the top, to listen to my Supernova. When I finally made that first Welcome call, it went quite well. I was quite impressed with myself. It wasn't too difficult thanking someone for their support. But there was more to it than just thanking them. You had to confirm several details with them – such as, which charity they were supporting, how much they donated each month, quarterly, biannually or yearly, say a little about the charity and tell them how much their support would help. We also had to ask how they found the Fundraiser(s) and if they enjoyed the information that was left and most important, for data protection reasons, if it would be okay for the charity to keep in touch. Finally, we finished off with a freephone number in case they wanted to call and then thanked them again.

A nice warm and friendly welcome call. This would be what I would have to say, repeatedly, every single day.

I really started getting into the swing of things at Premier Contact and started meeting a whole lot of new people. Colin sat next to me quite a lot when I started. He was quite tall and quite large, with dark hair. He used to talk to me a lot in the first few weeks and as much as I wanted to talk with him, I had to really concentrate on my work, as it was very hard listening to my Supernova, listening for the phone ringing and listening to a colleague as well. And, of course, I was on work placement so I had to concentrate as best as I could so that I would be taken on permanently. There was a smoking area out the back where people went to have a cigarette but I didn't bother at first, as smoking still embarrassed me, so I stayed in the kitchen with the others. I didn't really get to know many people in my first few weeks at work, apart from Colin. There were quite a few there, though, and the majority of them were women. Most of the agents were in their teens or early twenties but Kath and Nina were in their early fifties. Most of the girls were attractive and seemed very nice people.

One of the first female agents I talked to was Nicky. She was very friendly, average height, with blonde hair and had a nice cheeky smile. I talked to her in the kitchen one day during break-time. I always had a cup of coffee from the coffee machine during breaks but I always had to ask someone to fetch it for me, as I couldn't see well enough to use it. By now, it was extremely difficult to make people out so I had to learn to recognise people's voices. I had started learning voice recognition at the Blind College and now I had to do it with every person that worked at Premier. It wasn't easy as there were so many of them and what made things worse was that nobody, except me, sat in the same seat all of the time. There was a seating plan on the wall at the start of every shift, the idea being that people took turns in all the different positions. This wasn't so bad, because, eventually, it allowed me to get to know all the agents on my shift – and their voices. I started going outside for a smoke, once I felt comfortable. I still went out with Ian and the boys at night, for a drink, and then – often went into work feeling rough.

I don't know when it started but Wednesdays became a regular night for me going to Mum's for tea. Every Wednesday afternoon I'd walk down to The Ship for a glass of coke and Mum would pick me up there, at four. Dae was always at Mum's on a Wednesday too so he usually took me home. Before I knew it, I was going to Mum's for tea on a Thursday night as well. It was nice knowing my tea was on the table when I came home from work. One Friday night, when Dad was away, Mum asked me if I wanted to come across for tea. That turned into every Friday, whether Dad was away or not. It was good to know that I was getting fed properly, especially as I was doing a good bit of drinking. I was able to dry out for a couple of weeks when Ian was away. I still drank some nights during the week, but it was just a couple.

In April, Maxine, my friend from Shetland, was going to visit her Mum in Newcastle and Malky was going with her. Malky was driving as Maxine didn't have a licence and they were stopping off at my place for a couple of nights. They were coming on a Friday so I told them they might have to hang around till I got home. They were sitting outside my flat when Alex and I drew up. Malky was tall - over six feet, with a shaved head. Maxine, on the other hand, was quite small - yet large - and had very long brown hair, down to her bum. The last time they'd visited, they'd had Maxine's daughter with them but this time they were by themselves. While I was working, Malky and Maxine had been down at the harbour eating a fish supper. They'd seen Mum and Auntie Julie there but didn't know who they were until later that night when we all met up at my flat. I had invited some family and friends round to meet them.

Malky had both his walking sticks tucked down the side of the settee. He kept asking Maxine to go and get him a beer from the fridge and everyone kept looking at him, wondering why he didn't get it himself. Unlike me his back and legs were quite straight and no one could have guessed that he had a disability. Not until he got up to go to the toilet anyway! Then their chins all dropped when he slid his sticks out and made for the wee room. After the rest of my visitors left, Malky, Maxine and I talked for a long time before going to bed.

I took Malky out for a few drinks in The Ship on the Saturday night. Maxine wasn't much of a drinker so she stayed in and watched the tele. We sat in The Ship most of the night, drinking and chatting with my friends and some of the regulars. We had a good time, but I knew by the way Ian and some other people were talking that there was something not quite right. Mum had phoned me that afternoon to invite Malky and Maxine round for lunch on the Sunday so that's what we did before they left for Newcastle. I really enjoyed having them for the weekend. They were two lovely people, and Malky said if I wanted to go up to Shetland to visit them, he would travel down on the ferry to Aberdeen and then take me back with him. I was really pleased at his offer and said that if I couldn't get tickets for the Carling Weekend Festival in August I would go up then.

May was fast approaching and my work placement was coming to an end. I was about to start work for real but I was going to need some financial help. I phoned Anne at the Job Centre to see what was available. She said that if I came off Incapacity Benefit, I would get £200 from them because I was going into paid employment. I was entitled to Working Tax Credits and Anne said I could also get help from the Shaw Trust. I contacted the Trust and arranged a visit. A man there explained about the Trust and what they did. The long and short was that if I signed up to the Trust before I started work, they would give me £100 and if I was still in employment after three months, they would give me another £100. This was all a huge help to get me started, and all my computer equipment would be paid for and provided by Access To Work, who would also pay my travel costs. Eddie wanted Alex to continue driving me but I would have preferred Scott and Stuart at S & S Taxis. They seemed interested when I had a word with them but - Alex got the contract. Everything was now in place and I was ready to start work. I was lucky to get the job when I did because if I had stayed on benefits much longer I would have had to give up my flat and move back into Mum's and I didn't want to do that. I always wanted to work, but now I had to. I had to work for 16 hours or more so I needed another afternoon. I was already working Monday, Thursday and Friday and Gayle said it was up to me whether I took Tuesday or Wednesday. I chose the Tuesday so that I would have Wednesday in the middle of the week to do my bits and bobs, like the Bank and the Post Office and a bit of shopping. When I started at Premier Contact I was registered with Fife Employability, which meant I could have support at work if I needed it and someone would visit me every six months to discuss my progress. Everything was falling into place just nicely and after the first week at Premier Contact, I got my very first payslip. What more could I ask for at this stage in my life; I was now a working man, living on my own, doing all my household chores on my own and having a drink with my mates in the pub. Brilliant!

Chapter 28

A VISIT TO SHETLAND

I really enjoyed working for Premier Contact. The work was very satisfying and I enjoyed the banter with my colleagues. I often went home happy at night, knowing that I had thanked people for giving up a few pounds a month to help a worthwhile cause, and knowing that, after my phone call, they were happy to help. I often went for a run when I got home from work. I'd have my tea first and then go out for a run around the town, on my crutches, stopping off for a juice in the pub, and then home again. I felt that this was my best chance of keeping fit. The Gym was out of the question as I still had pain in the wound from my hernia operation.

We were overloaded with work by the end of May and I was asked if I wanted to work a couple of extra shifts. Great! However, that meant getting home about half past nine some nights and I didn't realise that such a late finish wouldn't be covered by Alex's contract. Eddie said Alex couldn't take me home at that time of night but I didn't want to lose out on the extra work so I said I would prefer a taxi firm that could manage the late finishes. Access to Work then asked me to provide three new taxi quotes to replace Alex. I wanted S & S from the start so I arranged for them to quote against two really expensive firms and – hey presto, S & S got the contract! I did like Alex though. He was a lovely, friendly man and had driven me for quite some time so I invited him and his wife through to Anstruther for a drink. They booked themselves in to a local B & B so that neither of them would have to drive afterwards. They picked me up from work on a Friday, which was to be Alex's last run, and we drove through to Anstruther. We had a good drink together, after tea, and I introduced them to Ian and some of the lads at The Ship. Alex and his wife didn't stay late but left me to finish the night off with the boys.

I can't remember if it was Scott or Stuart that picked me up on my first journey with them. As brothers, they were quite close and both were keen on motorbikes. However, they had very different tastes in music. Dance music was Scott's favourite while Stuart preferred rock and punk. I thought I would get on better with Stuart, the older brother, as I was into rock music too but I enjoyed the banter with Scott so much that I was equally comfortable with either one. They had two cars on the road - a four-seater Mondeo and a six-seater Mazda. I liked the Mazda better. For me, it was much easier to get into. I've never been good at getting in and out of cars and I always have to get in the left side as left is my weaker side. I knew I was never going to be bored, travelling, with S & S.

During the summer I met a lovely family in The Ship, who I'll call, The Donaldsons. There was Jim and Theresa, and their daughters, Allie and Lynn. They were from Livingston but Jim had a boat that he kept in Anstruther harbour. It turned out that they came through to stay on the boat, most weekends. My friend, Ian, had met them some time before me and had often wound me up about the older daughter, Allie. Allie was eighteen and Lynn, who they called 'Bucket' was two years younger. Ian had told me that Allie was quite a feisty little person who was a black belt in karate and drank pints of Guinness. I started to wonder what this 'Allie' was like and had built up quite a picture of her in my head. How wrong I was. When I finally met her, I got a surprise. She was, sure enough, a black belt, quite small and drank pints of Guinness, but what Ian hadn't told me was that she was very pretty. She was also disabled. A car had hit her when she was very young and she sustained some brain damage. She was often quite tired and grumpy but she was a cracking girl and I started to fall for her. Some Sunday afternoons I would sit on the boat with Jim and Theresa just so that I could see Allie – and it wasn't easy getting on that boat, with my sense of balance!

One night, Ian and I were drinking in The Ship with Jim and Theresa and they invited us down to their boat for a drink. Allie wasn't out that night; she had stayed on the boat to have an early night. We had a few drinks on the boat and were enjoying a bit of banter but when it started to get a bit loud I was concerned about waking up the 'grumpy' Allie, as we were right alongside the sleeping berths. It was quite late when we finally left the boat and started to wander home. Ian walked with me just to make sure I got home safely but it still took about an hour and a half to walk, or should that be, crawl, up the road but I made it eventually. Ian must have been fed up trying to get me home some nights, with the speed I walked at. After that night on the boat, I started to get quite close to the Donaldsons and looked forward to their weekend visits.

I decided to hold my first Race Night in August that year, to raise funds for glaucoma; the condition I suffer from. I knew that organising the Race Night wouldn't be easy and I'd need plenty of time in which to do it, so I started planning three months ahead. As I drank regularly in The Ship, I decided to hold the event there. I had to start by selling the horses for the races. I prepared a table on my computer for the horses' names, the punters' names, their addresses and telephone numbers etc. I also had to arrange prizes and advertising flyers for the night. I knew that I had a lot of work ahead of me but reckoned I would get some help from the pub owner. In the event, I didn't get much help from anyone and had to organise virtually the whole thing on my own. However, I managed to have everything ready in time. All the horses were sold in advance so that I could sort them out into a series of races. Chris, from across the road helped me with this. I had done the advertising, collected the prizes - for races and raffles - and drawn up a programme for the night, which my employers kindly printed out for me. Everything was set and ready to go. I just needed to get some people in, to bet on the horses. I didn't anticipate any problem there, as The Ship was usually quite busy at that time. I invited some people from the Blind Society to come along and give their support. A number of them did and Jim, Theresa and Allie came along as well.

I started the night off by explaining how the races worked and what the Race Night was in aid of. After my little speech, I handed the 'mike' over to one of the regulars, who I had asked to compére - reading out the horses' names so that people could go up and bet on a horse of their choice. The night was a great success, as I knew it would be. Despite being in quite a small venue, I still managed to raise £450 for the International Glaucoma Association and - even better - I was able to enjoy every second of the night sitting with the Donaldsons. Allie and I talked for quite a while after the 'racing' was finished and I told her how I felt about her and asked her if anything could happen between us. She said, "I'd like for something to happen between us, but just not right now, maybe sometime soon." I was happy enough with that and we kissed a little before she went back to the boat with her Mum and Dad.

In August, after the Race Night, I decided to visit Maxine and Malky. I had promised Malky that I would go there if I couldn't get tickets for the Carling Weekend Festival. When no tickets materialised, I put in for some days holiday from work and set about arranging the trip. Malky would travel down on the ferry from Shetland to Aberdeen and take me back to Shetland, with him. He knew it would be too difficult for me to do the whole journey on my own, given the state of my eyesight. Mum took me to Dundee to get the Aberdeen bus, avoiding the need for me to change buses at St Andrews. Malky said he would wait for me at the bus station in Aberdeen. Everything went to plan and as we pulled into the bus station, Malky was waiting, as promised, propped up on his walking sticks, and a cigarette hanging from his lower lip. I had told him that I could follow shapes if there were clear contrasts so he wore his blue jeans and white trainers. Following those trainers was dead easy. As we had a while to wait for the ferry, we decided to have a stroll around Aberdeen city centre. I followed Malky's feet while he carried the bags, walking as best he could with his sticks. A few hours later, we made our way to the ferry port. We checked in as foot passengers and I didn't have to pay when I showed my 'blind certificate'. In fact, I was able to do the whole journey to Shetland and back for free as I had a 'free' bus pass as well.

As foot passengers we slept on one of the long benches in the canteen area – we didn't want to pay a hefty charge for a cabin. We sat in the bar for most of the night, with Malky drinking tins of Tennants and me on pints of Carlsberg. Malky had been on the ferries quite a lot so he knew most of the staff and they helped carry our drinks across to the table. If we wanted a smoke, we had to go outside onto the deck and with Malky being a heavy smoker we were outside quite a lot. Once we'd had a few drinks, we started taking our drinks outside with us. It was very different, with Malky guiding me. He seemed to know better than anyone else, how to do it. I think it must have been difficult for him but he had a lot of patience with me. When we finally turned in for the night, I hardly slept a wink, though Malky slept all night. Once the bar had closed, at three in the morning, all I could hear was the clinking of glasses being washed and then all the preparations being made for breakfast, in the morning. This was my first trip on a ferry and it was quite a calm voyage but for the twelve hours on board, I think I only got about two hours sleep.

We arrived in the Shetlands around seven in the morning. It took another hour in Malky's little three-door Toyota before we reached their house. When we arrived there, Maxine was in bed; her son, Michael, was sitting in the living room, playing a game through Sky television and the house dog, Goggles, a cross-german shepherd-collie, came to greet me. Maxine soon came downstairs and we all sat down to a cup of tea and a cigarette. Maxine said she'd been up most of the night cleaning and tidying for me coming. I then had to go for a lie down, as I was shattered after the long journey. Maxine showed me to her daughter Jessica's room and I lay on her bed for a while. Malky's Mum was expected a few days later, for her first stay in Shetland so there was going to be a houseful. Although I had an hour's kip on Jessica's bed, I was going to be sharing a room with Michael, a tall, big-built boy of seventeen. On my first night in the Shetlands, Maxine, Malky, Michael and I, all went down the road a bit, to a pub called The Westings, for a quick drink and a game of pool. Malky couldn't play, as he couldn't balance well enough so I had a few games with Michael.

I went to the Shetlands for a break. I wasn't too

bothered about the history or the scenery. I couldn't see that, anyway! But when Malky's mum arrived she wanted to see it all and Malky had to drive her everywhere. I went with them because it got me out of the house and got me involved. Malky's mum was in her late seventies and was quite deaf so we had to shout quite loudly for her to hear us. We drove all over Shetland that week and I didn't see a bit of it! Maxine often came with us and we would stop off at a café for a cup of tea. The highlight of my visit, was visiting Aith Social Club, a couple of miles up the road. I had a lot of fun there. It was only open at weekends but as I was in Shetland over two weekends, I was able to go two weekends running. I played pool with one of the locals and almost beat him. When we had finished, Malky said to him, "Do you realise Billy's blind?" The guy was amazed and quickly apologised for taking advantage. But I said, "There's no need to apologise. This blind man almost beat you!" The three of us went to Aith Social club on our own, leaving Maxine and Malky's mum in the house on their own. Malky's mum was never late going to bed. I think the latest she went was about eleven and left us to have a few drinks before we turned in. Actually, Maxine didn't really drink - she'd rather have a cup of tea, Michael didn't drink much and I had never been a heavy drinker. But Malky - could drink lager like water. He'd have two tins to my every one and could drink all night. As much as I knew how Malky could drink, he took it easy while his mum was staying. I liked staying there. Although the three bedrooms, and the bathroom, were all upstairs, they had a stair lift. The bathroom was a wet-floor shower room – the type of thing I was waiting to have installed in my house. Every lunchtime we had a sandwich of some kind - sausage, bacon, salad or toastie, and we ate it off a plate on our lap. When it came to teatime though, I asked to eat at the dining room table because that was easier for me. I also asked everyone not to smoke while we were eating – the smell puts me off my food. Maxine kept forgetting and when she would light up at the table, Malky would shake his head and say, "She's got a short memory!" When Malky's mum finally went home, the day before me, I was left at home with Michael and the dog, while Malky and Maxine took his mum to the airport.

When it came my turn to leave I was really sad. I'd had such a great time with Malky and his family, and Jessica had come through a couple of times for her tea so I got to meet her as well. I still had most of the day to enjoy Shetland, as the ferry wasn't leaving till seven at night. Again, Malky went with me for the whole journey and I said my goodbyes to Maxine, Michael and Goggles, the dog. As we were leaving at teatime, Maxine had made some sandwiches for us to eat on the way down on the ferry. The return ferry voyage was a little rockier and we were regularly out on deck for a cigarette. I think we had a little more to drink too but I still couldn't sleep properly, for the noise in the bar, again. As the ferry arrived in Aberdeen at seven in the morning, we had a while to wait for my bus. I chose the three o'clock bus because I didn't want to leave Malky hanging around for hours until he got the ferry back. After leaving our bags in lockers at the bus station, we browsed the shops for a while and then went to MacDonalds for lunch and then on to a couple of pubs before returning to the bus station. I thanked Malky for having me and he waited to make sure I got safely on the bus. I slept most of the way from Aberdeen to Dundee, where Mum was waiting for me when the bus pulled in. When she asked if I would go back to the Shetlands again, I didn't hesitate, "Yes - I think I will!"

In September of 2005 Premier Contact, was put

forward for the Fife Diversity Awards. These awards were for companies employing disabled people. I was to attend the awards ceremony at the Balbirnie House Hotel in Markinch, with Gayle, my supervisor. I went to work in my Sunday best that day, as I wasn't going to do any work. I dressed in my black suit and black shirt, with Scotland cufflinks. Scott drove me to work that afternoon - Stuart was to pick me up after the event. I was struggling with my cufflinks in the house and was running out of time so I took them with me and fiddled about with them in the car, on the way. It took me most of the journey to get the cufflinks in, as I had never worn them before, but I finally managed. Well, I thought I had until Scott asked to see them and noticed they were in upside down! He managed to fix them for me in no time, as he knew what he was doing - and he could see! I had a little while to wait before heading for the ceremony, so I went and sat with a couple of colleagues but Gayle saw me and said that if I sat and spoke to them I would have to get on the phones and work for a while. Mmm - I went out the back for a cigarette instead! We finally left Premier Contact in a taxi and when we got to the hotel, we stopped for a cigarette - just to settle the nerves. The hotel was very posh. We were given name tags and directed to our designated table. The table seated eight and was laid out with flashy place mats and cutlery - a bit swanky by our standards. We had a lovely four-course meal and then the award ceremony began. There were two categories, which were the Sustainment award and the Employment award. Premier Contact won an Employment Award and resolved to try again, the following year, for a Sustainment Award. Gayle accepted the award on behalf of Premier Contact and after all the awards had been made we all preened ourselves for the massive photo shoot that followed. It was a great night and I really enjoyed Gayle's company. She had a lot of time and patience for me. After the awards Gayle and I stood and chatted outside, waiting for Stuart to collect me. When he did arrive, he was quite late. He said he might have been there quicker if I had given him the correct directions. A tip for my readers, never ask a blind man for directions! At work the next day, everyone was asking how my 'date' with Gayle had gone. I just smiled and said, "Fine."

A works night out was to be held in September in the local bowling alley for the new call agents and for some others that were leaving to go back to university. Premier Contact was a popular place for students to work in the summer. The night out was to be held on a Saturday, a week that East Fife were playing at home. My dad wasn't home for this match so my uncle took me along to the game and then took me to Glenrothes bus station afterwards, to meet up with Colin. Colin was going to look after me for the night. Colin and I were early so we settled in the bar until the others arrived. I got through a few Carlsberg Special Brews and was quite drunk after the third bottle so that I could hardly play by the time we went down stairs to the alleys. There were a lot of hot girls at Premier Contact and Colin said he couldn't help noticing me eyeing them up as they swept their balls down the alley. Each time it was my turn, I walked up to the bowling line and one of the girls brought the ball to me, to save me having to carry it. Inevitably, I came last on our team and was presented with the boobie prize - a set of children's skittles and two little plastic bowling balls! When we left the bowling alley, Colin was a little drunk and kept wandering off, while Gayle and Lynne held back and waited on me. At one point, I thought I'd be clever and jump up a kerb, not realising that the kerb actually went down. I got quite a 'drop' and I landed flat on my front, scraping my entire finger on the ground. I picked myself up again and headed for the pub with Gayle and Lynne. It was in one of the pubs that I told a couple of the girls I had the hots for them. Unfortunately I chose to tell them when they were together - not very smart! In my defence, I must say, by then I was very drunk and – really should have been home. I asked Gayle to phone me a taxi. When it came I got a bit of a shock. It was going to cost about £30! I got another surprise when several people chipped in to help pay for my journey home. The driver was a lovely blonde lady and I told her the reason for the night out, and a bit about myself. This was my first work's night out since I had worked at the Waid Centre and I loved it. I was socialising with my work mates, and getting away from life at home.

I can't quite remember when it was but I was out drinking in Anstruther one Wednesday night with John and Eck, when we met up with some people on our way from The Sally to The Ship and they sort of tagged along with us. To begin with, there was Eck, John, Eck's mate and me, then a girl about eighteen who fancied Eck, joined us - and then a few more. Well, Eck took it upon himself to invite them up to my flat. I wasn't keen, as I was working the next day but they came anyway. They helped themselves to drink in the kitchen and then went through to the living room. The music was on and cranked up loud so that the whole block would hear and I knew that wasn't going to go down too well with the girl next door. There was much smoking and drinking in the kitchen and the living room and I was quite drunk by the time I heard the knock at my front door. When I opened the door, a very large police officer was standing there. My friendly girl next door had complained! The policeman came in and talked to me about the disturbance and told me to keep the noise down. On top of that, he had to take my personal details, "for the record". That was the first time I'd ever had to provide my details to the police. After the officer left, we tried to keep the noise down but the partying carried on for hours and I started to get very tired – and very grumpy. I didn't even get into my bed that night - Eck slept in it with our eighteen-year-old 'tag-along'. Around about six in the morning, I finally clambered onto my two-seater sofa and grabbed a couple of hours sleep before I had to get up again, for work.

When I did get up, I had to clear up all the mess from the night before. While I was doing this, Eck woke up. He'd heard the noise and thought it was his mate (who had slept on my three-seater sofa!) that was doing the clearing up. When he got up and discovered it was me, he gave his mate a right rollicking for not helping. Then he cleared up the rest of the mess, himself. Finally, the three of them went home and left me to have some time to myself, before I went to work. It was about a week later when Dad was in that he noticed three burns on my living room carpet. I assumed that they were from the party. After that I said I would never have a party in the flat again unless I knew everybody and could trust them not to make such a mess.

I finally got word of when the work was to start on my wet-floor shower. There had been a delay because there was asbestos to be removed first. I had to vacate the flat while the work was done so I moved back in with Mum for a week. The asbestos crew removed all the asbestos on the Monday and the contractors then started on the shower work the following day and were finished by Friday afternoon. I popped across a couple of times during the week to see how the work was progressing. I'd previously told my Occupational

Therapist about my eyesight and explained the need for contrasts in the shower room. I knew that it was going to be basic white tiles on the walls where the shower and sink were, but the shower controls were white and so was the sink. I knew this would be a problem so I asked if I could have blue tiles where the shower controls were and a line of blue tiles above the sink to identify where the sink was. The contractors were happy to do this but when I went to check I felt something wasn't quite right. I had chosen a yellow floor, but the yellow floor and white tiles clashed too much so I got the workmen to put a line of blue tiles at the bottom of each wall, to emphasis the boundary between the walls and the floor. When I moved back into my flat on the Friday the difference was amazing. I no longer had a bath to struggle in and out of. Now I just had to walk into my shower and walk out again. I was now able to shower in about ten minutes whereas, previously, a bath took about forty-five minutes. There was a bit of tiling still to be done (which wasn't contracted for) but my mate Morris was a plumber and said he would do it for me before Christmas. And - he would do it for a reduced rate as I was a mate and didn't have a big budget! Thanks, Morris.

October was quite quiet. My job was going well and I was paying regular visits to The Ship. Morris started work in my bathroom – mainly at nights and weekends as his plumbing business kept him busy during the daytime. My Dad left Standby Boats and bought a fish-round for himself. He'd never been a salesman before, having been at sea most of his life, but now he fancied being at home at nights and so he bought the fish round, selling fish all around Fife – and now he would be home with Mum, every night.

As Christmas approached, an Office Christmas Party was arranged and was to be held in Pinkertons, in

Glenrothes. I was really looking forward to another staff night out but I was concerned that I might not get looked after properly if everyone else was drinking heavily. Quite a lot of my colleagues liked to arrive at a night out, already drunk – I suppose it saved time – but it left me a bit anxious about being on nights out with them. As it turned out, I needn't have worried; the night went well. And – yes, almost everyone *was* drunk by the end of the night, including me. Even so, I had enough awareness to know that Gayle was looking out for me all night which was really nice of her. There was a lovely buffet meal and a disco afterwards – and I had a great time!

Chapter 29

WEDDINGS, FUNERALS & FALL-OUTS

The year 2006 was a very mixed year for me, with three funerals, two weddings, another trip to Shetland and some sad fall-outs. I woke up one cold January Monday morning and was getting myself ready for my support worker, Ann, coming in, when the phone rang. It was my dad. He told me that my granny had passed away that morning. I said, "I didn't realise she was ill!" Dad said she'd had a stroke, overnight, and hadn't managed to pull through. I was devastated and when I hung up the phone, I bottled it all up inside. Like with my granddad, I didn't cry for my granny's loss, although I wanted to; it just didn't happen. The funeral was a few days later. I didn't take a chord for Granny's coffin; by that time my eyesight was too poor. I can remember having a tear in my eye during the lovely service and I heard some things about my granny that I hadn't known. Granny wrote a lot of lovely poems, which a member of the congregation read out. Granny was a bit like me in a way, as she couldn't see very well. Her glasses were like the bottoms of milk bottles; they were so thick. However, her hearing was superb. Although I didn't see her a lot, I still loved Granny and I knew I was going to miss her. The service at the cemetery, was the first time in a long time, I saw my dad cry. It must have been hard for him, now losing his mum, as well as his dad. They both died round about seventy years old.

It was early 2006 when I decided to see about getting the cataract removed from my right eye. Not that it would improve my sight, as I was blind in my right eye anyway. I wanted the cataract removed because of the difference between my eyes. My left one looked normal but my right eye looked murky and strange. I was also fed up with kids playing around the flats, questioning me about it. Sometimes I'd hear them saying, "Look, there's the boy with the blue eye – let's go and see him." Even close friends, like Eck's son, picked on me because of my blue eye, so I asked for the cataract to be removed. However, the consultant told me he couldn't remove it at this stage. He said my eye was far too weak and if he was to remove the cataract, my eye would collapse. He suggested giving me a new eye by cutting the front off it and replacing it with an artificial one, or giving me a cosmetic shield. The cosmetic shield would be like a contact lens that I would slide in every morning but it would be coloured to make both eyes look the same. I decided to go with the cosmetic shield option - I didn't want my eye cut away. I had to practice with a clear contact lens first, learning how to wear it. I had to build up tolerance to it by wearing it for a short time to begin with and gradually increasing the time until I could wear it all day. It was during this process that I fell out with Ian one night, in The Ship. He was chatting to a couple of women when I joined in and invited all three of them back to my place, for a drink. I arranged a taxi but when we arrived outside the flats and I walked up to open the security door, they all got back in the taxi and drove off. I was boiling and went inside, really angry. I roughly knew where they were heading so I phoned the same taxi firm to pick me up and take me to that address. I asked the taxi driver to take me up to the door, as I couldn't see where I was going. When he knocked on the kitchen window and told Ian that I was there, I heard Ian swear. I think I had spoiled his plans.

He was trying to get rid of me so that he could go home with one of the women. I just thought mates don't ditch each other like that, but I shouldn't have gone; because I finished up walking all the way home, about three in the morning! Ian walked with me to make sure I got home safely. When I took my contact lens out that night, my eye felt like a golf ball – the lens had been in for far too long.

It was a Monday morning again, in April this time, when I was getting myself ready for Ann, and the phone rang. Again, it was my dad; my dae had passed away. Dad said Dae had fallen out of bed and punctured his lung and as he was quite a frail man, he didn't pull through. When I hung up the phone, I just broke down – crying more than I had cried in my entire life. As much as Dae was a moaner and burped over everyone's tea when he visited, I loved him to bits and he had a lot of time for me. He went along to the football with us to see East Fife and every time they lost a game he would say, "That's it, I'll no be back!" Of course he was always back at the next game – but this time he wouldn't be back. I had to phone my work and arrange for a week off. Lynne said she would send Gayle an e-mail to let her know. That same afternoon, Gayle phoned, asking where I was, as I wasn't in work and I told her about Dae. She apologised, saying Lynne hadn't sent the e-mail, and told me to take as much time off as I wanted. That night Mum phoned and asked me to go down to Helen's house as she and Auntie Julie were there. At Helen's, I sat all quiet, trying to put on a brave face and when Mum asked if I was okay. I said, "Aye, I'm fine." But she wasn't taken in, and said, "You're not really, are you"? I broke down in tears - I couldn't keep it in any longer. That night, I didn't go out - I stayed in and had an early bed - and Dae came to see me, while I slept. I still experienced the Charles Bonnet Syndrome from time to time but this night, it was definitely Dae. He sat down beside my bed and although he didn't say anything, it was as if he was assuring me that he would always be there for me. For the rest of that week, I didn't do much more than laze about thinking about Dae and how much I was going to miss him. The funeral was on the Friday. Everyone had been in to see Dae, lying in his coffin - apart from me, and my cousin John. I didn't really want to see him that way but Dad eventually persuaded me that I should go. Dae looked so peaceful lying there; it was like he was in a deep sleep. He was seventy-seven years old and my longest-living grandparent. He'd had his troubles in later life, with two heart attacks, a replacement hip and chronic gout amongst them. He got so lazy and hardly ever exercised. If he could've got his car into your house, he would have, to save him walking any distance. He was a much-loved wee man in the community and almost everyone knew who he was. The funeral was a Masonic service held in his house. His small bungalow was crammed to bursting so that a lot of mourners had to stand outside. After the service we took him to the graveyard where he would be buried in the same grave as my granny. It was too far for me to walk so I went in the limousine with Mum, Auntie Julie and Auntie May. At the graveyard, there were over three hundred mourners paying their respects and when Mum saw how many there were, she started to sob. I had been brave all week but I couldn't keep it together either. It was hard for Mum and Dad – and on top of everything, they had to guide me through the graveyard. After the burial, we were all invited back to the Craw's Nest Hotel for something to eat. Dae had always liked fish so Mum had made sure that fish was on the menu. There was, of course, a choice but I, in respect for Dae, had the fish. Most of the cousins wanted to get together that night, to celebrate Dae's life, and it was decided we do this in The Bank House. We had a few drinks and talked about Dae most of the night, and the things he did and said. There was a karaoke on but I was in no mood for singing. There were about ten of us cousin's altogether and I really enjoyed being in their company. I had planned to go to the Shetlands again, about ten days after the funeral, but now I was swithering. Was it the right time?

I was starting to frequent other pubs. The Ship was fine but I liked The Bank House, too. Sometimes I would race John up the road. This John was a Geordie and I knew him, from drinking in The Ship. Sometimes we would bump into each other in The Ship and agree to meet later, in The Bank House. He never expected me to get to The Bank House before him but I often did. During the week before I went to Shetland I popped into The Bank House and found Richard serving. He'd heard about my dae dying and noticed that I was very quiet and tried to comfort me. I nearly let myself go again, but I was in a pub and I didn't want to cry in front of the customers – even though there were only five there.

My uncle Jock was going to sea, the same day I was heading off to the Shetlands, but still he gave me a lift to Aberdeen and Malky met me there, as he had done before. After putting my bags into the bus station left-luggage we had a drink in the pub across from the Ferry Terminal. Later, at the ferry check-in, the woman at the desk was asking Malky, not me, all the relevant questions, as if I wasn't there. When she asked if I required a cabin, Malky wanted to know how much it would be. Without even a glance in my direction, the woman said, "It's free if he's registered blind." I was irritated by her manner – but we took the cabin! The trip was smooth enough and when we got to Malky's place, I discovered that I had a room to myself this time as Maxine's son had gone back down south. Her daughter, Jessica, though, stayed with us a few nights.

I didn't do much in Shetland this time, apart from visiting the Aith Social Club and hanging around the house. This time Malky was drinking a lot more and I was beginning to be a little concerned. One night, on our way back from Aith Social Club we didn't go straight home but instead, went to someone else's house along the street. I suspected that he was cheating on Maxine and when we arrived home, Maxine asked if we had been at the woman's house. I couldn't lie – and that was the start of my fall out with Malky. To make matters worse, I then was sick on the living room carpet. Malky and I argued – as drunks often do, and I swore at him – also, as drunks often do! I told him, "If you're going to be like that, I'm going home!" It was near the end of my stay, anyway. He said, "On you go then, sailor," knowing well it was impossible for me to go on my own. I didn't sleep well that night and when I went downstairs in the morning, Malky was already there. I thought he had just got up but unbeknown to me he had stayed up all night – and he was still drinking. I couldn't face more alcohol and even the orange juice that I took with my breakfast, came right back up. I went back to bed. Eventually, I heard Malky coming up the stairs – on his chair lift – a thing he never did. A few hours later I felt a bit better and came downstairs, expecting Malky to be there but he didn't make an appearance until teatime. I made up with him then but that same night he started drinking again. Jessica got quite upset and ran away and I went for a walk. There was a lot of tension between Malky and Maxine, after this fall-out and I was glad to be going home. I didn't want to get in between them!

On the return journey, we were given a cabin again.

We had a good drink on the ferry and Malky started chatting up a woman in the bar. By this time, I was very tired and he helped me back to our cabin, before returning to the bar. He said he wouldn't be long but I suspected differently. When I got fed up waiting for him, I locked the door and when he returned – he wanted to bring 'the woman' into the cabin. "No way, José!" I told him and the woman went off – somewhere. I liked the woman but I didn't want to see Malky cheating on Maxine. There were parts of that holiday I did enjoy but I was glad to be on my way home - going back to my work colleagues and a drink with my mates in the pub. Ian and the rest of the guys in The Ship didn't like Malky. In fact, very few people in Anstruther liked Malky – but I did. He was a really good friend to me and he understood me like no one else ever did, so I stuck by him. Maxine kicked him out of the house a few weeks later and he stayed at one of the old ladies' houses that he did some gardening for until he was given a house from the Council. He also lost his driver's licence, for drink driving – informed on by a very stressed out Jessica.

When I got back from Shetland, a letter was waiting for me. My cosmetic shield was ready for fitting – well ahead of schedule. The shield was amazing. It was identical to my other eye. Lots of people commented on it, saying it looked great. As with the clear contact lens, I had to build up my tolerance to the shield, wearing it for only an hour or so to begin with and then, day by day, gradually increasing the time. Sometimes I'd take it out at work and put it on a colleague's desk to freak them out –it was very life-like! Before long, I was wearing it all day. It made a huge difference to my features and soon, people that didn't know me, didn't realise it was fake.

Scott and Stuart, my taxi drivers, were both bikers

and round about May, that year, they both came off their bikes - within two weeks of each other. Scott had his accident first, and while he was laid up in hospital, Stuart employed his own girlfriend, Valerie to drive in his place. Valerie, better known as Val was the same age as my mum and had been in the same year at school. Val was a very friendly woman and I was in the same year at school, with her eldest son. After Stuart's accident, Val ran the business on her own until one of the brothers was fit to return to work. With me being as blind as I am, I get a fright very easily and Stuart and Scott picked up on this. Stuart would always wait until I was almost at the taxi door and then he would honk the horn and watch me jump. I knew he was going to do it but it still made me jump!

I had two wedding invitations this year. My cousin, Hayley, got married in June and, in July I was to be best man at my brother's wedding. Gayle, from work, was to be my partner at Michael's wedding. I liked Gayle; she was very good to me and knew how to guide me, so she seemed an obvious choice. Hayley's wedding was really good and a great day but I often felt left out, sitting on my own, not being able to get involved in the dancing and other celebrations.

I had a big fall-out in The Ship, at the beginning of July and stormed out. It all started out, as a joke; certain people putting beer mats on top of my glass, knowing I wouldn't see it. When I rumbled their trick, I started drinking straight from the bottle. It didn't take long before they came up with a new angle – they started rolling up the beer mats and sticking them in the neck of the bottle. (What a hoot!) Or, they would pass me a beer bottle with just water in it - or a bottle with the top still on. I'd been having a few problems in The Ship for a while and things came to a head that night. I quite often got a lift home from the bar staff when they finished work but recently the owner had told me I couldn't expect a lift all the time. Then it was suggested that I was stalking Ian, and tracking him down in The Boat or The Ship. Sometimes, in The Ship, when I'd ask if someone – Ian or Bill, for example – was in, the owner would say, "No, I haven't seen them," and then have a big laugh. Of course, the person in question was invariably standing behind me. That might sound funny to some people but as far as I was concerned it felt like he was taking the piss out of my poor eyesight and I'd had just about enough. The final straw came as I was leaving that night and the owner and a customer started throwing ice at me, on the way out. I told him to shove his pub up his arse - I wouldn't be back. He said I wouldn't get the same treatment anywhere else and I said, "That's true – it's bound to be better than this!" I was sad to leave The Ship – I had a lot of friends there - but I was never setting foot in that place again. When I told Malky what had happened, he said that if they were true friends, they would follow me.

Still, I had my brother's wedding to look forward to and a best man's speech to prepare. I also had to organise a 'stag do' but not having been on many stag nights myself, I didn't really know what to do, so I just organised a pub-crawl in Anstruther. My brother's wife-to-be had her hen party on the same night and also in Anstruther. I think that was because the aunties wanted to be close at hand to make sure the uncles didn't get up to any mischief! We all went from pub to pub and then back to Mum's for sandwiches and more drink. By the time I got to Mum's I was really drunk so I ordered a taxi and quietly slipped off home.

We had to go for a service rehearsal, the night before the wedding. Dad picked me up from work and we drove to the hotel, which was in Edinburgh. The venue for the wedding was down several flights of stairs, like an old dungeon, and at first, I didn't think I would manage. However, I made it and the rehearsal went fine. After the rehearsal, I went to The Sally for a few drinks with Michael and a few of my cousins and uncles, and then on to The Old Bank House. We had round after round and then I invited them all back to mine. Manuella was in that night, so I asked her to join us. We had a few drinks at mine and then Michael went and crawled into my bed while the rest of us carried on drinking till the wee hours. By the time most people were starting to leave, it was so late, Dad decided to stay, as he would have to get up again in only a couple of hours.

The day came for Michael's wedding. Michael was driving through to Edinburgh with me, the pageboy and Gayle. The rest of the guests were going by private coach. Michael had a few things to do before he got into his kilt so I had a drink and a chat with Gayle while I waited for him. When he got back, we both went upstairs and got dressed in our kilts. When I came downstairs again, I introduced Gayle to my family. At the beginning of the wedding ceremony, I was standing proudly beside Michael when I suddenly heard the bagpipes playing. The hairs stood up on the back of my neck and I turned round in time to see Lecia sweeping in, stunning in her wedding dress. My young cousins were the bridesmaids and they looked lovely, too. The service was beautiful. When it came to the exchanging of rings I just handed the box over – no way was I going to struggle, trying to free them from the box, not with my eyesight. Once the ceremony was over, we had to go back upstairs for the photos and some champagne. This gave the hotel staff time to rearrange the tables downstairs for the meal. The meal was lovely - and then it was time for the speeches. When it was my turn, I thanked everyone for coming and everyone that helped to make the day happen. I also said that some relatives, who weren't there, would have been proud of Michael, particularly our 'Dae'. It was one of the proudest days of my life and of course, in true best-man tradition, I then proceeded to slate Michael mercilessly, highlighting and embellishing incidents from our childhood. When the speeches were finished I asked Dad to read the cards – another thing that my poor eyesight prevented me doing. After all that, we had to clear the hall again while the staff got it ready for the dancing, to follow. The whole celebration went really well and, although all the stair climbing was hard on me, I still enjoyed the day as much as anyone – and now I had an official sister-in-law. Gayle was a great partner but, of course, I had to give her up at the end of the day when she went home to her boyfriend.

After I had 'abandoned The Ship', I started drinking in The Royal. After only a few visits there I recalled the words I'd last heard in The Ship – "…you won't get the same treatment anywhere else." The reason was – I was already being treated a lot better! The only downside to not frequenting The Ship was that I wasn't going to see the Donaldsons as much. However, even this wasn't so bad when they agreed to meet me in The Royal. It was about this time when I realised that Geordie John was ill, in hospital. I hadn't seen him for a while and it turned out that he had developed a brain tumour and had been in hospital for most of the summer. I had found a new second home in The Royal. There was a lovely young barmaid there, called Laura. She was a bit like my ex-girlfriend, Carrie, small, with long dark hair and a great personality. We became really good friends and when I wasn't working on a Monday night, I would often walk down to The Royal, see Laura, and have a few soft drinks before heading home again.

Another 'Stars in Their Eyes' event was held that summer and through travelling to work with Scott, a great Country and Western fan, I decided to perform as Johnny Cash. One of the reasons Scott liked C & W was that a lot of them were funny and gave him a laugh. But that wasn't the only thing he laughed at as we drove back and forth to Markinch. He and his brother were equally guilty of catching me unawares and stamping on the brakes just as I was taking a slug from my juice bottle. They got a few chuckles at juice splashing all over me. I was all set to learn 'Ring of Fire' but then I came across another Johnny Cash song and decided to sing that instead. I hadn't listened to much of Johnny Cash or many Country songs at all but 'Folsom Prison Blues' sounded like a good match for my voice so I gave it a go. After I'd learned the words, Scott gave me a CD cover with a photo of Cash on it and Auntie Julie used this likeness to trim a wig I'd bought to look like Cash's hair. I got my cousin Arlene, who was also performing, to paint eyebrows on me as Johnny Cash had bushy eyebrows. All I needed then, was a white shirt and a black suit - after all, Johnny was The Man in Black. On the big night, all the contestants did their introductions and then we went off to get changed. Michael went as the lead singer from Thin Lizzy this time. When it was my turn, I poured out Folsom Prison Blues with, as much feeling as I could muster and I thought it was the best performance I'd given. We had a long wait for the results but finally Eck came running in and told me to make my way to the stage. I realised straightaway that I had won something, but what? Well, I hadn't won the competition but I was chuffed when Eck said,"And in second place, it's – Johnny Cash!" I had actually won a prize for singing - something I never thought I would do. After the presentation, I had to do my turn again and I loved every minute of it. After that night, I really got into Johnny Cash and landed up buying lots of the great man's CDs.

After my fall-out with The Ship, I spent a lot of time in The Royal and The Bank House. Richard told me he held a Quiz night every Tuesday in The Bank House but was thinking of changing it to a Thursday night, to accommodate the Darts League. I liked a quiz night and said I would go along if it was on Thursday nights. On one of my first nights at The Bank House, I was heading down the stairs when a little cocker spaniel suddenly appeared and started barking furiously at me. It seemed to be quite upset at the sight of my crutches. Luckily Richard appeared on the scene and picked it up, saying, "Don't be daft, Megan, it's only Billy. C'mon let him past." Turned out, Megan was Richard's dog and as daft as a brush. She certainly gave me a bit of a start that night but she didn't take long to get used to me and we were soon the best of pals.

In August I decided that I wanted a move. I was fed up having buggies outside my door all the time and too many noisy kids with bikes lying all over the place. Ann said she had noticed that I wasn't keeping my flat tidy – I had just lost interest and wanted to move somewhere better. I put an application in to the Council for a move and got a phone call response only a few weeks later, offering me a move. The area-housing officer offered me a one bedroomed bungalow in the west side of Anstruther. She said it would be a lot quieter and was just up the road from my mum. I went to have a look, with the officer and my mum. The house had front and back doors and the back door had a ramp. The bathroom was a wet-floor shower, just like my old flat, but was a lot bigger. I was a little reluctant to take the house as I had my heart set on another area but went for a second look and this time, took my dad.

The house was nice and I finally agreed to take it. However, I had to tell the housing officer that I would need to stay in the flat until I had the house ready to move in, as I wouldn't manage to climb over boxes! While all this was going on, I was busy organising another Race Night for Charity. This time it was in the Legends Bar and I was raising money for 'Scope,' a charity for people with Cerebral Palsy. It was a bigger affair this time as there was a lot more room in Legends Bar. There was a good turn out – including sixteen of my work colleagues – and we had a really good time, with £750 being raised for 'Scope'.

I had been a bit worried that the Race Night might clash with my house removal but as it turned out there was a problem with the water system and the Race Night had come and gone by the time the house was ready. I never intended taking my living room suite to the new house. It was far too big for the new place so I advertised it for sale, in the local paper. If it didn't sell, I would give it to Michael and Lecia. My bedroom carpet was going to be a good fit for my new bedroom so that would save a bit on expenses and I could use my living room carpet for the hall. I had Michael put laminate flooring down in the kitchen and living room, to set off the new brown suite I'd bought. The walls of my living room and hall were all cream and my kitchen was painted green so, like the flat, there were some colour contrasts. I didn't need the ramp so the council removed it. By the time I was ready to move, I hadn't had any offers for my suite so it looked like it would be going to Michael, for laying my floors. When I finally left, on a Sunday night, I breathed a sigh of relief and gave a little chant, "Cheerio, Cheerio, Cheerio!" At that point, I thought I had seen the last of the flat but before the night was out, I got a phone call from someone interested in the suite so – back I had to go. As it happened, Michael still got it. I had just agreed a price for it with the prospective buyers when we heard my dad calling from the kitchen, "No, you're not getting it for that price!" The couple just got up - and walked out. This time, when we walked out of the flat it was, finally, the last time. It was the first week in October.

I met Stan and Christine, a couple in their sixties, in The Royal, towards the end of September, beginning of October. Stan had known me most of his life but it was only then that we became friends. It was around this time that Geordie John died. I wanted to go to his funeral but it was down in Johnstone Bridge and I had no way of getting there. Stan and Christine offered to take me, as they were going by car. When the car arrived, on the day, Christine came to the front door. I tended to use the back door so I indicated to her to go around the back and they picked me up there. Later, on the journey, Christine wondered why I had a sock stuck in my letterbox. The flap had been clattering in the wind for a couple of nights! Christine had volunteered to sit in the back so that I could sit in front with Stan. Throughout the journey, she was kept busy, lighting cigarettes and handing them over to Stan. She forgot that I smoked but that was all right with me, as I don't like smoking in cars when they are on the move. When we stopped at Annan Water Service Station, though, I had a smoke outside with Christine, while Stan parked the car. They both knew I didn't have much sight and weren't very sure how to guide me so I said to Stan, "Just walk in front and I'll follow you!" He looked a bit baffled at that so I explained, "You're wearing steel heel tips - I can hear you walking - I'll just follow the sound of your shoes!" There weren't that many people attending the funeral but there were a few from Anstruther, including the Bank House crew, Richard,

Jeannette and Manuela and the Donaldsons had travelled from Livingston. (I had the hots for Manuela at that time!) The funeral wasn't far from the service station but it was a bit out of the way so most of us got a little lost before we eventually found it. Although it was quite bright and sunny, it was a bit on the chilly side, with a slight breeze. At the graveside I couldn't hear Stan's feet on the grass so had to rely on my very hazy eyesight but I managed. After the funeral we were all invited back for drinks and snacks. It was a really sad day for John's family, and us, his friends, but it was nice that a few from Anstruther were able to go and pay their respects.

While I frequented The Bank House, there was a barmaid working there that grabbed my attention. I knew I had heard her voice before but it took me some time to realise that it was Tanya, who I had known at playgroup. Of course, I'd also gone through High School with her and hung around with her and her friends at the Youth Club but because of my sight loss I didn't realise it was her.

One night, in The Haven, a pub in Cellardyke, I was drinking with my cousins, John and Eck, when I heard the news on the television that a boat called the Maridian owned by a local man from Anstruther had sunk. There were three local men and an Aberdonian on board. The next day, it was all over the news. Three men were lost at sea and the body of one of the Anstruther men had been recovered from the water. Anstruther was very different then. It was a busy fishing port and the whole community felt it when men were lost at sea. It took a long time for them to get over the loss of those men.

I had a bit of an accident, one night, in The Royal. Before I'd even had much to drink, I had to go to the toilet. Of course I wasn't familiar with the layout yet and managed to bump my head against a wall. Luckily, someone came to my rescue with some ice, wrapped in a cloth, and I spent the rest of the night, clutching this to my eye. This was the night that I met John and Brian. John was in his mid-fifties, with white hair while Brian was in his forties and a little bald. The three of us had a great laugh that night and from then on we spent a lot of time in each other's company. I was beginning to enjoy life away from The Ship, meeting new people. Bill and Morris had both moved away and I rarely saw Ian after I left The Ship. He moved away in October to live with his girlfriend. John, Brian and I would often go from pub to pub and end up in The Smugglers. One Friday night we arrived there when Stan, Christine and Michael were playing Dominoes, and John joined in. I asked if I could join in, too. Michael Dick had been nicknamed Spawney Dick, as he was so lucky. Stan explained that the double blank now counted as thirteen as Spawney used to keep hold of it all the time. I had to ask everybody to tell me what they played each time so that I could try and remember who played what. If, say, the double-six was down, the player next to me might say, "I've played the six-five," and the next player might say, "I've played the double-five," and so on. This would be my Friday night from now on as they played every week and John would walk me home as he was going that direction, anyway.

I started going to The Bank House on Thursdays for the quiz night. Richard was already in a team with a boy called Mark, who was a barman in The Bank House, and Mark's girlfriend and her mum. Not long after I started going to the Quiz, I paired up with Richard, Alan and another man called Mark that I used to drink in The Ship with. We called ourselves 'My Turn'. The quizmasters were Colin and John, known as

C & J entertainment, who also ran the karaoke in The Bank House. The team from The Smugglers called themselves 'The Smug Bastards'. Our team didn't bother if we won or not, as long as them Smug Bastards didn't win, we were happy.

Later in the year, as Christmas was approaching, our works outing was arranged for the same venue as the previous year. John, a colleague at work, said I could stay at his house, overnight, to save me going home so late. He finished early on a Friday so he came back to work to walk me along to his house. He showed me around his house and made sure I was familiar with the surroundings as I would (probably!) be drunk when I came back. We had a couple of drinks and then got dressed to go out. We went to Emma and Sarah's house before going to the night-out. They were his nieces and worked with us. The women were taking ages so John and I played cards till they were ready. The night was better than the year before with great food and music, and when it was finished we went back to Emma's. John fell asleep there and we couldn't wake him. I didn't want to stay at Emma's, as I didn't know my way around. In any case, I needed to go back to John's as my medication and stuff for my cosmetic shield were in my rucksack at his place. When we couldn't rouse John, I phoned Val to come and get me but thought I'd be a sorry state, without my medication and contact lens for a couple of days. I was just on my way out when John appeared, he had been sleeping on Sarah's bed and had finally woken up – too late I was on my way home. He tried to persuade me to stay but I was having none of it – so he hopped in the taxi with me, to pick up my bag from his house. On the following Monday, at work, I apologised for my behaviour. It was nice of Sarah offering me her bed for the night but it was a strange place and I didn't feel confident enough to stay.

Mikey, my new nephew was born in early December so I was now an uncle to two. Unlike the case with Lecia's first child, I held Mikey within a week or two and vividly remember holding him in my arms over Christmas, at my auntie's. He was so content lying there in my arms, and it made me wonder - if or when, I would be a dad.

Chapter 30

NEGLECTED IN LONDON

The year 2007 wasn't a very good year for me – in fact, a year I'd rather forget. In January, I made my working hours permanent at 22 per week and a few new staff were taken on, including Annie, Ashley, Craig and Nicola. There were already a number of established staff, including Nina, Kath, Colin, Lesley, Kim, Sarah, Kerry and Nicky and they were a great bunch to work with. We had a works night-out in Dundee at the end of January, the day after my birthday. There were about fifty of us, and this was when I was introduced to Jonny, another boy who worked at the call centre. Jonny was quite tall and had 'not a lot of hair'! He was one of a group that looked after me that night and made sure I was always okay. Our previous visits to Dundee had been in September 2005 and September 2006 to mark the occasion of summer staff going back to university. I really enjoyed our Dundee nights, especially going to Starz, a karaoke bar. The place was brilliant and the bouncers let me smoke on the landing at the top of the stairs so that I didn't have to negotiate the stairs each time I wanted a smoke. They said, as far as I was concerned, they counted the landing as 'outside'.

Things started to go wrong in March. I tried to buy tickets for the Carling Weekend Festival in Leeds. I couldn't get through on the phone so I tried to buy the tickets online. By sheer chance, I stumbled onto the wrong website. It was a broker's site and having put my details in and clicked pay; I received an e-mail receipt for £1185. For four tickets! I expected to pay about

£500 so nearly died when this amount came up. My speech software hadn't read out the amount and the website wasn't very compatible for a screen reader. I went on the phone to the broker the next morning and explained what had happened – and asked them to cancel the order. A lady in their office, offered to refund my money, less 25% administration fee. A few days later, no money had been put back into my account so I called them again. This time, another lady told me that under no circumstances would they give refunds. She said that they had put my tickets up for re-sale, so if and when the tickets were sold I would receive my money back less the 25% administration fee. I had lost all that money with one click of a button!

The following day, I told my workmates what had happened and John offered to help me get my money back. He contacted everyone he could think of - Trading Standards, Disability Rights Commission, my MP and all the major newspapers. It was then just a case of waiting for responses.

There had been a few changes at work, with Gayle moving departments and her successor in our department leaving as well. This meant the Team Manager's position was up for grabs. I decided to apply for it. There were only two candidates - Jonny and me. When I was invited for a meeting with Gayle, Emma and another member of staff, I didn't realise it was an interview – no one said as much – and so I wasn't prepared. Not surprisingly, I didn't get the job – that went to Jonny. Later, at a leaving do in Jamie's Bar, in Markinch, I congratulated Jonny on his success and discovered that he was quite upset that his getting the position meant I had to lose out, as we had always got on well together. Soon after this, the Supervisor's position was advertised so I tried for that. Gayle declined my application this time and told me that I wasn't able for that position yet, and why. She also explained why I was unsuccessful with my previous application. But she said she would train me in development skills so that I could be ready for Supervisor or Team Manager in the future and would be able to do Cash Calling. Kyle, quite a large boy, got the Supervisor's job this time - unfortunately! He was a very cheeky young man in his late twenties, and was always having a laugh at someone.

John was still trying his best to help me retrieve my money from the online broker but had got no response from most of his letters – only the DRC and Trading Standards had replied and they couldn't help. I was fed up waiting so I arranged help from a lawyer through legal aid, but in view of the poor response up to this point, I wasn't getting my hopes up.

Michelle was a new start round about June. She was a nice girl - very quiet to begin with but once she started talking, you couldn't shut her up. Even so, I enjoyed working with her. She was lovely, with long brown hair and we got on really well together.

In July the company took on a new Call Centre Manager. He was about seven feet tall and made a lot of changes. A short time after that, a few members of staff were let go, including Gayle, John and Emma and no replacements were brought in. It was about this time that data started to get quite low.

One morning in May, a few weeks before the Great Scottish Walk in Edinburgh, I answered my mobile. I couldn't see the display screen, but it turned out to be my cousin, Eck. He had bought tickets to see Metallica at Wembley Stadium, in London and was phoning to ask if I wanted to go. I accepted, without hesitation. Eck gave me the disability number to phone so that I could get a Disabled Ticket. I then suggested that we should ask Michael if he'd like to go, as he had mumped and moaned about the last Metallica gig we had been to, and he wasn't invited. Eck was okay with that. I then reminded him that I would be entitled to a free carer's ticket and that I could give that to Michael. Eck wasn't okay with that. He wanted to go 'halfers' on the tickets as he had bought an extra ticket, which would have been for me. I didn't really understand what he meant at the time - but it all made sense later!

The Metallica Gig was quite a while away so we had plenty of time to prepare for the trip. Before that, we had to do a sponsored walk, for charity. The Metallica concert wasn't until the 8th of July and it was still only May. John, Eck and I had a pow-wow over a few drinks and discussed how best we could get to London. John wanted to fly and Eck wanted to hire a mini-bus for the weekend. I wasn't bothered how we got there - as long as we did. At work, I was talking to Kirsty, and telling her the exciting news about going to see Metallica and she asked how we were getting there. When I said I didn't know, she said, "Why not get the bus?" I said, "The bus? All the way down to London? You must be joking!" I didn't realise that she meant there was a coach travelled to London daily, and back, but you had to book in advance. She also said that if we booked it well in advance we could travel for as little as a pound, each. When I told John and Eck, they were sceptical but agreed that it was worth checking out. We did - and secured the tickets in plenty of time. It was a bit of a bonus when we discovered that our bus travelled overnight so we would be able to get a bit of sleep on the journey and arrive fresh for the gig.

With tickets, and travel sorted, we then concentrated on the Great Scottish Walk. This was to be a twelve-mile walk through Edinburgh. John and Eck had done one before but this one would be my first attempt. Obviously I wouldn't be able to walk the full twelve miles but they had suggested that one of them would push me around in my wheelchair for the first eleven miles and then I could get out and walk the last mile. It would be a challenge for one of them to push me that distance and even the last mile would be a challenge for me. When it was all agreed, Eck gave me a sponsor form. I had to raise money for *his* charity. I took my sponsor form everywhere I went - to the pubs, to my work and on family visits. All told, I managed to raise over £200 for the walk. I didn't do an awful lot of training for it – though I should have. Apart from that, that was me fund-raised and ready to walk – well, be pushed and then walk. A few days before the walk, Eck sent me a text, telling me where we were leaving from and what time to be there for. As I had my wheelchair to take, it was agreed that I would get picked up first and be taken to the rendezvous point. I didn't go out on the night before the walk. I wanted to be fresh, fit and ready so I went to bed quite early on the Saturday night and had a good sleep.

In the morning, I got a text message asking if I was up and ready to go. I replied, saying, yes, I was up and, yes, I was ready to go. I was having some teething problems with my new phone and for some reason, the message didn't get sent. However, John phoned me a little later, on my landline to make sure that I had received the message. By this time, he was panicking – and having visions of me still lying in bed. I assured him I was ready and a short while later, he arrived to pick me up, but when he got out the back of his car, I wondered why? It turned out, he had been out most of the night - and wasn't fit to drive. Luckily, Carra and her boyfriend were also doing the walk so Carra drove us through to Edinburgh, in John's car. Once my chair was in the boot of the car we set off to meet everyone else at the rendezvous point, which was outside

Legends.

We were first there. Eck and Jeanette arrived next with Eck's son and his niece. Once all four cars were there, we set off for Edinburgh. We were again the first to set off and we reached Edinburgh well ahead of the rest, and decided to pop into MacDonalds for a breakfast. When Eck finally arrived in Edinburgh, he sent John a text, asking where we were. By the time Eck and the others arrived at MacDonalds, we had finished our breakfast and Eck was urging us to get a move on. Eventually, we got clear of MacDonald's and were within sight of the starting line by five minutes to eleven. The Walk was due to start at eleven, prompt. Late or not, some of us needed the toilet and that wouldn't wait! That was the fastest toilet stop I've ever done. Not fast enough, though, because, we were still short of the start line, when we heard the gun go off, to start the Walk.

To begin with, John was pushing me but he soon got tired and Eck took over. Crikes – not long started and John was struggling. Yet, it didn't take us long to catch up to the crowds of walkers and we started to weave in and out of them, to get past. Eck's plan was to get a bit in front as it would obviously take me a while to cover the last mile under my own steam. John and Jeanette stayed with us for most of the walk. Carra and her boyfriend started lagging behind so we left them to go at their own pace, while we bashed on. We caught up with Ann, my support worker, and her daughter, around 40 minutes into the Walk. We talked with them for a while, wishing them the best of luck and then horsed on. In a short time we came to a set of steps. It was obvious we couldn't take the wheelchair up them. Luckily, there was a steward nearby who pointed out an alternative route to the top. Great - but when Eck saw how steep the path was, he wasn't amused. I think a mountain goat might not have been amused either! Eck's a big strong lad though and pretty soon he had us at the top of the slope – and the steps. We took a rest there, waiting for the rest of our group to catch up with us. However, when we started recognising people in the passing crowd, that we had passed earlier, we decided to get moving again. About five minutes later, Eck was pushing me up another hill when the handle came off my wheelchair. We had to stop and fix it - more time lost. Once we got going again, Eck stepped up a gear and phoned John to ask where he was. Turned out they were just a few hundred yards ahead and we soon caught up with them. Just as well because they were carrying my crutches. About two miles from the finish disaster struck again. One of the tyres came off my wheelchair as we were crossing a section of cobbles. I thought that was the end of our walk but Eck was determined and after a bit of a struggle he managed to get the tyre back on again. One mile after that, I clambered out of my chair and got my crutches from Jeanette. Eck looked mighty relieved. No wonder! I decided to follow John for the last mile. His trainers were very white – quite easy to see. So, off went our little procession - Jeanette in front with the wheelchair, followed by Eck, then John, then myself. There were lots of water stations throughout the walk and I had collected a bottle along the way. About half an hour in to my mile walk, I had to ask John for the water – that distance was quite far for me and it was a hot day. I knew there wasn't far to go when I heard music coming from Meadowbank Stadium, the site of the finishing line so I started to go a little faster. Just as I was entering the stadium, Ann passed me – but was looking shattered. I felt proud as I crossed the finish line and went to collect my medal, with John and Eck. When a radio presenter rushed over and asked me if I had just walked twelve miles on crutches, I was tempted to say yes, but still being in a bit of a daze, I answered honestly, " No, just the last mile!" He applauded me anyway, as did the crowd sitting in the stadium. I was on cloud nine for hours afterwards but all I could think of now was, Metallica.

We all went home, intending to have a night out to celebrate. First, though, John and I got a Chinese Take-Away and took it back to my house. John left my place about seven-thirty to get spruced up for the night out. We had arranged to meet up again at The Sally and as I was feeling quite fit after the walk, I decided to walk down there. Carra and her boyfriend weren't planning on going out, as they were quite tired but as I was walking into The Sally, they arrived behind me. We'd already finished our first round by the time John turned up, twenty minutes late. After a few drinks in The Sally, we headed for The Royal and then on to The Bank House. After that, we finished the night off at Legends - where we eventually got thrown out! Eck then wanted us to continue at his house but I had Ann coming in the morning and decided to call it a night. However - on the way home I fell and split my chin on the pavement. It all happened so quickly – walking, falling down, car brakes screeching – then, the next thing I knew, I was waking up. I must have knocked myself out – maybe just a few seconds. One of my cousins bundled me into his car and took me home. In the morning, when I felt my chin, it was covered in dried blood and my nose was aching. Ann arrived before I had a chance to go in the shower and when she noticed the damage, she examined my nose and chin and told me that it wasn't a deep cut - it just looked bad because of the dried blood. After I had a shower, my chin looked a lot better. Mum and Dad were on holiday at the time and I was praying that my chin healed and the bruising round my nose and eyes disappeared before they came home. This little fall would remain my secret.

Once I'd got over the hype of the walk and the celebrations afterwards, it was time to look forward to Metallica and London. A few days before the trip, I tried to arrange for time off work. Unfortunately, the dates weren't available and so I had to arrange a shift-swap with a colleague. The coach for London was leaving Dundee at twenty-past-eight on the Friday evening so our group arranged to have a Chinese buffet there, before travelling. John took Eck, Michael and me to Dundee, by car. Two friends of Eck's went to Dundee by train as they were coming from a different direction. After the buffet, we headed for Tesco's to buy some beer for the journey. After John had transported the beer to the bus station, he went to find somewhere to dump his car for the weekend. About half-an-hour later, he arrived at the bus stance, sweating like a horse as he had just run a mile to get there in time. It was a downer when we were told that alcohol was not allowed inside the bus and the luggage, including the beer, had to be stowed in the baggage compartment.

Somehow, as usual, John and Eck managed to smuggle their beers onto the bus – but Michael and I didn't. We didn't all get to sit together on the bus, either. We were all upstairs but I was at the back, Michael was sitting in front of me, while John, Eck and the other two were scattered about at the front of the bus. I had some stranger sitting next to me on the window seat. I couldn't sleep on the journey. There were too many people talking all around me, and people opening tins, one after another. I think I was jealous because they were drinking and I wasn't. A short way into the journey I realised I needed the toilet.

Problem! I couldn't go on my own and Michael was asleep. I decided to phone Eck, at the front of the bus. He wasn't pleased and told me to wake Michael. I did – and he wasn't pleased! And then – Michael had just helped me to my feet when my mobile rang. Eck was wondering if I had managed to wake Michael – knowing damn well I had - and with my phone ringing, he'd woken everybody else around me. That was the start of things to come!

The bus was supposed to arrive in London at quarter-past six and it did, on the dot. Dragging our luggage behind us, we wandered a few hundred yards up the road and stopped outside a café. By this time, I was due to take my medication so asked Michael to get it from my bag. After a few minutes rummaging around amongst the bags he came over and said my bag wasn't there. I thought he was kidding but Eck said, "He's not joking – it's not there." Michael went off, heading back to the bus station and Eck started to quiz me about when I had last seen my bag and what was in it. I could feel my stomach churning at the prospect of my bag being lost. Everything I needed for the weekend was in it - my tickets, my medication, my eye, and camera - my clothes. What was I going to do? Bad enough that my weekend would be ruined without the tickets and clothes but how was I going to manage without my medication? I could almost touch the gloom descending on me when Michael suddenly strolled in, carrying my 'lost' bag. What a relief! It had been left on a luggage trolley at the bus station. Who'd have thought!

It was just after seven-o'clock now and we tried to phone the Youth Hostel where we were booked. Eck's friends had booked it for us – not far from the bus station and not too far from Wembley Stadium. Unfortunately, no one was answering the phone at seven in the morning so we decided to go into the café to get some breakfast. Again, just like on the bus, Michael and I were left on our own at one table while the others all settled down around another one. Once we'd all had enough to eat, we piled into two taxis and headed for the hostel. It was only a couple of miles away but with the 'Tour de France' on that week and some roads blocked off, the journey took more than half-an-hour – and cost a fortune!

When we arrived at the hostel, it wasn't open, so we had to hang around outside for a while. Weary from the long bus journey and feeling a cold coming on, I asked Michael to get a beer for me, from my bag. He started on the vodka and was getting drunk quite quickly. I started to worry. I was sitting in my wheelchair, trying to keep my eyes open but kept nodding off. John was lying on the steps of the pub, underneath the hostel, doing the same. Eck and his friends went for a wander to some nearby shops. That left me, in my chair, John lying on the steps and Michael sitting beside him, knocking back the vodka. Suddenly, I needed the toilet again so I asked Michael to take me round the corner somewhere, which meant we had to wake John to look after the bags. When Michael took me to the toilet I asked him to slow down a bit on the drink, as I had to depend on him to look after me. I didn't think the others would do it, after the way they had been treating us, so far. Michael was annoyed when I said this. He said, "Do you think I'd leave you, like?" Well – I was thinking, 'you never know what someone will do when they are drunk'. 'It could happen!' I thought it was very possible he could have got drunk and left me somewhere and forgotten all about me. When we got back to the hostel, John then went to the toilet so Michael had to look after the bags. I lit up a cigarette but was still dozing off while I was smoking it. Once I had finished I dropped the butt on the ground and nodded off.

I woke up when the other four came back. By this time, the pub was open so we all bundled in and started ordering drink. I think Michael stayed on the vodka while I started on the whisky and the rest were on pints. We weren't getting the keys for the hostel until two o'clock so we had time for a good few rounds before then. Eck knew a girl from Luton and was swithering whether he should go and visit her. When the barman told him it wasn't far and gave him directions, he decided to go. But before he went, he had a word for Michael. He said, "It's your job to look after Billy – you've got the Carer's ticket." That sparked me off. I reminded Eck that I had offered to go 'halfers' with the tickets but he was having none of it. He said "No - it's alright, it's done now!" When Eck left, I had a play fight with John on the floor - John isn't the smallest of guys! After that, I wanted to go up stairs to wash my eye and put it in, as I felt lost without it. Michael wasn't too keen but eventually gave in and took me upstairs, washed my eye and put it in for me. I felt a lot more confident when we headed back downstairs. As the day went on, my cold started to get worse and drinking all day wasn't helping matters. We had hardly eaten all day and the rest of them weren't planning to either - they just wanted to drink. I didn't. I needed to eat and I told them that I couldn't cope with drinking on an empty stomach. We eventually left the pub that night after taking a few Pro-Pluses to keep ourselves going.

We took a bus to a nightclub but the bus driver got irritated about something, stopped the bus and told everyone to get off. We headed straight across the road to another pub. Michael told the others that he and I were going to find something to eat. That didn't take long as we found a MacDonald's about a hundred yards along the road. And the meal didn't take long, either. Fast food! When we got back to the pub, the others were nowhere to be seen. What a surprise. I suspected they wouldn't be there when we got back - I thought the moment that we were out of sight they would be off. We had an idea that they would go back to the hostel, as there was a disco on there, that night, so we got a bus back to the hostel. When we got back, there was a huge bouncer standing outside the pub - and we didn't have our room key. Michael started arguing with him but then thought better of it as he was twice Michael's size. We had to pay to get back in. Once we were inside Michael started looking around for John and the others. I was tired, drained and developing a thumping headache and the last thing I wanted to hear was Rihanna's song 'Umbrella', blasting out. That just made matters worse. Michael found 'the gang,' all sitting together, around one table, wheeled me in beside them and went to the bar for some drinks. I hardly touched mine and asked Michael to take me upstairs. It didn't take him long to get me settled in and then he went back downstairs to drink with the others. I wasn't caring. I just wanted to put my head down and sleep. John and another of the guys came upstairs after me and went straight to bed. Michael and the other guy stayed up for a while and then came upstairs giggling and went on giggling right up to the moment they lay down to sleep. In the morning, we asked them what all the giggling was about. They said Michael had been videoing a fight on his mobile phone and doing a running commentary and a policeman told them to, "Move along!" Michael then started to video the policeman, who then said, "Get away, you terrorist!"

I wasn't in a good mood on the Sunday - my cold was getting worse. I didn't really feel like going to the concert now but I tried to refresh myself by going for a shower. The showers – downstairs and difficult for me to get to - weren't the best - they kept flooding and the whole floor was soaking wet. By mid-day, we were already dressed for the gig but there was no sign of Eck. His bag, with the tickets, was still in the room and as long as we had the tickets, we were going to the gig – Eck or no Eck. We were just about to leave when in burst Eck. Now we had to wait on him having a shower and getting changed. Twenty minutes later, we were heading for Wembley to see Metallica.

Although we had no idea how long it would take, we set out for Wembley on foot. It wasn't long before John produced a bottle of Slow Gin and Lemonade to drink on the way. None of us was particularly fond of gin but John insisted that Slow Gin was different and it was true - it was great. It didn't last long, as there were six of us, and we soon started on beers and, surprise, surprise, Michael had a bottle of vodka with him. During the walk I needed to pee but when I got out of my chair, I noticed that the bottom of one of my crutches had fallen off. Apart from being an immediate problem, it meant I would have to manage with one crutch for the rest of the weekend. We weren't getting anywhere fast and didn't really know how far we had to go. Then somebody spotted a bus – for Wembley. We all hopped on and in only a few minutes, we were there. When we got to Wembley, Michael was already pissed. I was starting to worry for my safety; Michael was pissed and nobody else was bothering about me. However, once we got inside the stadium we got to see the best band on the planet.

Michael and I were seated on the Disabled Platform while the rest of them sat in the stand. They had come in their shorts, expecting to get on the pitch with the crowds but they couldn't get anywhere near it. The support bands were really good. I was looking forward to seeing HIM before Metallica, as I was a big fan, but they got booed off the stage. Not many people wanted to hear them – what they wanted, was to see Metallica. Again I was nodding off, I wasn't coping with my cold and just wanted to sleep. I actually did fall asleep for a few minutes, while I was waiting for Metallica and Michael didn't even notice. When the AC-DC song 'If you wanna make it to the top, you got to rock 'n' roll,' came on, I got excited, shook Michael and said "Here we go – Here we go!" He said, "How do you know?" I said, "That's always the song that plays before they come on."

Wembley erupted when Metallica finally came onstage. They were amazing - and we loved every minute of it. I had seen them before, in Glasgow, and knew what to expect. I wasn't disappointed - they were just as I expected – only better. They played for about three hours - playing all their best songs, including Enter Sand Man, Nothing Else Matters, The Unforgiven, One, and Seek and Destroy. I like all their songs, but one I always look forward to is 'One' as it's really long and there are always loads of fireworks. I took my camera with me and asked Michael to capture a few photos. All he managed to catch - was the sky! The show was great and, even after a few encores; we were all still shouting for more. When it all finally ended and the crowd was leaving the stadium, Michael was holding back, hoping to link up with Eck and the others but couldn't spot them amongst the thousands of people packed into the ground. As Michael was drunk when we came in, he didn't know how to get out and I was beginning to panic by this stage. I wouldn't have been surprised if the rest of them had abandoned us at Wembley. My worries were unfounded though - we eventually found them.

We caught a bus back to the hostel and headed

straight for the bar, the last thing Michael needed but we had a few drinks anyway. This time I opted for half pints of lager - everyone else was on pints. When Eck went to the toilet, John decided it would be funny to dip his dick in Eck's pint and we were all still laughing when Eck got back. Inevitably, he asked what we were laughing at - though I think he had a good idea. While we were all in hysterics, Michael got up and went to the toilet. The pint was duly swapped around and when Michael came back, he drank it! When we were eventually asked to leave, we headed upstairs and continued drinking in the kitchen - me, still with a stinking cold. Michael, Eck and I all put our mobile phones on charge and we weren't going to bed until they were fully charged. While we were still drinking, I began to feel ill and asked Michael to take me to the toilet. By the time we got there I was in agony. We started arguing and Michael got impatient and shouted at me, "What's wrong with you?" I'd been feeling sick all night and this was the last straw. I yelled back at him, "I'm not well, for fuck sake!" I told him to go back upstairs and I'd come up when I was ready. When I was finished I headed upstairs, collected my mobile and went to bed. John was already in bed. Michael and Eck, and another guy, who was staying in the hostel, were still drinking and from our room, we could hear everything they said. About an hour later, Eck finally came through. Somebody had dropped a tube of toothpaste on the floor and when Eck stood on it, he decided to squeeze it over John's hair. Sometime later, John woke up and went ballistic! For some reason, he thought Michael was the guilty party and flew at him, in a rage. Michael was terrified - it took a while for him to get back to sleep. John had to have a shower in the middle of the night. He was not a happy bunny! Michael eventually got to sleep and some time afterwards I needed the toilet again. After the night's events, I didn't want to wake anyone so decided to go under my own steam. Thankfully, I managed and didn't have to go again, for the rest of the night. In the morning, I was the first one up. I didn't want to sleep in – I was desperate to go home. I set about waking the rest of them up – some, by slapping them about the head. No way was I staying in London any longer than necessary! I had a shower while the rest scrambled out of their beds. Some had showers, some didn't. About an hour later, everybody was as ready as they were going to be and we headed for the bus station. I didn't like London much but one thing I'll say for it; every bus in London had a wheelchair ramp.

The bus journey through London was slow and we began to get anxious that we might miss our Dundee bus. Eck thought it left at mid-day but luckily, it was actually half past twelve. When we arrived at the bus station most of us got something to eat, but I wasn't hungry. Michael wanted to buy some presents for his children but after standing in a long shop queue he eventually gave up, put the stuff back on the counter and headed for the bus. By then, we had lost the rest of the group again and couldn't find the coach. We were getting really worried at this point but eventually, with seconds to spare, we found the stance and, lo and behold, the rest of our group were there, standing by the bus.

On the coach, I was able to sit next to Michael, at the front, and again the rest of them headed up the other end, away from us. Leaving London in early afternoon, we had a long journey ahead of us. Around teatime, we stopped at a Burger King. By this time I was hungry! I asked Michael to bring me a couple of burgers. While I waited, I got off the bus to stretch my legs and have a cigarette – managing it all on only one crutch. After this stop we had only one more rest-break. We were to be allowed only five minutes but one of the passengers didn't return in that time and was going to be left behind. His girlfriend, who was foreign, was quite distressed and came off the bus, as she didn't want to leave without him. She pleaded with the driver to wait for him and when the miscreant eventually returned, the driver gave him a rollicking. Maybe he deserved it - but I felt sorry for the woman.

We had a change of drivers, and a delay of forty-five minutes in Glasgow, and eventually arrived in Dundee about one o'clock in the morning. John collected his car and we got some filled rolls from an all-night bakery before leaving Dundee. When we eventually got home I went straight to bed. I felt shattered and ill, and just wanted to sleep.

I had the Monday off work so had a very, very long lie-in. I hated London. Maybe it would have been different if I hadn't been ill. I'll never know. I did love Metallica though, that was worth making the journey for. I didn't quite know how to handle John and Eck after that weekend. A whole week later I cornered them and told them what I thought of their behaviour. I thought it was well out of order, especially over something like a ticket. After that, I didn't speak to them for weeks.

Chapter 31

DELIGHTED, DEVASTATED & DISCIPLINED

WHAT A YEAR

The Leeds festival was past and I hadn't seen any tickets or money back from the online broker. You may recall - I had lost all that money with one click of a button! Still, life at home was great. I was attending the quiz every week with my team, 'My Turn', and although most weeks we managed to win the quiz we never did pick up the jackpot. We were nicknamed 'The Fivers' as we kept picking the Fiver. Richard didn't like people going out the front door for a smoke during the quiz as his neighbours often complained, but he let me go out the front, as it was easier for me. The toilet was downstairs and it was difficult for me to negotiate the stairs but even there I worked out ways to make life easier. People used to wonder why I always wore a tracksuit to the pub. That was easy - easier when I needed the toilet, to pull tracky bottoms down than fighting with buttons or a zip on a pair of jeans. I could have peed myself by the time I struggled with buttons or a zip! I loved The Old Bank, and not just for the quiz. I started to become really good friends with Richard, the owner. Sometimes, when he worked behind the bar, Stan and I would sit and drink until the wee hours of the morning. Richard had a few lock ins at weekends as well - after the Karaokes. Not planned, you understand - they just happened. I don't think Richard knew that he helped to change my life – in his company I began to realise that there were better places to drink in and friendlier people to drink with. Richard was a very good friend to me.

I really enjoyed the times I spent with John and Brian. They both drank Magners Cider so I decided to try it, too. I became a (very) social drinker - whatever someone in my company was drinking, I would drink something similar. If they were drinking lager, I would drink lager. If they were drinking Vodka, I would drink Whisky. I would meet Brian in The Royal on a Friday night after tea at my mum's. After a quick one there, we would meet up with John at The Bank House and then go on to The Smugglers where we would meet Michael, Stan and Christine to play Dominoes. It took me a while to get into the Dominoes but once I learned to play the game properly, I started to win a few games. A Saturday night was different, but only a little - John and Brian would start in The Ship, work their way up via The Sally, to The Royal where I would meet up with them, and then we would all go on to The Bank House and The Smugglers. After a while though, I decided to walk down to The Sally to meet up with them there. By this time I had stopped going into The Ship altogether.

I started singing in the Open Mike nights in The Bank House, singing country songs. John, from C&J entertainments, who was also a distant relative of mine, started to come to my place almost every week to practice for the Open Mike nights. He played the guitar while I sang. I started singing a few Johnny Cash songs and then learned a few other country songs. It was great, finding a kind of music that I could sing to. After a quiz night, Open Night or Karaoke, I'd often walk home with John, Colin and Barbara, Colin's wife, who worked in The Bank House. On the way, I'd walk on the road, beside the pavement, following the double yellow lines. They'd often tell me to get on the pavement but it was easier for me to walk on the road as it was smoother and I often fell off the pavement. I usually had the road to myself late at night as there was not a lot of traffic then, and with my great hearing, I could hear a car a mile away, which gave me plenty of time to get on to the pavement, if need be.

Stan was like a big brother to me. Although he was a good bit older, he had a lot of time for me and I really enjoyed drinking with him. He once said to me, "Billy, Christine and I really like your company, but I think you should drink with people more your own age." I told him that I had nobody 'more my age' to drink with - they would stay with me for a little while then forget about me. Stan said he understood that. That's why I like being in older people's company. They are a lot more mature and don't abandon me. I would often meet Stan in The Royal when I came home from work on a Monday night and then we'd walk the short distance to The Bank House. I went through a phase of fancying a few of the barmaids in The Bank House and The Royal. Jeanette, the manageress of The Bank House was one that I fancied, although she was older than my mum. But, I really had the hots for Amanda who worked in the Bank House. Better known as Mindy, she wasn't very tall but she was beautiful, with long brown hair. She often played for another team in the quiz night at The Bank House. That's how I met her and I had the hots for her for ages.

Scott left S&S taxis and Stuart took over the business, with Val. I knew I'd miss Scott as he was a great guy and easy to get on with. I was going to miss the laughs we had over country music and the chats we had, in general. But I also got on really well with Stuart and Val. Stuart was still doing the thing about waiting till my hand was on the car door handle and then peeping his horn – really loud. He even started to creep into my house and surprise me – making me jump. He liked quizzing me on songs he played in the car, but most of them were before my time and I could never get them right. He bought a 37-inch LCD television and took me to his house to check if I could see the picture. I always fancied a big 'tele' but they were always a bit pricey. He got his one off eBay and gave me the item number for the exact television that he bought, so I went ahead, ordered it and paid for it with my credit card. When it was delivered, Stuart came along and set it up for me while I was at work. What a difference! The picture was a little bright but the quality was amazing. I could actually see things that I was never able to see on my old television. I bought surround sound speakers so that I got an even better sound experience as well.

During work, in October, something a colleague said, made me ask if she knew Tasha from college and she said, "Tasha's my cousin, how do you know her"? When I explained, she said she would get Tasha's number for me. Tasha was delighted to hear from me and we had quite a long conversation. This was around the same time when Ashley, from work, announced that she was pregnant. You have to watch the quiet ones.

We lost another member of our extended family, in this year, when my mum's cousin's boat went down off the Dorset coast. A lifeboat managed to rescue two crew members but Mum's cousin, the skipper, was never found. Unlike the Maridian, I went to the funeral - it was family. I didn't know him too well but it was another great loss to the community.

With Gayle and Emma both gone, the supervisor's position was advertised internally again, and I decided to have another go for it. Gayle hadn't been able to give me any development skills as the new Call Centre

Manager had come in and she was never able to find the time. For weeks, I wondered why some of my colleagues were doing Call Listening and the jobs that Kyle and Jonny did and it finally clicked - they were going for the supervisor's job. Six of us were in for the job - Kath, Annie, Ashley, Kerry, Colin and myself. As the interviews were only a couple of weeks away, I had to get trained up pretty quickly. Yet again, I didn't get the job. It was given to Kerry and Colin, my best mate at Premier Contact. I didn't mind who got it - I was happy for them both. This was just before Christmas and I thought they would take up their new positions in January but they started right away.

I was given a ticket to join in the New Year celebrations in The Bank House. I had always spent New Year with my family but I decided to have a change and accepted The Bank House invitation. John and Brian were going as well. Brian told me that he spent most New Years in the pub and I said, "Brian, I feel a burden on you and John some nights and think I should let you drink on your own some weekends." Brian looked a bit surprised and said, "Billy, you're not a burden on us, well, not on me anyway. I enjoy your company and if you were a burden, I would tell you!" That Hogmany was great. I really enjoyed myself with all my friends, the music and the grub. Anyone who knows me, knows that I'm a bottomless pit where food is concerned. I ate about three platefuls that night. The reason I do eat so much is that I use up a lot of energy walking - more than most people do. The night went off with a bang and it was an excellent start to 2008.

I had talked to Tasha a few times on the phone and I invited her through for my birthday party, which was being held in The Bank House as there was an Open Mike night, that night, and I was singing. Tasha said she would come but I wasn't getting my hopes up.

Anyway, on the Friday before my birthday, she phoned to ask how to get through to my place. She also asked if she would be staying overnight with me, or going home. When I said, "You'll have to go home," she was a bit surprised. But then, when I said, "I'm only joking. I'll sleep on the couch and you can get my bed," she said, "Don't be silly, we can share the bed. We're good friends and I'll only take up a small corner." I was so excited. I hadn't seen Tasha since college. She said she finished work at four on the Saturday so she would come through right after that. I still wasn't convinced. I spent most of Saturday cleaning and tidying, as I didn't want her to come in to an untidy house. When the phone rang, it was Tasha telling me that she was lost and asking me for more directions. Again, I say, never ask a blind man for directions. I told her the best I could, and also that I would meet her at the bus stop, in Anstruther. Once I got to the bus stop I only waited five minutes and she drove up. Everything was a bit strange at first. We hadn't seen each other for years and didn't know what to say to each other. I had my hair all swept back at the time – having just been Feargal Sharkey at the last Stars in Their Eyes. Tasha was quite small but she wasn't the tomboyish person I had known at College. She was all grown up. We had our tea, but as I had an ongoing problem with excess stomach acid, then, I struggled through it. I bought the tea as a treat as I hadn't seen Tasha for such a long time. As I was singing in The Bank House that night I wanted to be there fairly early. Tasha looked very pretty that night with a fresh hair-do and dressed in women's clothes rather than the boyish stuff she had worn at college. I had invited my mum and dad, my Auntie Julie, Uncle Eck and my mate Craig, from Cupar because I was singing but also because I wanted them to meet Tasha, too. Craig and my mum remembered her from my 20th birthday party but Tasha didn't remember them. The night was brilliant. I really enjoyed myself and everyone was buying me drinks for my birthday. I didn't want to get too drunk before my spot in the singing - I was doing two sets this time, instead of one. I sang three songs to start with and intended singing another three, later on in the night. I sang the best I could - I really loved singing the Johnny Cash songs, always putting my heart and soul into them. At the end of the night my cousin John and his friend both bought me a double whisky, which I couldn't drink, and so Tasha took them, discreetly, back to the bar. I knew that if Jeannette, Richard or any of the bar staff had known that the doubles were for me, they wouldn't have given them to John and his friend. They knew I couldn't handle doubles. When everyone started heading home, Richard offered to give Tasha and me a lift, to save us walking. When we finally got home, Tasha read out all my birthday cards for me and helped put some of my presents away. Then, we got our jammies on and got into bed. We talked for a long while, lying in bed, until Tasha couldn't keep her eyes open any longer, and fell fast asleep. I hardly slept a wink. I wasn't used to having someone lying next to me in bed.

Mum invited us down to her house for lunch on the Sunday. I could have walked but we took the car. It was only when Tasha was sitting in Mum's that she finally remembered Mum's house from her previous visit. Afterwards, when Tasha drove us back to my place, she collected her things, thanked me for a great night, gave me a kiss and left. I suddenly felt lost. Was I already getting used to her being around? I thought about her the whole day and night - thinking that she might walk back through the door, but she never did.

I wasn't my usual self at work for the next few days.

All I could think about was Tasha and I got easily upset. I said a few sharp words to Kyle as he was taking the piss about her. When I spoke to Jonny about Tasha, our talk lasted most of the day because I was too upset to work. I don't know what it was about Tasha that was getting me so upset. Of course, I used to fancy her when we were at college but when she came through I just thought of her as a friend. Yet, something was different when she was around me. Strong feelings for her were coming back again. Sometimes I expected her to have borrowed a key from my mum and be waiting for me when I came home from work or the pub. Why was I even thinking that would happen?

At the end of January, new owners took over The Smugglers. On their opening night, I thought I'd go along for a look. It was packed. Raymond, the new owner, spent most of the night standing at the end of the bar. I told the bar staff about my eyesight and explained to them how I liked my change placed in my hand. Raymond was a beast of a man; big and solid, but underneath, he was a Teddy Bear. He had previously been a bouncer at a nightclub. I told him that we liked to play Dominoes on a Friday night and asked if that was still okay and Raymond, being a Domino player himself, said that was fine with him. After meeting the new owners, I went back through to The Bank House, to finish the night off there.

Early in February, I got a phone call from Colin, my supervisor, to ask me what size of font I worked with because he wanted to try me on a Cash Campaign. This job was different from Welcomes, which was just phoning donors to thank them for their support. On Cash Campaigns we had to ask donors for more money. There were three types of Cash Campaign's and they were all upgrades. Colin was going to train me to ask existing customers to increase their donations to charity. Reactivation was asking donors to sign up again; Conversion involved switching donors from standing order to direct debit. Cash Campaigns was something I don't think I would ever have been allowed to do under Gayle or Emma but both Jonny and Colin believed in me and knew I was capable of doing the job. I took longer than everyone else to learn Cash Calling but on Cash Campaigns I hit the jackpot straight away. On my very first attempt, I got an upgrade - and - a Paperless Direct Debit, which we called a PDD. When Jonny saw it, he stopped the whole team at work and announced, "For three years, working for Premier Contact, Billy has never been on a cash campaign, and with his very first attempt, he has managed to get a PDD!" He was very proud of me but was also disappointed that I hadn't been given the opportunity earlier. I went on to romp that campaign and won Employee of the Week, for my efforts.

It was early in 2008 when Jeanette left The Bank House to go back home. Manuela had left, the year before, so Richard was now on his own. I really liked Jeanette. Sometimes she was a little nippy with me - if I was slow to leave at closing time - but mostly we got on really well. We'd often sing a duet at the karaoke – usually 'Jackson' the song more famously sung by Johnny Cash and June Carter. We had great fun singing that song and we had a lot of laughs together. One time, when I was sitting on a bar stool, she playfully pushed my shoulder and knocked me off the stool. Then, instead of picking me up, she sprayed me with wine, and couldn't stop laughing. Happy days – I was sad to see her go.

I can't remember exactly when, but I started getting friendlier with Ashley, at work. By then, she was pregnant and wasn't getting along with her boyfriend. I told her how I would love to have a family but didn't see it happening anytime soon. I was envious of my brother – watching his kids growing up and so much wanting a family of my own. Since Ashley was having problems with her boyfriend, I suggested to her that I might help her with her child. I was thinking that, even if it wasn't mine, I could love it as my own. I suppose I was just getting worried that I might never meet someone to settle down with and have a family of my own.

After I was so successful on my first Cash Campaign, Jonny gave me another one. It was another upgrade campaign and it involved one of Scotlands biggest wildlife charities. This campaign was a little more difficult but as Jonny and Colin had faith in me I persevered with it and again I got the PDDs and as part of working for this charity, we went on a client visit to one of their visitor centres, near Dunkeld, in Perthshire. There were about ten of us on the visit and the bus ride was quite bumpy. I didn't have my seatbelt on and I began thinking that one more bump and I would land in the aisle. And I did. I couldn't help laughing at the time and some of my colleagues chuckled along with me. Some others were concerned in case I had hurt myself but I was fine. I took my own wheelchair with me in case there was a lot of walking to do. The main organisers of the charity gave a presentation on what they did and told us about all the other facilities they ran, across the country. Their main focus was on the ospreys, which come back to Scotland to nest, every year. I couldn't *see* anything on the visit but being on the campaign, it was really good to hear all about what they did.

In the same month of the Client Visit, my football team, East Fife, won the Third Division and got promoted as champions, to the Second Division. A few of us went along to the match that clinched the championship. I had heard, the day before, that my friend, Malky, had died. My uncle had phoned the news to my mum. I was devastated but I didn't show any emotion when Mum told me - I just said, "Well what can I do, the man's dead." That night, after my usual Friday night out with John and Brian, and playing Dominoes, I phoned Maxine on the way home to talk about Malky. I could hardly speak, for crying. What made it worse was that Malky had died on the Tuesday and I didn't find out from my uncle until the Friday. I thought Maxine could have phoned me to tell me. I knew Malky had a drink problem but I didn't think it was as serious as that, but that's what killed him - he drank too much. I often wonder if we could have done anything to help him, but it would have taken a lot to help Malky. He died only a couple of months after his 40th birthday. I tried to put thoughts of Malky to the back of my mind on the Saturday, and focus on football. The game was away to East Stirling. The ground was packed with supporters – some, like us, who went every week – and a lot that hadn't seen them for years! There were a lot more East Fife supporters than East Stirling fans and we made that clear by our chanting, throughout the game. I don't usually have lunch before I go to a game. I just have a scotch pie and a cup of tea at the football. On this particular day, though, I didn't get my pie – it was so busy, the pie stand ran out of them – twice. It was a great day out and East Fife won three-nil to clinch the title, the first time in sixty years, I just wished Dae had been there to celebrate with us.

I'd almost given up hope of getting my ticket money back from the online broker when Ann, my support worker, suggested that I should contact the Sunday Post's 'Raw Deal' column. I sent them an email and got a phone call from Paul Johnson, the chief reporter in the paper's Edinburgh office. We talked for about half an hour - me telling Paul what happened and him asking me questions. I wasn't encouraged by his comments and I eventually said, "I'm not going to get my money back, am I?" He replied, "No, I don't think so!" I was left deflated, thinking that I had no hope at all. But then, Paul did something that nobody else had done – he kept in touch and updated me on any progress. As he knew I was almost blind, he always communicated by phone and one day he came back with some good news. Someone from the ticket vendor had looked into my situation and realised that my money should have been paid back into my account. They were sending me a cheque for the full amount plus an extra £100 for my inconvenience. Paul said that the cheque should arrive on the Friday but I was still not getting my hopes up. He arranged for a photographer to be at my house on the Friday and ten minutes after he arrived, the postman called, with the mail - including my cheque. I couldn't believe it. I had tried for fourteen months to get that money back and Paul had managed to get it back within two weeks. After the photographer finished taking photos I phoned my mum and dad, who were on holiday, to tell them the good news. Dad was delighted and Mum grabbed the phone off of him, to say that she was over the moon. I had a spring in my step all the way to the bank.

That night, in the Smugglers, playing Dominoes with Stan, Christine, Spawney Dick, John, Brian and Raymond, I got very drunk. I was just delighted to get that money back.

When we left The Smugglers in the small hours, I had a cigarette outside, with Christine and Stan before heading for home. I told them that they should go on home – that I would be okay and would walk home on my own after I'd finished my cigarette. But – they were only gone a few minutes when I slowly slumped to the ground and fell asleep. Some time later, a passing lorry wakened me. I was too tired – and too drunk to move and just sat there until some kind person in a car, stopped and took me home.

The article was printed that weekend and in our small town everyone was stopping me in the street to congratulate me. Raymond said I was a superstar. If I had only known about Raw Deal and gone to them first instead of trying to go through lawyers and other companies, I could have had that money back a lot quicker. Thanks to The Sunday Post and Paul Johnson, he made that happen.

Around the same time, I received a File Note at work - a verbal warning - and I had a little bother with Michelle. The File Note was, allegedly, for being idle, away from the phones. At the time of this alleged incident a supervisor should have supported me but the supervisors weren't even in the room. I'd had a problem with one of the donors and had been trying to write up a comment after the call so, yes, I may have been off the phones for a few minutes, but I needed help from my supervisors and none of them were there. No one would listen and so I just had to give in and accept the File Note. The Note would just be a written note on my file, outlining what I had done wrong. Not a big deal but I was absolutely livid with them, that day.

At that time there weren't many of us in on a daily basis. The company had cut back on people's hours, as there wasn't much business. One day, there was just Nicky, Craig and me in the office and we were given our instructions before the supervisors and managers went to a meeting. Nicky was given a certain campaign to work on, as was I, while Craig was told to do a Reactivation Campaign, something he wasn't trained for. Understandably, he didn't want to do the

Reactivation so we decided to swap. In fact I hadn't been trained up for Reactivations at that point, either, but I thought I could manage and just wanted to help. Craig read the script out to me and I typed it in to my computer. All the time we were doing this, Nicky kept telling us we shouldn't. It took about forty minutes altogether, to type and revise the script and get it on the system and then I made a few calls. That's when Colin came in and Craig and I told him that we were swapping our tasks. Later, the same day, Craig and I were pulled in to the office and had to provide statements, explaining why we swapped campaigns. My reason was simply that I was just trying to help out and we had agreed to swap. The matter went to a disciplinary hearing with a conference call between our office and Premier Contact's main office in London. I was allowed to invite someone along, for support, so I invited my Fife Employability person. She couldn't intervene but she was there if any questions were put to her and she could help me with any questions that I didn't understand. Someone from Premier Contact asked me questions and I answered them as best as I could, with the head of Human Resources on the other end of the conference call, typing my answers up on her computer. She also asked me some additional questions. After the hearing was over, we were asked to leave the room and we went for coffee while they made their decision. It was just what I expected - a warning for not following management instructions and it was to stay on my file for six months. Craig didn't go through a disciplinary hearing - he had left for another job, the day before.

When the calling team was very small, I was often working beside Michelle and sometimes, on a Friday, it was just the two of us. We'd often have a bit of playful banter as we got on really well together. One day, she gently restrained me with her hand, from interrupting when she was on a call. When she came off the call, she realised she was still holding my hand and promptly let go – I think, a little embarrassed. Some time after that I was involved in a slightly suggestive conversation with my colleagues in the kitchen, and Michelle's name came into it. When Michelle heard about this, she told Jonny and got her shift pattern changed so that she wasn't in on the same days as I was. It was my turn to be embarrassed and I had a number of in-depth conversations with Jonny and Kerry about the situation. After that, I was in tears for days, as I never intended to hurt Michelle. It was then, after the incident with Michelle, that I was an emotional wreck and I opened up to Jonny and Kerry and told them things about the problems I had with women. Ever since I started losing my eyesight, I can't see what women look like anymore and have to go entirely on personality, and maybe sometimes I try just a little bit too hard. I talked to Jonny and Kerry about a lot of things that day, things that I'd never told anyone else in my life.

Chapter 32

I WOKE UP

Too many people were talking at once, and most of them were asking questions.

"What's Wrong with your legs?"
"Is there nothing can be done?"
"What can you see?"
"Is there nothing they can do?"
"You can see more than you let on!"
"You're an inspiration."

I woke up with a start – and all those words going around in my head. It was early on a Sunday morning and everything seemed very still and quiet. My face was bathed by the sunshine flooding through my window and all I could hear from outside were a few chirping birds. I lay awake in bed, thinking back over my 26 years and the things that I had gone through in my life, when the realisation struck me! I couldn't walk by the time I was supposed to - when everyone else could. I crawled on my hands and knees for the first three years of my life before I was strong enough to stand up and I had gone through a lot of operations to improve my legs and posture. I thought back to second year at school, to the time when Louise asked me when I would be able to walk properly and I've lost count of the number of people that have asked, "Is there anything else that can be done?" The answer to that is, 'Probably not.' My legs may never be any better than they are now but hey, I can still get around - with great difficulty sometimes - but I manage.

I've been through the pain barrier – many times. Some people may never have suffered much pain in their life and others may have suffered quite a bit. I've suffered pain in a lot of different ways. I've suffered physical and emotional pain with operations, relationship troubles and countless other things in my life. I've worked my way through mainstream schools and colleges and a special college for the blind. I've had lots of friends and girlfriends and I've learned to live independently, on my own. When I was young and my eyesight started to go, I never thought these things would be possible for me. As if my mobility problems weren't enough, now I had this additional disability and everything became so much more difficult. Yet, I came through that as well.

One question I have difficulty with, is, "What can you see?" I just don't know how to answer that question, as I don't know really. If someone should ask me a similar question, like, "How *much* can you see?" This question is very different and my answer is, "Not a lot!"

Many people have told me, "You're an inspiration!" I don't think I am. Sometimes I don't even see myself with a disability, although I do have disabilities, I just see myself like anyone else – going out for a drink, visiting places and generally just trying to enjoy my life. I just try not to let my disability get in the way. Some people, even my mum, have said to me, "you can see more than you let on," and I hate people saying that to me because it's not true. I can't see very much at all and I made sure my mum knew that, and she's never said it again. When anyone else says it to me now, I set them straight too. But it's not just my sight - people also suggest that I can *do* more than I let on. Believe me, if I could do more, I would! I'm not one for sitting back and letting someone else do everything for me. I try to do as much for myself as I can. I'm stubborn that way. Something that really annoys me is people who can work but won't. While it's true that some people are not able to work there are some who just sit on their backsides all day, claiming all the benefits they can, although they're more than capable of working – but just choose not to. Here am I, someone who gave up benefits so that I can hold down a job and be self supporting while there are still people, much more able than me, who are still on benefits. I'd like to see these people coming off benefits and going out to work – disabled people too. A number of disabled people already have jobs and I'd like to see that number increase.

Some people have suggested that I deserve a medal for what I have been through in my life but I don't see it that way. I'm just me. I just get on with things – doing what I have to do. If any medals were to be handed out, they should be given to my family - my mum, dad and brother - for what they have had to put up with over the years and for getting me to where I am today. My physiotherapist deserves a lot of credit too. She was the one who managed to get me walking. If it hadn't been for her, I'd probably still be in a wheelchair now. So I don't deserve a medal. I'm just trying to live a normal life, like anyone else. I just happen to have a few different problems to deal with.

Still in bed, I lay thinking about my brother and his wife – them having two kids and me still single, with no children. I'd love to have a family, but for a few years now, I've been thinking that my time for that might be running out. I heard the words in my head again - people saying, "You're still young enough yet Billy!" I, on the other hand, was not so sure. Then I thought, 'I wonder how many people have had the experiences I've had?' And now, at 26, I've only lived a small portion of my life – with plenty years to go. I have all the friends I need and no doubt I'll meet plenty more. I may not have a family of my own and even if I never do, I still have, Mum and Dad, Michael, Lecia, Mya and Mikey. Plenty family for anyone!

With all these thoughts running round and round in my head, it was still early on a Sunday morning and I wasn't nearly ready to get up so I rolled over and drifted off into a deep sleep but just before I did, I thought to myself.

'It's a life – it's my life, and it's a life I just have to get on with!'